Living Language™

CONVERSATIONAL
GERMAN

REVISED AND UPDATED

W0009031

THE LIVING LANGUAGE™ SERIES

LIVING LANGUAGE™ Complete Courses, Revised & Updated

French*
German*
Inglés/English for Spanish Speakers
Italian*
Japanese*

Portuguese (Brazilian)
Portuguese (Continental)
Russian
Spanish*

*Also available on Compact Disc

LIVING LANGUAGE™ Complete Courses

Advanced French
Advanced Spanish
Children's French
Children's Spanish
English for Chinese Speakers

English for French Speakers
English for German Speakers
English for Italian Speakers
Hebrew

LIVING LANGUAGE IN-TENSE™ Verb Practice

French, German, Italian, Spanish

LIVING LANGUAGE PLUS®

French, German, Italian, Spanish

LIVING LANGUAGE TRAVELTALK™

French, German, Italian, Japanese
Portuguese, Russian, Spanish

LIVING LANGUAGE™ SPEAK UP!® Accent Elimination Courses

American Regional
Spanish
Asian, Indian, and Middle Eastern

LIVING LANGUAGE™ FAST & EASY

Arabic
Czech
French
German
Hebrew
Hungarian
Inglés/English
  for Spanish Speakers

Italian
Japanese
Korean
Mandarin Chinese
Polish
Portuguese
Russian
Spanish

Living Language™
CONVERSATIONAL
GERMAN

REVISED AND UPDATED

Revised by Walter Kleinmann
Coordinator of Foreign Languages and
English as a Second Language
Sewanhaka Central High School District

Based on the original by
Genevieve A. Martin
and
Theodor Bertram

CROWN PUBLISHERS, INC., NEW YORK

This work was previously published under the titles *Conversation Manual German* and *Living Language™ Conversational German* by Genevieve A. Martin and Theodor Bertram, based on the method devised by Ralph Weiman.

Copyright © 1956, 1985, 1993 by Crown Publishers, Inc.

Published by Crown Publishers, Inc., 201 East 50th Street, New York, New York 10022. Member of the Crown Publishing Group.

Random House, Inc. New York, Toronto, London, Sydney, Auckland

LIVING LANGUAGE and colophon are trademarks of Crown Publishers, Inc.

Manufactured in the United States of America

Library of Congress Catalog Card Number: 56-9319

ISBN 0-517-59043-3

10   9   8   7

CONTENTS

Living Language™
CONVERSATIONAL
GERMAN
REVISED AND UPDATED

INTRODUCTION

Living Language™ *Conversational German* makes it easy to learn how to speak, read, and write German. This course is a thoroughly revised and updated version of *Living German: The Complete Living Language Course*®. The same highly effective method of language instruction is still used, but the content has been updated to reflect modern usage and the format has been clarified. In this course, the basic elements of the language have been carefully selected and condensed into forty short lessons. If you can study about thirty minutes a day, you can master this course and learn to speak German in a few weeks.

You'll learn German the way you have learned English, starting with simple words and progressing to more complex phrases. Just listen and repeat after the native instructors on the recordings. To help you immerse yourself in the language, you'll hear only German spoken. Hear it, say it, absorb it through use and repetition.

This *Living Language*™ *Conversational German* manual provides English translations and brief explanations for each lesson. The first five lessons cover pronunciation, laying the foundation for learning the vocabulary, phrases, and grammar, which are explained in the later chapters. If you already know a little German, you can use the book as a phrase book and reference. In addition to the forty lessons, there is a Summary of German Grammar, plus verb conjugations and a section on writing letters.

Also included in the course package is the *Living Language™ German Dictionary*. It contains more than 20,000 entries, with many of the definitions illustrated by phrases and idiomatic expressions. More than 1,000 of the most essential words are capitalized to make them easy to find. You can increase your vocabulary and range of expression just by browsing through the dictionary.

Practice your German as much as possible. Even if you can't manage a trip abroad, watching German movies, reading German magazines, eating at German restaurants, and talking with German-speaking friends are enjoyable ways to help reinforce what you have learned with *Living Language™ Conversational German*. Now, let's begin.

The following instructions will tell you what to do. *Viel Glück!* Good luck!

COURSE MATERIAL

1. Two 90-minute cassettes or three 60-minute compact discs.

2. *Living Language™ Conversational German* manual. This book is designed for use with the recorded lessons, but it may also be used alone as a reference. It contains the following sections:

   Basic German in 40 Lessons
   Summary of German Grammar
   Verb Conjugations
   Letter Writing

3. *Living Language™ German Dictionary*. The German / English–English / German dictionary contains more than 20,000 entries. Phrases and

idiomatic expressions illustrate many of the definitions. Over 1,000 of the most essential words are capitalized.

INSTRUCTIONS

1. Look at page 1. The words in **boldface** type are the ones you will hear on the recording.

2. Now read Lesson 1 all the way through. Note the points to listen for when you play the recording. The first word you will hear is **Albert.**

3. Start the recording, listen carefully, and say the words aloud in the pauses provided. Go through the lesson once and don't worry if you can't pronounce everything correctly the first time around. Try it again and keep repeating the lesson until you are comfortable with it. The more often you listen and repeat, the longer you will remember the material.

4. Now go on to the next lesson. If you take a break between lessons, it's always good to review the previous lesson before starting on a new one.

5. In the manual, there are two kinds of quizzes. With matching quizzes, you must select the English translation of the German sentence. The other type requires you to fill in the blanks with the correct German word chosen from the three given directly below the sentence. If you make any mistakes, reread the section.

6. Even after you have finished the forty lessons and achieved a perfect score on the Final Quiz,

keep practicing your German by listening to the recordings and speaking with German-speaking friends. For further study, try *Living Language Plus*® *German, Living Language In-Tense*™ *German Verb Practice,* and *Living Language Traveltalk*™ *German.*

LESSON 1

A. SOUNDS OF THE GERMAN LANGUAGE

Many German sounds are like English. Listen to and repeat the following German names, and notice which sounds are similar and which are different:

Albert	Gustav	Minna
Anton	Hans	Otto
Anna	Heinrich	Paul
Bernhard	Jakob	Paula
Emma	Josef	Richard
Erich	Katharina	Rudolf
Franz	Lotte	Stefan
Friedrich	Ludwig	Thomas
Georg	Martha	Wilhelm

NOTES

1. Each sound is pronounced clearly and distinctly; sounds are not slurred over as they often are in English.
2. Simple words have one stressed syllable, generally the first one.
3. The *Umlaut* (¨) is placed at times on the letters *a, o, u,* and changes their pronunciation. Contrast the following examples: *über*—over, *unter*—under.
4. All nouns are written with a capital letter.

B. COGNATES: WORDS SIMILAR IN ENGLISH AND GERMAN

Now listen to and repeat the following words which are similar in English and German. These words are called "cognates" and are descended from the same root. Notice how German spelling and pronunciation differ from English:

Adresse	address
Alkohol	alcohol
Amerikaner	American
Bank	bank
Bad	bath
Bett	bed
Bier	beer
Butter	butter
Charakter	character
Direktor	director
Doktor	doctor
Drama	drama
Ende	end
Export	export
Film	film
Garage	garage
Gas	gas
hier	here
Hotel	hotel
Hunger	hunger
Lampe	lamp
lang	long
Linie	line
Maschine	machine
Nation	nation

national	national
Oper	opera
Operette	operetta
Papier	paper
Person	person
parken	(to) park
Prinz	prince
Problem	problem
Publikum	public
Radio	radio
Restaurant	restaurant
Signal	signal
Station	station
Telefon	telephone
Tee	tea
Theater	theater
Tempel	temple
Triumph	triumph
Tunnel	tunnel
Wolf	wolf
Zone	zone

LESSON 2

A. Vowels

The following groups of words will give you some additional practice in spelling and pronunciation:

    1. The sound long *a* in the English "ah" or "father":

sagen	to say	**Laden**	shop
Datum	date	**Tafel**	board

2. The sound short *a* is similar to the English "o" in "hot:"

kann	can	**was?**	what?
Mann	man	**Pfanne**	pan

3. The sound long *ä* is similar to the English "ai" in "fair":

spät	late	**Währung**	currency
Erklärung	explanation	**Ernährung**	nutrition

4. The sound short *ä* is similar to the "e" in "bet":

Männer   men

5a. The sound long *e* is similar to the "ay" in "may":

geben	(to) give	**stehen**	(to) stand

b. The sounds *ee* and *eh* are also long, as in the "a" in "care":

mehr	more	**Heer**	army

6. Short *e* is similar to the "e" in "bent":

Adresse	address	**wetten**	to bet
Moment	moment	**rennen**	to run

7. The sound *e* at the end of a word is similar to "e" in "pocket":

beide	both	**Karte**	card
heute	today	**seine**	his

8. The sound long *i* is pronounced "ee" as in "see":

Miete	rent	**Liebe**	love
dienen	to serve	**Dieb**	thief

9. The sound short *i* is said like "i" as in "ship":

mit	with	**Witz**	joke
Sitte	custom	**mittags**	at noon

10. The sound long *o* is like the "o" in "lone":

oben	above	**Boden**	floor
Obst	fruit	**holen**	(to) fetch

11. The sound short *o* is similar to the "o" in "love":

oft	often	**Stoff**	material
kommen	(to) come	**Loch**	hole

12. The sound long *ö* is somewhat similar to the German "e" in "*geben*," and is pronounced by rounding the lips and saying long *e*:

König	king	**hören**	(to) hear
Löwe	lion	**böse**	angry

13. Short *ö* is said like a short *u* with rounded lips, as in "pup":

können	(to) be able to	**möchte**	would like
Töchter	daughters	**Röcke**	skirts

14. The sound long *u* is like the English "oo" in "noon":

Blume	flower	**Hut**	hat
Huhn	chicken	**gut**	good

15. The sound short *u* is similar to the "u" in "bush":

muss	has to	**bummeln**	(to) stroll
dumm	dumb	**Russland**	Russia

16. Long *ü* is said like "ee" as in "see," but with rounded lips:

über	over	**früher**	sooner
drüben	over there	**Frühstück**	breakfast

17. The sound short *ü* is pronounced by keeping the tongue in the same position as for short *i* but with rounded lips:

Stück	piece	**dünn**	thin
Brücke	bridge	**müssen**	(to) have to

18. The same sound is used to pronounce *y*:

typisch	typical	**Lyrik**	lyrics

B. DIPHTHONGS

1. The sounds *ai* and *ei* are pronounced almost like the "y" in "by," only with greater emphasis:

Mai	may	**Heimat**	homeland
Ei	egg		

2. The sound *au* is pronounced almost like the "ou" in "house":

Haus	house	**Baum**	tree
Maus	mouse	**Pflaume**	plum

3. The sounds *äu, eu,* are pronounced somewhat like the English *oy* in "boy":

Häuser	houses	**Leute**	people
träumen	(to) dream	**heute**	today

LESSON 3

A. CONSONANTS

1. *B* is generally pronounced like the English *b*:

Bett	bed	**Gabe**	gift

However, *b* at the end of a word is pronounced like *p* in the English word "trap."

Grab	tomb	**Trab**	trot

2. *C* before *e, i, ä, ö, y,* is pronounced like *ts*: however, this is a rather rare combination. Generally *z* precedes these letters.

   C before *a, o, u* is pronounced like *k*, but the letter *k* is generally substituted. These two pronunciations of the *c* occur mostly in foreign words:

Cäsar	Caesar	**Cato**	Cato

3. *D* is generally pronounced like the English *d*:

Datum	date	**Norden**	Nord

However, *d* at the end of a word is pronounced like *t* in the English word "but":

Bad	bath	**Hund**	dog

4. *F* is like the English *f*:

Fliege	fly	**Fluss**	river

5. *G* is generally pronounced as in the English word "garden"; as in the English "general" only in words of foreign origin:

Garten	garden	**Garage**	garage
General	general		

6. *H* is pronounced like the English *h* at the beginning of a word, or before an accented syllable.

hundert	hundred	**Geheimnis**	secret
Heimat	native country	**behalten**	keep

In other cases, it is not pronounced:

Schuh	shoe	**fröhlich**	merry

7. *J* is pronounced like the English *y* as in "York":

Jahr	year	**jemand**	someone

8. *K* is pronounced like the English *c* before *a, o, u* ("canal," "corn," "cut"):

Katze	cat	**Keller**	cellar
Kind	child	**Kunde**	customer

9. *L* is pronounced as in the English "land," "life," "million":

Land	land	**Leben**	life
Wolf	wolf		

10. *M* and *N* are pronounced as in English:

Meile	mile	**nur**	only
Maler	painter	**Neffe**	nephew

11a. *P* is pronounced like the English *p*:

Preis	price	**Papier**	paper

b. The cluster *pf* is pronounced as one sound and has no English equivalent:

Pfanne	pan	**Pferd**	horse
Pfennig	penny		

12. *Q*, always used in combination with *u*, is similar to the English *q*:

Quelle	spring	**Qualität**	quality

13. *R* is more rolled than in English and always strongly pronounced:

Rede	speech	**reine**	clean

14. *S* before a vowel is pronounced like the English *z* in "zoo":

süss	sweet	**Sahne**	cream

At the end of a word or a syllable, it is pronounced as in the English "son":

Maus	mouse	**Eis**	ice

15. *T* is pronounced as in the English "tea":

Tanz	dance	**Tasse**	cup

There is no sound equivalent to the English *th*. This combination is simply pronounced like *t*:

Theater	theater	**Thron**	throne

16. *V* is pronounced, except in a few cases, like the English *f* in "fair":

Vogel	bird	**Vater**	father

The exceptions are a few Latin roots:

Vase	vase	**Vulkan**	volcano

17. *W* is pronounced like the English *v* in "vain," never like the English *w* in "want":

Wein	wine	**Waffe**	weapon

18. *X* is pronounced as in English:

Axt	axe	**Hexe**	witch

19. *Z* is pronounced like the English combination *ts*:

Zahn	tooth	**Zauber**	magic

B. SPECIAL GERMAN SOUNDS

Practice the following sounds which have as equivalents in English:

1. The German combination *ch* has three different sounds:

   a) The sound as pronounced in the English "character":

Christ   Christian   **Charakter**   character
Chor   Chorus

When followed by an *s*, this combination has generally the sound of *ks*:

Fuchs   fox   **Wachs**   wax

   b) A sound near the English *h* in "hue":

China   China   **mich**   me
Kirche   church   **sicher**   certain

   c) A guttural sound which does not exist in English but can be only approximated to the Scotch "loch":

Ach!   ah!   **Dach**   roof
Bach   brook   **Buch**   book

2. When in final position, the combination -*ig* approximates the -*ch* sound as in the word *ich*:

ewig   eternal   **männlich**   manly
König   king   **persönlich**   personally

When the -*ig* sound is followed by -*lich* or -*e* it is pronounced like hard *g* or hard *k*:

wenigstens	at least	(pronounced like *k*)
richtige	correct	(pronounced like *g*)
königlich	royally	(pronounced like *g*)

3. Note the following combinations containing *s*:
   a) *sch*, equivalent to the English *sh* in "shoe":

Kirsche	cherry	**amerikanisch**	American
Schuh	shoe		

   b) *sp* or *st* at the beginning of a word, with the *s* sounded like *sh*:

stehen	(to) stand	**Spanien**	Spain
Stahl	steel	**Spiegel**	mirror

4. The combination *ng* is pronounced like the English *ng* in "sing"; the two letters are never pronounced separately:

bringen	(to) bring	**anfangen**	(to) begin

5. The combination *tz* is similar to the English *ts*:

Mütze	cap	**Blitz**	lightning

6. The combination -*er* occurring at the end of a word is similar to the English sound of "a" in "father":

kleiner	smaller	**Vater**	father
schöner	nicer	**Wetter**	weather

LESSON 4

A. THE GERMAN ALPHABET

LETTER	NAME	LETTER	NAME	LETTER	NAME
a	ah	j	yot	s	ess
b	beh	k	kah	t	teh
c	tseh	l	ell	u	oo
d	deh	m	em	v	fau
e	eh	n	en	w	veh
f	eff	o	oh	x	iks
g	gay	p	peh	y	üpsilonn
h	hah	q	ku	z	tsett
i	ee	r	err		

ä	(ah-Umlaut)
ö	(oh-Umlaut)
ü	(oo-Umlaut)

B. MORE ENGLISH-GERMAN COGNATES

Building up a German vocabulary is a rather easy matter since, as you have already seen, a great number of words are similar in German and English. Many are spelled almost the same, though they may differ considerably in pronunciation.

diagonal	diagonal	**Drama**	drama
Platz	place	**Material**	material
Land	land	**Süden**	South
Zentrum	center	**Park**	park

direkt	direct	**Juwelen**	jewels
Frucht	fruit	**Wolf**	wolf
original	original	**Priester**	priest
Problem	problem	**Datum**	date
Idee	idea	**Intelligenz**	intelligence
Leder	leather	**Automobil**	automobile
Sekunde	second	**Minute**	minute
Appetit	appetite	**Konversa-**	conversation
		tion	
Kapitel	chapter	**Instruktion**	instruction
Medizin	medicine	**General**	general
Norden	North	**spezial**	special
Westen	West	**Präsident**	president
Polizei	police	**Akt**	act
Revolution	revolution	**modern**	modern
Methode	method	**Klasse**	class
blond	blonde		

LESSON 5

A. General Spelling Equivalents

1. German *k*—English *c*:

Kanal	canal	**Respekt**	respect
Kolonie	colony	**Direktor**	director

2. German *-ik*—English *-ic (s)*:

Musik	music	**Politik**	politics
Physik	physics	**Lyrik**	lyrics

3. German -*ekt*—English -*ect*:

Effekt	effect	**Objekt**	object
Projekt	project	**Subjekt**	subject

4. German -*heit, -keit, -tät*—English ending -*ty*:

Freiheit	liberty	**Schwierigkeit**	difficulty
Schönheit	beauty	**Notwendigkeit**	necessity
Autorität	authority	**Qualität**	quality

5. German -*enz*—English -*ncy*:

Frequenz	frequency	**Tendenz**	tendency

6. German -*ie*—English -*y*:

Geographie	geography	**Industrie**	industry
Kopie	copy	**Philosophie**	philosophy

7. German -*tie*—English -*cy*:

Demokratie	democracy	**Diplomatie**	diplomacy

8. German -*ist*—English -*ist*:

Journalist	journalist	**Artist**	artist
Pianist	pianist		

9. German *sch*—English *sh*:

Schiff	ship	**Wäsche**	washing
Schuh	shoe	**Schilling**	shilling

10. German *-voll*—English *-ful*:

wundervoll wonderful **gedankenvoll** thoughtful

11. German *-los*—English *-less*:

herzlos heartless **geruchlos** odorless

12. German *-wärts*—English *-ward*:

westwärts westward **vorwärts** forward

LESSON 6

A. DAYS AND MONTHS

Montag	Monday
Dienstag	Tuesday
Mittwoch	Wednesday
Donnerstag	Thursday
Freitag	Friday
Samstag, or **Sonnabend**	Saturday
Sonntag	Sunday
Januar	January
Februar	February
März	March
April	April
Mai	May
Juni	June
Juli	July
August	August
September	September
Oktober	October
November	November
Dezember	December

B. NUMBERS 1–10

eins	one
zwei	two
drei	three
vier	four
fünf	five
sechs	six
sieben	seven
acht	eight
neun	nine
zehn	ten

C. COLORS

blau	blue
rot	red
gelb	yellow
grün	green
weiss	white
schwarz	black
braun	brown
grau	gray
rosa	pink

D. NORTH, SOUTH, EAST, WEST

Norden	North
Süden	South
Osten	East
Westen	West

QUIZ 1

Try matching the following two columns:

1. *Sonntag*	a. Thursday
2. *August*	b. brown
3. *Mittwoch*	c. ten
4. *grau*	d. Sunday
5. *Donnerstag*	e. red
6. *neun*	f. August
7. *braun*	g. Monday
8. *acht*	h. July
9. *Juli*	i. five
10. *gelb*	j. white
11. *rot*	k. gray
12. *Montag*	l. nine
13. *fünf*	m. Wednesday
14. *weiss*	n. yellow
15. *zehn*	o. eight

ANSWERS

1—d; 2—f; 3—m; 4—k; 5—a; 6—l; 7—b; 8—o;
9—h; 10—n; 11—e; 12—g; 13—i; 14—j; 15—c.

LESSON 7

A. GREETINGS

Guten Morgen!	Hello! Good morning.
Herr	Mr.
Herr Wagner	Mr. Wagner
Guten Morgen, Herr Wagner.	Good morning, Mr. Wagner.
Guten Tag.	Good afternoon (Good day).

Guten Abend.	Good evening.
Frau	Mrs.
Frau Wagner	Mrs. Wagner
Guten Abend, Frau Wagner.	Good evening, Mrs. Wagner.
Gute Nacht.	Good night.
Gute Nacht, Frau Wagner.	Good night, Mrs. Wagner.
Wie geht es Ihnen?	How are you? How do you do? ("How is it going with you?")
Wie geht's?[1]	How are you?
Wie geht es dir?	How are you? (*fam.*)
Wie geht es Ihnen, Frau Wagner?	How do you do, Mrs. Wagner?
sehr	very
gut	well
Sehr gut.	Very well.
Danke.	Thank you. Thanks.
Danke schön	Thank you.
Sehr gut, danke.	Very well, thanks.
Sprechen Sie!	Speak!
langsam	slowly
Sprechen Sie langsam!	Speak slowly!
Sprechen Sie langsam, bitte.	Speak slowly, please.
Wiederholen Sie!	Repeat!
Wiederholen Sie, bitte.	Please repeat.
danke	thanks
vielmals	much, a lot
Danke vielmals.	Thank you very much. Thanks a lot.

---

[1]*geht's* is a contraction of *geht es.*

Keine Ursache.	Not at all.
Ich danke Ihnen.	Thank you.
Ich danke Ihnen dafür.	Thank you for it.
Gern geschehen.	It was a pleasure.
Bis morgen.	Till tomorrow. See you tomorrow.
Bis Samstag.	Till Saturday. See you Saturday.
Bis Montag.	Till Monday. See you Monday.
Bis Donnerstag.	Till Thursday. See you Thursday.
Bis heute abend.	Till this evening. See you this evening.
Bis morgen abend.	Till tomorrow evening. See you tomorrow evening.
Bis nächste Woche.	Till next week. See you next week.
Bis später.	See you later.
Bis gleich.	See you in a little while.
Auf Wiedersehen.	Good-bye.

B. HOW'S THE WEATHER?

Wie ist das Wetter heute?	How's the weather today?
Es ist kalt.	It's cold.
Es ist heiß.	It's hot.
Es ist kühl.	It's cool.
Es ist warm.	It's warm.
Es ist windig.	It's windy.
Es ist sonnig.	It's sunny.
Es regnet.	It's raining.

Es schneit.	It's snowing.
Das ist ein Hundewet-	That's dog's (terrible)
ter!	weather!
Ein herrlicher Tag,	A lovely day, isn't it?
nicht wahr?	

QUIZ 2

1. *sehr gut*	a. speak . . .
2. *Guten Abend.*	b. how . . .
3. *Sprechen Sie . . .*	c. much, a lot
4. *Danke.*	d. See you tomorrow.
	(Till tomorrow.)
5. *wie . . .*	e. How are you?
6. *Bitte.*	f. very well
7. *viel*	g. It's raining.
8. *Bis morgen.*	h. Thank you.
9. *Wie geht es Ihnen?*	i. please
10. *Es regnet.*	j. Good evening.

ANSWERS
1—f; 2—j; 3—a; 4—h; 5—b; 6—i; 7—c; 8—d; 9—e;
10—g.

C. WORD STUDY

The Word Studies point out words which are almost
similar in German and English.

Form	form	*Liste*	list
Post	mail	*Gruppe*	group
reich	rich	*Sorte*	sort
Suppe	soup	*Kapitän*	captain
Operation	operation	*Admiral*	admiral
Note	note (musical)	*Orange*	orange

Diamant	diamond	*Ratte*	rat
Pilot	pilot	*Kamel*	camel
Pflanze	plant	*Pirat*	pirate
Sport	sport	*November*	November

LESSON 8

A. DO YOU HAVE ... ?

Haben Sie ... ?	Do you have ... ?
Wasser	water
Zigaretten	some (any) cigarettes
Feuer	a light
Streichhölzer	some matches
Schreibpapier	notepaper
Papier	paper
etwas zu trinken	something to drink
einen Stadtplan	a map of the city
noch Zimmer frei	any vacancies
einen Reiseführer	a guidebook

B. IN A RESTAURANT

das Frühstück	breakfast
das Mittagessen	lunch
das Abendessen	dinner, supper
Was wünschen Sie, mein Herr?	What will you have? (''What do you wish, sir?'')
Guten Tag, mein Herr. Was wünschen Sie?	Good afternoon. What would you like? (''Good day, sir. What do you wish?'')

Bringen Sie mir . . .	Give me . . .
Bringen Sie mir die Speisekarte, bitte.	Please bring me a menu.
Die Speisekarte, bitte.	The menu, please.
Ich möchte . . .	I'd like . . .
Brot	bread
Butter	butter
Suppe	soup
Fleisch	meat
Rindfleisch	beef
Eier	eggs
Gemüse	vegetables
Kartoffeln	potatoes
Salat	salad
Milch	milk
Wein	wine
Zucker	sugar
Salz	salt
Pfeffer	pepper

Bringen Sie mir . . .	Bring me . . .
einen Löffel	a spoon
einen Teelöffel	a teaspoon
eine Gabel	a fork
ein Messer	a knife
eine Serviette	a napkin
einen Teller	a plate
ein Glas	a glass

Ich möchte . . .	I'd like . . .
ein Glas Wasser	a glass of water
ein (Glas) Bier	a beer
eine Tasse Tee	a cup of tea
eine Tasse Kaffee	a cup of coffee
eine Flasche Wein	a bottle of wine

eine Flasche Mineral-wasser	a bottle of mineral water
eine Flasche Weiss-wein	a bottle of white wine
eine Flasche Rotwein	a bottle of red wine
noch ein Ei	another egg
ein wenig davon	a little of that
noch ein wenig davon	a little more of that
noch etwas Brot	some more bread
noch ein wenig Brot	a little more bread
noch etwas Fleisch	some more meat
noch ein wenig Fleisch	a little more meat
Die Rechnung, bitte.	The check, please.

QUIZ 3

1. *Fleisch*	a. Bring me ...
2. *Rotwein*	b. matches
3. *Haben Sie ... ?*	c. Give me ...
4. *Milch*	d. meat
5. *Butter*	e. some water
6. *Geben Sie mir ...*	f. a light
7. *Streichhölzer*	g. milk
8. *noch etwas Brot*	h. eggs
9. *Bringen Sie mir ...*	i. red wine
10. *Wasser*	j. The check, please
11. *Feuer*	k. Do you have ... ?
12. *einen Reiseführer*	l. Butter
13. *Eier*	m. a cup of coffee
14. *eine Tasse Kaffee*	n. some more bread
15. *Die Rechnung, bitte.*	o. a guidebook

ANSWERS

1—d; 2—i; 3—k; 4—g; 5—l; 6—c; 7—b; 8—n; 9—a;
10—e; 11—f; 12—o; 13—h; 14—m; 15—j.

LESSON 9

In German there are two kinds of verbs:

1. The weak (*schwache Zeitwörter*) or regular verbs.
2. The strong (*starke Zeitwörter*) or irregular verbs.

A. To Learn: *Lernen* (WEAK)

1. I learn.

ich lerne	I learn, I do learn, I'm learning
du lernst	you (*fam.*) learn, you do learn, you are learning
er (*sie, es*) **lernt**	he (she, it) learns, he does learn, he is learning
wir lernen	we learn, we do learn, we are learning
ihr lernt	you (*fam. pl.*) learn, you do learn, you are learning
Sie lernen	you (*polite*) learn, you do learn, you are learning
sie lernen	they learn, they do learn, they are learning

NOTES

a. Notice the verb endings:

ich	-e
du	-st
er (*sie, es*)	-t
wir	-en
ihr	-t
Sie, sie	-en

b. These forms, which make up the present-tense, translate English "I learn," "I'm learning," and "I do learn."

c. *du lernst* and *ihr lernt*

The singular and the plural of these forms are used when you address one or several close friends. These *du* and *ihr* forms are called "familiar" forms. Notice the capital S in *Sie*. It is used to address one or several persons you don't know very well (whom you would not call by first name in English.) This *Sie* form is called the "polite" or "formal" form used either in direct speech or writing. This distinction is indicated throughout the course by (*pol.*) and (*fam.*).

d. *Er lernt* means "he learns"; *sie lernt* means "she learns"; *es lernt* means "it learns"; *sie lernen* means "they learn" just as in English for all genders.

2. Learn!

Lerne!   Learn (the familiar form used to a person one knows well; compare *du lernst* above)

Lernt!	Learn (the familiar plural form; compare *ihr lernt* above)
Lernen Sie!	Learn! (the polite form; compare *Sie lernen* above)
Lerne nicht!	Don't learn! (*fam.*)
Lernt nicht!	Don't learn! (*fam. pl.*)
Lernen Sie nicht!	Don't learn! (*pol.*)

This form of the verb which is used in commands and requests is called "the imperative."

B. To Give: *Geben* (strong)

1. I give.

ich gebe	I give, I do give, I'm giving
du gibst	you (*fam.*) give, you do give; you're giving
er (*sie, es*) **gibt**	he (she, it) gives, he does give, he's giving
wir geben	we give, we do give, we're giving
ihr gebt	you (*fam. plu.*) give, you do give, you're giving
Sie geben	you (*pol.*) give, you do give, you're giving
sie geben	they give, they do give, they're giving

2. Give!

Gib!	Give! (*fam.*)
Gebt!	Give! (*fam. pl.*)
Geben Sie!	Give! (*pol.*)

Notice that in the case of the strong verb, the endings are the same as those of the weak verb, but the vowel of the stem changes in the second and third person singular. Some common vowel changes are *e* to *i*; *e* to *ie*; *a* to *ä*.

C. NEGATION

To negate a statement, add the word *nicht*:

sprechen	to speak (strong)
ich spreche	I speak, I do speak, I'm speaking
ich spreche nicht	I don't speak, I'm not speaking
du sprichst nicht	you (*fam. s.*) don't speak, aren't speaking
er (*sie, es*) **spricht nicht**	he (she, it) doesn't speak, isn't speaking
wir sprechen nicht	we do not speak, aren't speaking
ihr sprecht nicht	you (*fam. pl.*) don't speak, are not speaking
Sie sprechen nicht	you (*pol. s. and pl.*) aren't speaking, don't speak
sie sprechen nicht	they do not speak, are not speaking

D. ASKING A QUESTION I

1. To ask a question, invert the word order so that the verb comes before the subject pronoun:

Sie lernen.	You learn. You're learning.
Lernen Sie?	Do you learn? Are you learning?
Lerne ich?	Do I learn? Am I learning?
Lernst du?	Do you learn? Are you learning?
Lernt er?	Does he learn? Is he learning?
Lernt sie?	Does she learn? Is she learning?
Lernen wir?	Do we learn? Are we learning?
Lernt ihr?	Do you learn? Are you learning?
Lernen Sie?	Do you learn? Are you learning?
Lernen sie?	Do they learn? Are they learning?

2. To ask a question in the negative form, also reverse the word order and use the negative *nicht*.

Lerne ich nicht?	Don't I learn?
Lernst du nicht?	Don't you learn?
Lernt er nicht?	Doesn't he learn?
Lernt sie nicht?	Doesn't she learn?
Lernen wir nicht?	Don't we learn?
Lernt ihr nicht?	Don't you learn?
Lernen Sie nicht?	Don't you learn?
Lernen sie nicht?	Don't they learn?

REVIEW QUIZ 1

Choose the correct German word equivalent to the English.

1. Five—
   a. *sechs*
   b. *sieben*
   c. *fünf*

2. Eight—
   a. *acht*
   b. *neun*
   c. *vier*

3. Tuesday—
   a. *Mittwoch*
   b. *Dienstag*
   c. *Freitag*

4. Sunday—
   a. *Sonntag*
   b. *Samstag*
   c. *Montag*

5. March—
   a. *März*
   b. *September*
   c. *April*

6. June—
   a. *Juli*
   b. *Juni*
   c. *Mai*

7. Red—
   a. *blau*
   b. *orange*
   c. *rot*

8. Green—
   a. *gelb*
   b. *grün*
   c. *grau*

9. Black—
   a. *schwarz*
   b. *braun*
   c. *weiss*

10. Brown—
    a. *schwarz*
    b. *rot*
    c. *braun*

11. Good morning—
    a. *Guten Morgen*
    b. *Guten Abend*
    c. *Guten Nacht*

12. Very well—
    a. *Danke*
    b. *sehr gut*
    c. *viel*

13. Thank you—
    a. *schon gut*
    b. *Danke*
    c. *sehr schön*

14. Please—
    a. *Sprechen Sie!*
    b. *danke*
    c. *bitte*

15. Good-bye—
    a. *Bis morgen*
    b. *Auf Wieder-
       sehen*
    c. *Guten Tag*

16. He gives—
    a. *er gibt*
    b. *sie gibt*
    c. *sie geben*

17. We are learning—
    a. *wir lernen*
    b. *Sie geben*
    c. *wir geben*

18. I don't speak—
    a. *er spricht nicht*
    b. *ich gebe*
    c. *ich spreche
       nicht*

19. Do you give?—
    a. *Geben Sie?*
    b. *Gibt er?*
    c. *Gibt sie?*

20. Do I give?—
    a. *Geben Sie?*
    b. *Gebe ich?*
    c. *Gibt er?*

ANSWERS

1—c; 2—a; 3—b; 4—a; 5—a; 6—b; 7—c; 8—b; 9—a; 10—c; 11—a; 12—b; 13—b; 14—c; 15—b; 16—a; 17—a; 18—c; 19—a; 20—b.

E. WORD STUDY

Anekdote	anecdote	*Detektiv*	detective
Patient	patient	*Talent*	talent
Film	film	*Religion*	religion
Patriot	patriot	*Liste*	list
Dialekt	dialect	*Experiment*	experiment

LESSON 10

A. THE GERMAN DECLENSION

In German, articles, nouns, adjectives, and pronouns undergo some changes in their endings. This variation is called "declension." There are four case declensions: nominative, genitive, dative, and accusative.

1. The nominative case is used for the subject.

Das Buch ist hier.   The book is here.

2. The genitive case is used to denote possession, and after certain prepositions.

der Name des Lehrers (*masc.*)	the name of the teacher
die Farbe der Blume (*fem.*)	the color of the flower
während des Tages	during the day

3. The dative case is used for the indirect object after certain prepositions, and after certain verbs.

der Mann mit dem Stock	the man with the stick
Der Fisch springt aus dem Wasser.	The fish jumps out of the water.
Er gibt dem Mädchen eine Puppe.	He gives the girl a doll.
Wir helfen dem Mann.	We help the man.
Er dankt der Frau.	We thank the woman.

4. The accusative case is used for the direct object and after certain prepositions.

Sie hält die Feder.	She is holding the pen.
Er geht durch den Wald.	He walks (goes) through the forest.

B. THE ARTICLE

In German there are three genders, masculine, feminine, and neuter. As already mentioned, the articles are declined in the four cases already given.

1. The definite article is declined as follows:

	MASC.	FEM.	NEUTER
Nom.	*der*	*die*	*das*
Gen.	*des*	*der*	*des*
Dat.	*dem*	*der*	*dem*
Acc.	*den*	*die*	*das*

	PLURAL (ALL GENDERS)
Nom.	*die*
Gen.	*der*
Dat.	*den*
Acc.	*die*

2. The indefinite article is declined as follows:

	MASC.	FEM.	NEUTER
Nom.	*ein*	*eine*	*ein*
Gen.	*eines*	*einer*	*eines*
Dat.	*einem*	*einer*	*einem*
Acc.	*einen*	*eine*	*ein*

C. DECLENSION OF NOUNS

1. Note that the endings of nouns in the singular undergo no changes except for the addition of *s* or *es* in the genitive singular of all neuter and most masculine nouns.
2. In the plural, an *n* should be added to the dative of all three genders.

D. PLURAL OF NOUNS

Although many noun plurals are irregular and must be learned individually, here are some guidelines for the formation of plural nouns in German:

1. MASCULINE NOUNS

a. Most nouns of one syllable form their plurals by adding -e. Most masculine and all feminine plural nouns add an Umlaut to the stem vowel:

der Hut	die Hüte	hat
der Stuhl	die Stühle	chair
der Brief	die Briefe	letter
der Freund	die Freunde	friend
die Frucht	die Früchte	fruit

b. Some masculine nouns end in -er and may take an Umlaut over the stem vowel:

der Mann	die Männer	man
der Geist	die Geister	spirit

c. Some masculine nouns with more than one syllable form their plural by adding -e:

der Abend	die Abende	evening
der Sonntag	die Sonntage	Sunday

d. Some masculine nouns ending in -e form their plural by adding an -n or -en:

der Junge	die Jungen	boy
der Mensch	die Menschen	person
der Diplomat	die Diplomaten	diplomat

e. Masculine nouns ending in -el, -en, -er do not change their endings. Some take an Umlaut:

der Apfel	die Äpfel	apple
der Acker	die Acker	acre
der Lehrer	die Lehrer	teacher (*masc.*)
der Kuchen	die Kuchen	cake
der Ofen	die Öfen	oven

2. FEMININE NOUNS

a. Most feminine nouns form their plurals by adding *-n* or *-en*:

die Tür	die Türen	door
die Frage	die Fragen	question
die Zeitung	die Zeitungen	newspaper

b. Some add an *-e* or *-e* and an Umlaut on the last vowel:

| die Kenntnis | die Kenntnisse | knowledge |
| die Frucht | die Früchte | fruit |

c. Feminine nouns ending in *-in* form their plurals by adding *-innen*:

| die Ärztin | die Ärztinnen | doctor |
| die Schülerin | die Schülerinnen | student |

NOTE: Feminine nouns are easily recognizable since they may end in *-e, -in, -ung, -heit, -keit,* and *-is*.

| **die Seite** side/page | **die Sauberkeit** cleanliness |
| **die Freiheit** freedom | **die Übung** exercise |

3. NEUTER NOUNS

a. Some neuter nouns form their plural by adding *-er* and/or an Umlaut on the stem vowel:

das Bild	**die Bilder**	picture
das Licht	**die Lichter**	light
das Bad	**die Bäder**	bath
das Dorf	**die Dörfer**	village
das Haus	**die Häuser**	house

b. Some neuter nouns add -*e*:

das Heft	**die Hefte**	notebook
das Brot	**die Brote**	bread
das Jahr	**die Jahre**	year

c. Some neuter nouns ending in an -*e* form their plural by adding -*n*:

das Auge	**die Augen**	eye
das Ohr	**die Ohren**	ear

d. Neuter nouns ending in -*el, -er, -en, -chen, -lein* remain unchanged in the plural:

das Mädchen	**die Mädchen**	girl
das Büchlein	**die Büchlein**	little book
das Fünftel	**die Fünftel**	one fifth

e. Some nouns have only a plural form:

die Ferien   vacation   **die Leute**   people

4. SOME NOUNS TO LEARN

Singular	Plural	Meaning (sing.)
der Herr	*die Herren*	gentleman, sir
das Datum	*die Daten*	date
das Gebäude	*die Gebäude*	building
die Mutter	*die Mütter*	mother
das Kino	*die Kinos*	movie theater

das Büro	*die Büros*	office
der Bürgersteig	*die Bürgersteige*	sidewalk
die Antwort	*die Antwort*	answer
der Verkäufer	*die Verkäufer*	salesperson
die Stadt	*die Städte*	city
das Hemd	*die Hemden*	shirt
der Anzug	*die Anzüge*	suit
der Fahrstuhl	*die Fahrstühle*	elevator
die Anweisung	*die Anweisungen*	direction
der Verkehr	———	traffic

E. DECLENSION OF ADJECTIVES

1. a. The possessive adjectives and the word *kein* (not any) are declined like the indefinite article:

das Buch meines Bruders   my brother's book
Er hat keinen Hut.   He has no hat.

b. An adjective used predicatively is not declined:

Das Wasser ist warm.   The water is warm.

2. Adjectives may be declined in three ways:

a. Without article or pronoun.
In this case the adjective takes the same case ending as the definite article, except in the masculine and neuter genitive, where it takes *en* instead of *es*:

	MASC.	FEM.
Nom.	*roter Wein*	*rote Tinte*
Gen.	*roten Weines*	*roter Tinte*
Dat.	*rotem Wein*	*roter Tinte*
Acc.	*roten Wein*	*rote Tinte*

	NEUTER	PLURAL (ALL GENDERS)
Nom.	*rotes Gold*	*rote Weine*
Gen.	*roten Goldes*	*roter Weine*
Dat.	*rotem Gold*	*roten Weinen*
Acc.	*rotes Gold*	*rote Weine*

Du darfst mit roter Tinte nicht schreiben.	You aren't allowed to write with red ink.
Roten Wein trinken unsere Gäste nicht.	Our guests don't drink red wine.

b. With the definite article the adjective takes an *e* in the following five cases:

Nominative singular: masculine, feminine, and neuter.

Accusative singular: feminine and neuter.

en in all other cases.

	MASC.	FEM.
Nom.	*der rote Wein*	*die rote Tinte*
Gen.	*des roten Weines*	*der roten Tinte*
Dat.	*dem roten Wein*	*der roten Tinte*
Acc.	*den roten Wein*	*die rote Tinte*

	NEUTER	PLURAL (ALL GENDERS)
Nom.	*das rote Gold*	*die roten Weine*
Gen.	*des roten Goldes*	*der roten Weine*
Dat.	*dem roten Gold*	*den roten Weinen*
Acc.	*das rote Gold*	*die roten Weine*

Ich möchte den roten Wein.	I'd like the red wine.
Er kommt mit dem roten Heft an.	He arrives with the red notebook.

c. Since the indefinite article has no ending in the masculine and neuter nominative and in the neu-

ter accusative, in these cases the adjective takes
the ending of the definite article. In the nominative and accusative feminine, it takes an *e*; in
all other cases *en*.

	MASC.		FEM.
Nom.	*ein* **roter** *Wein*	*seine* **rote** *Tinte*
Gen.	*eines* **roten** *Weines*	*seiner* **roten** *Tinte*
Dat.	*einem* **roten** *Wein*	*seiner* **roten** *Tinte*
Acc.	*einen* **roten** *Wein*	*seine* **rote** *Tinte*

	NEUTER		PLURAL (ALL GENDERS)
Nom.	*kein* **rotes** *Gold*	*meine* **roten** *Weine*
Gen.	*keines* **roten** *Goldes*	*meiner* **roten** *Weine*
Dat.	*keinem* **roten** *Gold*	*meinen* **roten** *Weinen*
Acc.	*kein* **rotes** *Gold*	*meine* **roten** *Weine*

Ein roter Wein würde   A red wine would taste
  gut schmecken.   good.
Meine roten Weine sind   My red wines are the
  die feinsten.   finest.

F. COMPARATIVE AND SUPERLATIVE

1. The comparative and the superlative are formed
   as in English by adding *er* for the comparative
   and *st* (or *est*) for the superlative to the adjective. Some short adjectives also take an Umlaut
   (¨) on their vowel.

schlecht, schlechter, schlechtest   bad, worse, worst
alt, älter, ältest   old, older, oldest

2. "Than" is translated by *als*.
3. The superlative is declined.
4. There are a few adjectives which have an irreg-

ular comparative. Here are the most common ones:

gern	*lieber*	*der (die, das) liebste, am liebsten*	gladly, preferably, like the most
gut	*besser*	*der (die, das) beste, am besten*	good, better, best
gross	*grösser*	*der (die, das) grösste, am grössten*	big, bigger, biggest
hoch	*höher*	*der (die, das) höchste, am höchsten*	high, higher, highest
nah	*näher*	*der (die, das) nächste, am nächsten*	close, closer, closest
viel	*mehr*	*der (die, das) meiste, am meisten*	much, more, the most

5. Examples:

Das Mädchen ist kleiner als der Junge.

The girl is smaller than the boy.

London ist die grösste Stadt in Europa.

London is the largest city in Europe.

G. PREPOSITIONS

1. The following prepositions always take the genitive:

während	during
wegen	because of
statt, anstatt	instead of
trotz	despite

während des Krieges	during the war
wegen der Leute	because of the people
anstatt einer Feder	instead of a pen
trotz der Kälte	despite the cold

2. The following always govern the accusative:

durch	through, by
für	for
gegen	against, toward
ohne	without
um	round, about, at (time)

durch die Stadt	through the city
für den Mann	for the man
gegen den Krieg	against the war
ohne einen Lehrer	without a teacher
um den See	around the lake

3. The following always govern the dative:

aus	from, out of
ausser	except for
bei	at, by, near
mit	with
nach	after, to (place)
seit	since
von	of, by, from
zu	to, at
gegenüber	across from, facing

aus der Schule	out of, from school
ausser den Gästen	except for the guests
bei meinen Eltern	at my parents'
mit gutem Appetit	with a good appetite
nach dem Frühstück	after breakfast
seit einem Jahr	for (since) one year
von dem Hafen	from the port
zu den Freunden	to the friends
gegenüber der Post	across from the post office

The following take the accusative if they denote motion toward a place. In this case they are used in reply to the question, "*Wohin?*" (Where to?) But they also can take the dative if they denote rest (or motion) at a place. In this latter case they are used in reply to the question, "*Wo?*" (Where?)

an	at, to
auf	on, upon, in
hinter	behind
in	in, into, at
neben	beside, near
über	over, across
unter	under, among
vor	before, ago
zwischen	between

an die Ecke	to the corner
an der Ecke	at the corner
auf dem Land	in the countryside
hinter dem Hotel	behind the hotel
in dem Wasser	in the water
neben der Kirche	next to the church
über den Wolken	over the clouds
unter dem Dach	under the roof
vor dem Rathaus	before the town hall
zwischen den Schultern	between the shoulders

Some of the above prepositions may be contracted
with the definite article in the following way:

am	for	*an dem*
im	for	*in dem*
beim	for	*bei dem*
vom	for	*von dem*
zum	for	*zu dem*
zur	for	*zu der*
ins	for	*in das*
ans	for	*an das*

Examples:

Wo liegt Rom?	Where does Rome lie?
Rom liegt am Tiber.	Rome lies on the Tiber.
Wohin fahren Sie heute?	Where are you going today?
Ich fahre an den Strand.	I am going to the beach.
Wo steht die Lampe?	Where is the lamp standing?
Auf dem Tisch.	On the table.
Wohin gehen die Touristen?	Where are the tourists going?
Sie gehen auf das Schiff.	They are going to the ship.
Wo liegt der Garten?	Where is the garden located?
Hinter dem Haus.	Behind the house.
Wohin stellen Sie den Schirm?	Where are you putting the umbrella?
Hinter die Tür.	Behind the door.
Wo wohnt Herr Müller?	Where does Mr. Müller live?

Er wohnt in dieser Strasse.	He lives in this street.
Wohin gehen die Leute?	Where are the people going?
Sie gehen ins Kino.	They are going to the movies.
Wo fliegt das Flugzeug?	Where is the plane flying?
Es fliegt gerade über den Bergen.	It is now flying over the mountains.
Wohin laufen die Kinder?	Where are the children running?
Sie laufen über die Brücke.	They are running over the bridge.
Wo ist die Katze?	Where is the cat?
Unter dem Bett.	Under the bed.
Wohin legt er das Heft?	Where is he putting the notebook?
Er legt es unter das Lineal.	He is putting it under the ruler.
Wo ist der Brunnen?	Where is the fountain?
Vor dem Schloss.	In front of the castle.
Wohin tragen Sie den Koffer?	Where are you carrying the suitcase?
Vor das Hotel.	In front of the hotel.
Wo liegt Luxemburg?	Where is Luxemburg located?
Es liegt zwischen Deutschland und Frankreich.	It is located between Germany and France.
Wohin legen Sie den Bleistift?	Where are you putting the pencil?
Zwischen die Seiten des Buches.	Between the pages of the book.

LESSON 11

A. WHERE?

Verzeihung, mein Herr.	Excuse me, sir.
wo	where
ist	is
Wo ist es?	Where is it?
das Hotel	the hotel
Wo ist das Hotel?	Where is the hotel?
Wo ist das Restaurant?	Where is the restaurant?
Wo ist das Telefon?	Where is the telephone?
Könnten Sie mir sagen . . . ?	Could you tell me . . . ?
Können Sie mir sagen . . . ?	Can you tell me . . . ?
Können Sie mir sagen, wo das Telefon ist?	Can you tell me where the telephone is?
Können Sie mir sagen, wo der Bahnhof ist?	Can you tell me where the (railroad) station is?

B. HERE AND THERE

hier	here
dort	there
dort drüben	over there
Welche Richtung ist es?	Which way is it?

hier entlang	this way
dort entlang	that way
hier hinunter	down this way
in die/der Richtung	over that way
dort hinunter	in that direction
Das ist dort entlang.	It's over that way.
Es ist nicht hier.	It's not here.
Es ist nicht dort.	It's not there.
Es ist hier.	It's here.
Es ist nicht hier.	It's not here.
Es ist dort.	It's there.
Es ist dort drüben.	It's over there.
Es ist dort oben.	It's up there.
Er ist hier.	He's here.
Kommen Sie hier!	Come here.
Bleiben Sie hier!	Stay here.
Warten Sie dort.	Wait there.
Gehen Sie hier entlang!	Go this way.
Gehen Sie dort entlang.	Go that way.
Wer ist dort?	Who's there?
Legen Sie es hierhin!	Put it (over) here.
Legen Sie es dorthin!	Put it (over) there.

C. THERE

dort, da	there
Ist er in Paris?	Is he in Paris?
Ja, er ist dort.	Yes, he is (there).
Ist Paul da?	Is Paul there?
Ja, er ist da.	Yes, he's there.
Fährt er nach Frankfurt?	Is he going to Frankfurt?
Ja, er fährt dorthin.	Yes, he's going there.

Ich fahre dorthin.	I'm going there.
Ich will nicht dorthin fahren.	I don't want to go there.
Ich wohne dort.	I live there.

D. To the Right, Etc.

rechts	to the right
links	to the left
rechts von Ihnen	to your right
zu Ihrer linken	to your left
auf der linken Seite	on your left
Das ist rechts.	It's to the right.
Das ist links.	It's to the left.
Biegen Sie rechts ab.	Turn right.
Biegen Sie links ab.	Turn left.
Gehen Sie geradeaus.	Keep straight on.
Das ist geradeaus.	It's straight ahead.
Gehen Sie geradeaus.	Go straight ahead.
Es ist direkt gegenüber.	It's directly opposite.
Es ist weiter oben.	It's farther up.
Es ist weiter unten.	It's below (farther down).
Es ist an der Ecke.	It's on the corner.

E. Near and Far

nah	near
nah bei	near here
sehr nahe	very near; quite close
in der Nähe des Denkmals	near the monument
in der Nähe der Hauptstrasse	near the main street
in seiner Nähe	near him
Es ist sehr nah.	It's very near.

Es ist ganz in der Nähe.	It's very near here.
weit	far
Ist es weit bis dorthin?	Is it far to get there?
Es ist weit.	It's far.
Es ist nicht weit.	It's not far.
Das ist weit von hier.	That's far from here.

QUIZ 4

1. *Können Sie mir sagen, wo das Telefon ist?*
2. *Wo befindet sich das Hotel?*
3. *Das ist hier entlang.*
4. *Das ist geradeaus.*
5. *Das ist zur rechten.*
6. *Er wohnt dort.*
7. *Warten Sie dort!*
8. *Gehen Sie hier entlang!*
9. *Biegen Sie links ab!*
10. *Das ist direkt gegenüber!*
11. *Das ist nicht weit.*

a. It's this way.

b. It's to the right.

c. Turn left!

d. That's directly opposite.

e. It's straight ahead.

f. Can you tell me where the telephone is?

g. Where is the hotel? (Where is the hotel situated?)

h. He lives there.

i. That's not here.

j. Stay here.

k. Wait there!

12. *Legen Sie es dort-hin!*	l. Go this way!
13. *Das ist nicht hier.*	m. Who's there?
14. *Bleiben Sie hier!*	n. Put it there.
15. *Wer ist dort?*	o. It's not far.

ANSWERS
1—f; 2—g; 3—a; 4—e; 5—b; 6—h; 7—k; 8—l; 9—c;
10—d; 11—o; 12—n; 13—i; 14—j; 15—m

LESSON 12

A. TO BE OR NOT TO BE: *SEIN*

1. I am

ich bin	I am
du bist	you are
er ist	he is
sie ist	she is
es ist	it is
wir sind	we are
ihr seid	you are
Sie sind	you are
sie sind	they are

2. I am not

ich bin nicht	I am not
du bist nicht	you are not
er ist nicht	he is not

sie ist nicht	she is not
es ist nicht	it is not
wir sind nicht	we are not
ihr seid nicht	you are not
Sie sind nicht	you are not
sie sind nicht	they are not

3. Be!

Seien Sie!	Be!
Seien Sie ruhig!	Be quiet. Don't worry!

4. Am I?

Bin ich?	Am I?
Bist du?	Are you?
Ist er?	Is he?
Ist sie?	Is she?
Ist es?	Is it?
Sind wir?	Are we?
Seid ihr?	Are you?
Sind Sie?	Are you?
Sind sie?	Are they?

5. Where am I?

Wo bin ich?	Where am I?
Wo bist du?	Where are you?
Wo ist er?	Where is he?
Wo ist sie?	Where is she?
Wo ist es?	Where is it?
Wo sind wir?	Where are we?
Wo seid ihr?	Where are you?
Wo sind Sie?	Where are you?
Wo sind sie?	Where are they?

6. Study these examples:

Ich bin Amerikaner.	I'm (an) American.
Ich bin im Zimmer.	I'm in the room.
Ich bin im Hotel.	I'm at the hotel.
Er ist hier.	He's here.
Sie sind hier.	They're here.
Sie sind dort drüben.	They're over there.
Ich bin bereit.	I'm ready.
Sie ist bereit.	She's ready.
Sie sind bereit.	They're ready.

Sind Sie sicher, mein Herr?	Are you certain, sir?
Sind Sie sicher, meine Dame?	Are you certain, madam?
Sind Sie sicher, mein Fräulein?	Are you certain, miss?
Sind Sie sicher, meine Herren?	Are you certain, gentlemen?
Sind Sie sicher, meine Damen?	Are you certain, ladies?

Sind Sie Engländer?	Are you English?
Ja, ich bin Engländer.	Yes, I'm English.
Nein, ich bin nicht Engländer.	No, I'm not English.

Wie spät ist es?	What time is it?
Wo sind Sie her?	Where are you from?
Ich bin aus Berlin.	I'm from Berlin.

B. MY, YOUR, HIS, ETC.

The possessive adjectives are declined like the article *ein*.

MASCULINE/NEUTER

Wo ist mein Buch?	Where is my book?
Wo ist dein Buch?	Where is your (*fam.*) book?
Wo ist sein Buch?	Where is his book?
Wo ist ihr Buch?	Where is her book?
Wo ist Ihr Buch?	Where is your (*pol. sing.*) book?
Wo ist ihr Buch?	Where is their book?

FEMININE

Wo ist meine Feder?	Where is my pen?
Wo ist deine Feder?	Where is your (*fam.*) pen?
Wo ist seine Feder?	Where is his pen?
Wo ist ihre Feder?	Where is her pen?
Wo ist Ihre Feder?	Where is your (*pol. sing.*) pen?
Wo ist unsere Feder?	Where is our pen?
Wo ist eure Feder?	Where is your (*fam.*) pen?
Wo ist Ihre Feder?	Where is your (*pol. pl.*) pen?
Wo ist ihre Feder?	Where is their pen?

PLURAL

Wo sind meine Bücher?	Where are my books?
Wo sind deine Bücher?	Where are your (*fam.*) books?
Wo sind seine Bücher?	Where are his books?

Wo sind ihre Bücher?	Where are her books?
Wo sind Ihre Bücher?	Where are your (*pol. sing.*) books?
Wo sind unsere Bücher?	Where are our books?
Wo sind eure Bücher?	Where are your (*fam.*) books?
Wo sind Ihre Bücher?	Where are your (*pol. pl.*) books?
Wo sind ihre Bücher?	Where are their books?

Note that the endings of the plural of the personal pronouns remain the same regardless of the gender of the noun.

Wo sind meine Federn?	Where are my pens?
Wo sind deine Federn?	Where are your (*fam.*) pens?
Wo sind seine Federn?	Where are his pens?
Wo sind Ihre Federn?	Where are your (*pol. sing.*) pens?
Wo sind ihre Federn?	Where are her pens?
Wo sind unsere Federn?	Where are our pens?
Wo sind eure Federn?	Where are your (*fam.*) pens?
Wo sind Ihre Federn?	Where are your (*pol. pl.*) pens?
Wo sind ihre Federn?	Where are their pens?

QUIZ 5

1. *Wo sind Sie her?*		a. What time is it?
2. *Wie spät ist es?*		b. Where are you from?
3. *Er ist hier.*		c. Where is he?
4. *Ich bin bereit.*		d. Where is her letter?
5. *Sind Sie sicher?*		e. They are ready.
6. *Wo ist er?*		f. Where are their books?
7. *Wo ist ihr Brief?*		g. I'm ready.
8. *Wo sind ihre Bücher?*		h. I'm at the hotel.
9. *Sie sind bereit.*		i. Are you certain?
10. *Seien Sie ruhig!*		j. He's here.
11. *Ich bin im Hotel.*		k. I'm (an) American.
12. *Ich bin Amerikaner.*		l. Be quiet.
13. *Ich bin nicht bereit.*		m. I'm from Berlin.
14. *Wir sind hier.*		n. I'm not ready.
15. *Ich bin aus Berlin.*		o. We are here.

ANSWERS

1—b; 2—a; 3—j; 4—g; 5—i; 6—c; 7—d; 8—f; 9—e; 10—l; 11—h; 12—k; 13—n; 14—o; 15—m.

C. WORD STUDY: COGNATES

Instruktion (die)	instruction
energisch	energetic
Instrument (das)	instrument
Regiment (das)	regiment
Violine (die)	violin
Palast (der)	palace

Terrasse (die)	terrace
national	national
Sardine (die)	sardine
Skandal (der)	scandal

LESSON 13

A. IT IS, THAT IS

Es ist gut.	It's good.
Das ist gut.	That's good.
Das ist nicht gut.	It's not good.
Das ist in Ordnung.	It's (that's) all right. (It's in order.)
Das ist nicht in Ordnung.	It's not very good (nice). It's not right (fair).
Das ist schlecht.	It's bad.
Das ist nicht schlecht.	It's not bad.
Das ist klein.	It's small.
Das ist gross.	It's big.
Das ist nichts.	It's nothing.
Das ist schwer.	It's hard (difficult).
Das ist leicht.	It's easy.
Das ist sehr leicht.	It's very easy.
Das ist leicht genug.	It's easy enough.
Das ist leichter.	It's easier.
Das ist weniger schwer.	It's less difficult.
Das ist weit.	It's far.
Das ist nicht sehr weit.	It's not very far.

Das ist in der Nähe.	It's near here.
Das ist sehr in der Nähe.	It's very near here.
Das ist wenig.	It's (a) little.
Das ist zu wenig.	It's too little.
Das ist genug.	It's enough.
Das ist viel.	It's a lot.
Das ist dort.	It's there.
Das ist nicht dort.	It's not there.
Das ist hier entlang.	It's this way.
Das ist dort entlang.	It's that way.
Das ist für mich.	It's for me.
Das ist für dich.	It's for you (*fam.*).
Das ist für ihn.	It's for him.
Das ist für sie.	It's for her.
Das ist für Sie.	It's for you (*pol. sing. and pl.*).
Das ist für uns.	It's for us.
Das ist für euch.	It's for you (*fam. pl.*).
Das ist für sie.	It's for them.
Das ist nicht für sie.	It's not for them.
Das ist für die Kinder.	It's for the children.
Das ist es.	That's it.

B. ASKING A QUESTION II

1. In German, a question is usually formed by placing the verb before the subject:

| STATEMENT: | *Er geht heute ins Kino.* | He's going to the movies today. |

QUESTION: *Geht er heute*   Is he going to
                ins Kino?   the movies to-
                                       day?

2. A question may also be formed by leaving the
   word order the same as in a statement and adding a question mark. In this case, the intonation
   of the speaker rises and the question is intended
   to show surprise.

Er geht heute ins   He's going to the mov-
Kino?   ies today?

3. In German statements, the subject comes before
   the verb. Questions usually have "inverted
   word order" (the verb comes before the subject), as you learned earlier.

When question words (interrogatives) are used, the
verb remains in second position in the sentence and
precedes the subject:

Wer kommt um zehn   Who's coming at ten
  Uhr?   o'clock?
Wohin fährst du   Where are you travel-
  heute nachmittag?   ing to this afternoon?

4. More questions:

Ist es das?   Is it that? Is it this?
Das ist es?   That is it?
Das ist wahr.   It's true.
Das ist wahr?   Is it true?
Wo ist es?   Where is it?
Sind Sie bereit?   Are you ready?

Sind sie bereit?	Are they ready?
Kommen Sie?	Are you coming?
Haben Sie Zigaretten?	Do you have any cigarettes?
Haben Sie Feuer?	Do you have a light?
Sprechen Sie Englisch?	Do you speak English?
Sprechen Sie Deutsch?	Do you speak German?

C. WORD STUDY

Asien (das)	Asia	*Lektion (die)*	lesson
alt	old	*Nase (die)*	nose
Feld (das)	field	*Bär (der)*	bear
Alpen (die)	Alps	*Tiger (der)*	tiger
August (der)	August	*Elefant (der)*	elephant

LESSON 14

A. TO HAVE AND HAVE NOT: *HABEN*

1. I have

ich habe	I have
du hast	you have
er hat	he has
wir haben	we have
ihr habt	you have
Sie haben	you have
sie haben	they have

2. I don't have

ich habe nicht	I don't have, I haven't
du hast nicht	you don't have, etc.
er hat nicht	he doesn't have
wir haben nicht	we don't have
ihr habt nicht	you don't have
Sie haben nicht	you don't have
sie haben nicht	they don't have

3. Study these phrases:

Ich habe etwas.	I have something. I've got something.
Ich habe nichts.	I have nothing. I don't have anything. There's nothing wrong with me.
Ich habe Geld.	I have money.
Ich habe genug Geld.	I have enough money.
Ich habe kein Geld.	I have no money. I haven't any money.
Ich habe genug Zeit.	I have enough time.
Sie haben keine Zeit.	They don't have any time.
Ich habe Hunger.	I'm hungry.
Er hat Hunger.	He's hungry.
Ich habe Durst.	I'm thirsty.
Er hat recht.	He's right.
Er hat unrecht.	He's wrong.
Sie haben recht.	You're right.
Sie hat Angst.	She's afraid.
Ich habe Zahnschmerzen.	I have a toothache.
Sie hat Kopfschmerzen.	She has a headache.

4. Do I have?

habe ich?	do I have?
hast du?	do you have?
hat er?	does he have?
haben wir?	do we have?
habt ihr?	do you have?
haben Sie?	do you have (*pol.*)?
haben sie?	do they have?

5. Don't I have?

habe ich nicht?	don't I have? haven't I?
hast du nicht?	don't you have?
hat er nicht?	doesn't he have?
haben wir nicht?	don't we have?
habt ihr nicht?	don't you have?
haben Sie nicht?	don't you have?
haben sie nicht?	don't they have?

6. Now study these sentences:

Hat er Geld?	Does he have any money?
Hat sie genug Geld?	Does she have enough money?
Hat er Freunde in Berlin?	Does he have (any) friends in Berlin?
Haben Sie einen Bleistift?	Do you have a pencil?
Haben Sie einen Kugelschreiber?	Do you have a pen?
Haben Sie eine Briefmarke?	Do you have a stamp?
Haben Sie etwas Papier?	Do you have any paper?

Haben Sie Zigaretten?	Do you have any cigarettes?
Haben Sie Feuer?	Do you have a light?
Haben Sie ein Streich-holz?	Do you have a match?
Haben Sie einen Stadtplan?	Do you have a map of the city?
Was haben Sie?	What's the matter with you?
Was hat er?	What's the matter with him?
Haben Sie Zeit, mit mir zu sprechen?	Do you have time to talk to me?

B. THERE IS

Es gibt . . .	There is . . .
Es gibt etwas.	There is something.
Es gibt nichts hier.	There is nothing here.
Es gibt nichts mehr.	There isn't any more.
Es gibt nichts mehr davon.	There isn't any more of that.
Es gibt keine Ant-wort.	There is no answer.
Es gibt keinen Unter-schied.	There's no difference.
Es gibt keine Schwierigkeit.	There's no difficulty.
Niemand ist dort.	No one is there.
Niemand ist hier.	No one is here.
Sind Briefe für mich da?	Are there any letters for me?
Ist Post da?	Is there any mail?
Ist Post für mich da?	Is there any mail for me?

Sind viele Menschen da?	Are there many people?
Gibt es ein Telefon hier?	Is there a telephone here?
Gibt es ein Restaurant in der Nähe?	Is there a restaurant nearby?
Gibt es eine Apotheke hier in der Nähe?	Is there a druggist nearby?
Gibt es ein Cafe in der Nähe?	Is there a cafe nearby?
Hier sind vier Personen.	There are four people here.

C. AGO

vor	ago
vor einer Stunde	an hour ago
vor zwei Stunden	two hours ago
vor drei Stunden	three hours ago
vor einem Tag	a day ago
vor zwei Tagen	two days ago
vor drei Wochen	three weeks ago
vor fünf Monaten	five months ago
vor fünf Jahren	five years ago
vor zehn Jahren	ten years ago
vor langer Zeit	a long time ago
vor ziemlich langer Zeit	a pretty long time ago
vor nicht langer Zeit	not so long ago
vor kurzer Zeit	a short time ago

D. ALSO, TOO

auch	also, too
ich auch	I also (too)
du auch	you also (too)

er auch	he also (too)
sie auch	she also (too)
wir auch	we also (too)
ihr auch	you also (too)
Sie auch	you also (too)
sie auch	they also (too)
Er kommt auch.	He's coming, too.
Sie kommen auch.	They're coming, too.
Er tut es auch.	He's doing it, too.
Ich komme auch.	I'm coming, too.
Sie sind so gross wie die andern.	They're as tall as the others.
Sie sind nicht so klein wie die andern.	They're not as small as the others.
Das ist nicht so gut wie das andere.	That's not as good as the other.
Das ist nicht so gross wie das andere.	That's not as large as the other.
Kommen Sie so schnell wie möglich!	Come as quickly as you can.
Tun Sie es so schnell wie möglich!	Do it as soon as possible.
Machen Sie es so gut wie möglich!	Do it as well as possible.

QUIZ 6

1. *Ich habe genug Zeit.*
2. *Er hat recht.*
3. *Ich brauche das.*
4. *Er hat unrecht.*
5. *Ihm ist kalt.*

a. Not at all. Don't mention it.
b. There's no answer.
c. There's no difference.
d. There's no difficulty.
e. Are there any letters for me?

6. *Ich habe Hunger.*

    f. There's nobody here.

7. *Ich bin zwanzig Jahre alt.*

    g. A day ago.

8. *Ich habe Durst.*

    h. Three weeks ago.

9. *Wie alt sind Sie?*

    i. A long time ago.

10. *Hat er Geld?*

    j. Come as quickly as you can.

11. *Wieviel haben Sie davon?*

    k. I have nothing. (I don't have anything.) There's nothing wrong with me.

12. *Hat er Freunde in Paris?*

    l. I have enough time.

13. *Ich habe nichts.*

    m. I'm hungry.

14. *Sie haben recht.*

    n. I'm thirsty.

15. *Was hat er?*

    o. He's cold.

16. *Seit drei Wochen.*

    p. He's right.

17. *Es gibt keinen Unterschied.*

    q. He's wrong.

18. *Es gibt keine Schwierigkeit.*

    r. You're right.

19. *Keine Ursache.*

    s. I need that.

20. *Seit langer Zeit.*

    t. I'm twenty (years old).

21. *Niemand ist hier.*

    u. Does he have (any) money?

22. *Kommen Sie so schnell wie möglich.*

    v. Does he have (any) friends in Paris?

23. *Sind Briefe für mich da?*

    w. What's the matter with him?

24. *Seit einem Tag.*

    x. How old are you?

25. *Keine Antwort.*

    y. How many of them do you have?

ANSWERS
1—l; 2—p; 3—s; 4—q; 5—o; 6—m; 7—t; 8—n;
9—x; 10—u; 11—y; 12—v; 13—k; 14—r; 15—w;
16—h; 17—c; 18—d; 19—a; 20—i; 21—f; 22—j;
23—e; 24—g; 25—b.

LESSON 15

A. DO YOU SPEAK GERMAN?

Sprechen Sie Deutsch?	Do you speak German?
Nein, ich spreche nicht Deutsch.	No, I don't speak German.
Ich spreche nicht gut Deutsch.	I don't speak German very well.
schlecht	poorly
sehr schlecht	very poorly
Ich spreche sehr schlecht.	I speak very poorly.
ein wenig	a little
Ja, ich spreche ein wenig.	Yes, I speak a little.
sehr wenig	very little
Ich spreche sehr wenig.	I speak very little.
Ein paar Wörter.	A few words.
Nur ein paar Wörter.	Only a few words.
Verstehen Sie?	Do you understand?
Nein, ich verstehe nicht.	No, I don't understand.
Ich verstehe nicht sehr gut.	I don't understand very well.

Ich verstehe Deutsch nicht sehr gut.	I don't understand German very well.
Ja, ich verstehe.	Yes, I understand.
Ja, ich verstehe ein wenig.	Yes, I understand a little.
Ich lese, aber ich kann nicht sprechen.	I read but I can't speak.
Verstehen Sie?	Do you understand?
Überhaupt nicht.	Not at all.
Schreiben Sie es!	Write it (down).
Wie schreiben Sie es?	How do you write (spell) it?
Ich kenne dieses Wort nicht.	I don't know this word.

B. PLEASE SPEAK MORE SLOWLY

würden Sie	would you . . . ?
sprechen	(to) speak
etwas langsamer	more slowly ("somewhat slower")
Würden Sie etwas langsamer sprechen?	Would you speak more slowly?
Wenn Sie langsam sprechen, kann ich Sie verstehen.	If you speak slowly, I can understand you, *or,* If you speak slowly, I'll be able to understand you.
bitte	please
Würden Sie bitte etwas langsamer sprechen?	Would you mind speaking a little more slowly, please?
ich bitte Sie	please ("I beg you")

Ich bitte Sie, etwas langsamer zu sprechen.	Would you mind speaking a little more slowly, please?
Würden Sie das bitte wiederholen?	Would you please say that again? ("Would you repeat that, please?")
Bitte, sprechen Sie langsam!	Please speak slowly!
Bitte, sprechen Sie langsamer.	Please speak more slowly.

C. What Did You Say?

Was haben Sie gesagt?	What did you say? You were saying? What was that?
Wiederholen Sie, bitte.	Repeat, please.
Wie bitte, was haben Sie gesagt?	What did you say? ("How, please, what did you say?")
Wie sagen Sie das auf Deutsch?	How do you say that in German?
Wie sagt man "Thank you" auf Deutsch?	How do you say "Thank you" in German?
Was wollen Sie sagen?	What do you want to say?

D. Thanks

Danke.	Thanks.
Ich danke Ihnen.	Thanks. ("I thank you.")

Ich danke Ihnen vielmals.	Thank you very much.
Keine Ursache.	Don't mention it.
Danke schön.	Thanks.
Bitte schön.	Not at all. You're welcome.
Entschuldigen Sie, bitte.	Excuse me.
Bitte sehr.	Certainly.
Gestatten Sie?	May I? ("You permit me?")
Bitte sehr!	Of course! Please do!
Ich bitte Sie.	Please do! ("I beg you.")
Wie bitte?	Pardon? What did you say?
Verzeihung, was sagen Sie?	Sorry. What are you saying?
Auf Wiedersehen!	Good-bye. See you soon.
Auf baldiges Wiedersehen!	See you soon. See you later.
Bis heute abend.	See you this evening. ("Until this evening.")

QUIZ 7

1. *Schreiben Sie!*	a. No, I don't speak German.
2. *Nein, ich spreche nicht Deutsch.*	b. A few words.
3. *Ich verstehe Deutsch nicht gut.*	c. Do you understand?

4. *Verstehen Sie?*	d. I don't understand German very well.
5. *Ein paar Wörter.*	e. Write!
6. *Möchten (Könnten) Sie das bitte wiederholen?*	f. How do you write it?
7. *Wie sagt man "Thank you" auf deutsch?*	g. I don't know that word.
8. *Was wollen Sie sagen?*	h. How do you say "Thank you" in German?
9. *Wie schreiben Sie es?*	i. What do you mean? ("What do you want to say?")
10. *Ich kenne das Wort nicht.*	j. Would (Could) you please repeat that?

ANSWERS
1—e; 2—a; 3—d; 4—c; 5—b; 6—j; 7—h; 8—i; 9—f; 10—g.

E. WORD STUDY

Äquator (der)	equator
backen	(to) bake
Ballon (der)	balloon
Gras (das)	grass
Problem (das)	problem
weise	wise
Arm (der)	arm
Honig (der)	honey
Winter (der)	winter
Sommer (der)	summer

LESSON 16

A. This and That

The demonstrative adjectives *dieser, diese, dieses* follow the same declension as *der, die, das*:[1]

dieser Anzug	this or that suit
diese Nacht	this night
dieses Wochenende	this weekend
dieser Mann	this man
diese Frau	this woman
dieses Kind	this child

To express "that one" in contrast with "this," German simply uses *der (die, das)* with a special emphasis in the pronunciation.

Dieser Tisch ist breit und der ist schmal.
This table is wide and that one is narrow.

Diese Wand ist dick und die ist dünn.
This wall is thick and that one is thin.

Dieses Kleid ist lang und das ist kurz.
This dress is long and that one is short.

Dieser and *der* are interchangeable, so that you could also say:

Der Tisch ist breit und dieser ist schmal.
Dieser Hund ist gross und der ist klein.

---

[1] See page 296 for more on demonstrative adjectives and pronouns.

Diese Katze ist grau und die ist schwarz.
Das Bild ist gut und dieses ist schlecht.

Note that both *dieser* and *der* can mean either "this"
or "that," although the basic meaning of *dieser* is
"this."

QUIZ 8

1. *Ich bevorzuge diesen (Ich ziehe diesen vor).*
2. *Was bedeutet das?*
3. *Geben Sie mir das!*
4. *Dieses gehört mir und das gehört Ihnen.*
5. *Das hängt davon ab.*
6. *Das ist es nicht.*
7. *Wie geht's?*
8. *Das ist selbstverständlich.*
9. *Das ist mir gleich.*
10. *Dieses gehört mir.*

a. What does this mean?
b. This is mine (This one belongs to me).
c. That goes without saying.
d. It's not that.
e. This one belongs to me and that one belongs to
   you.
f. Give me that.
g. It's all the same to me.
h. That all depends.
i. How are you?
j. I prefer that one (masc.).

ANSWERS
1—j; 2—a; 3—f; 4—e; 5—h; 6—d; 7—i; 8—c; 9—g;
10—b.

B. NOT, NOT ANY

Das ist nicht gut.	That's not good.
Es ist nicht schlecht.	It's not bad.
Das ist es nicht.	That's not it.
Es ist nicht hier.	It's not here.
Das ist nicht zuviel.	Not too much.
Nicht zu schnell.	Not too fast.
Nicht viel.	Not much.
Nicht viele.	Not many.
Nicht genug.	Not enough.
Nicht oft.	Not often.
Noch nicht.	Not yet.
Überhaupt nicht.	Not at all.
Er fährt nicht zu schnell.	He's not driving too fast.
Wir haben nicht viele.	We don't have many.
Das ist nicht genug.	That's not enough.
Ich gehe nicht oft.	I don't go often.
Er ist noch nicht hier.	He's not here yet.
Das ist überhaupt nicht wahr.	That's not true at all.
Ich habe keine Zeit.	I haven't any time. I have no time.
Ich weiss nicht wie.	I don't know how.
Ich weiss nicht wo.	I don't know where.
Ich weiss überhaupt nichts.	I don't know anything. I know nothing at all.
Er hat nichts gesagt.	He didn't say (hasn't said) anything.

C. NOTHING, NEVER, ONLY, ETC.

Nichts.	Nothing.
Ich habe nichts.	I haven't anything.
Niemals, nie.	Never.
Ich sehe ihn nie.	I never see him.
Er kommt nie(*mals*).	He never comes.
Wer ist gekommen?— Niemand.	Who came?—Nobody.
Ich sehe niemand.	I don't see anyone.
Ich gehe nicht mehr dorthin.	I don't go there anymore.
Er kommt nicht mehr.	He doesn't come anymore.
Ich habe nur hundert Mark.	I have only a hundred marks.
Du hast nur eine Stunde.	You have only one hour.
Er hat nur zehn davon.	He has only ten of them.

D. ISN'T IT? AREN'T YOU? ETC.

Nicht wahr?	Isn't that so?
Das ist schön, nicht wahr?	It's nice, isn't it?
Sie kommen, nicht wahr?	You're coming, aren't you (right)?
Sie haben genug davon, nicht wahr?	You have enough of it, haven't you?
Sie haben keine, nicht wahr?	You haven't any, have you?
Sie sind damit einverstanden, nicht wahr?	You agree, don't you?

QUIZ 9

1. *Das ist es nicht.*	a. I don't see anyone.
2. *Ich weiss nicht wann.*	b. I have only a hundred marks.
3. *Ich habe keine Zeit.*	c. You have only one hour.
4. *Er sieht nichts.*	d. You're coming, aren't you?
5. *Sie kommen, nicht wahr?*	e. You haven't any of it, have you?
6. *Sie haben nur eine Stunde.*	f. That's not it.
7. *Ich sehe niemand.*	g. I don't have any time. I have no time.
8. *Ich habe nur hundert Mark.*	h. I don't know when.
9. *Sie haben keine davon, nicht wahr?*	i. He didn't say (hasn't said) anything.
10. *Er hat nichts gesagt.*	j. He sees nothing/ doesn't see anything

ANSWERS
1—f; 2—h; 3—g; 4—j; 5—d; 6—c; 7—a; 8—b; 9—e; 10—i.

E. WORD STUDY

Sympatie (die)	sympathy
illustrieren	illustrate
Gymnastik (die)	gymnastics
Kristall (das)	crystal

frieren	(to) freeze
packen	(to) pack
Gott (der)	God
Brust (die)	breast
Lokomotive (die)	locomotive

LESSON 17

A. IT'S ME (I), YOU, ETC. (SUBJECT PRONOUNS)

Ich bin es.	It's me (I).
Du bist es.	It's you (*fam.*).
Er ist es.	It's him (he).
Sie ist es.	It's her (she).
Wir sind es.	It's us (we).
Ihr seid es.	It's you (*fam.*).
Sie sind es.	It's you (*pol.*).
Sie sind es.	It's they.

B. IT'S MINE, YOURS, ETC. (POSSESSIVE PRONOUNS)

Es ist meiner (*meine, meines*).	It's mine.
Es ist deiner (*-e, -es*).	It's yours (*fam.*).
Es ist seiner (*-e, es*).	It's his.
Es ist ihr (*-er, -e, es*).	It's hers.
Es ist unser (*-er, -e, -es*).	It's ours.
Es ist euer (*-er, -e, -es*).	It's yours (*fam. pl.*).

Es ist Ihr (*-er, -e, -es*).   It's yours (*pol.*).
Es ist ihr (*-er, -e, es*).   It's theirs.

C. HE SPEAKS TO ME, YOU, ETC.

1. Declension of the personal pronoun.

SINGULAR

Nom:	ich	du	er	sie, Sie	es
Dat:	mir	dir	ihm	ihr	ihm
Acc:	mich	dich	ihn	sie, Sie	sie, sie

PLURAL

Nom:	wir	ihr	sie, Sie	sie
Dat:	uns	euch	Ihnen	ihnen
Acc:	uns	euch	sie, Sie	sie

Examples:

Ich gebe dir ein Buch.	I give you a book.
Er spricht mit mir.	He is speaking to me.
Sie liebt mich.	She loves me.
Du sprichst mit ihm.	You are speaking with him.
Er hat dich gern.	He likes you.
Wir geben ihr Blumen.	We are giving her flowers.
Wir haben sie gesprochen.	We have spoken to her.
Ihr habt es ihm gegeben.	You have given it to him.
Er gibt Ihnen eine Feder.	He is giving you (*pol.*) a pen.
Sie haben ihnen Geld gegeben.	They have given them money.

Ich habe euch etwas gegeben.	I have given you (*fam. pl.*) something.
Er hat uns nicht sprechen lassen.	He did not let us speak.

2. Study these phrases:

Er spricht mit mir.	He speaks to me.
Er spricht mit dir.	He speaks to you (*fam. sing.*).
Er spricht mit ihm.	He speaks to him.
Er spricht mit uns.	He speaks to us.
Er spricht mit euch.	He speaks to you (*fam.*).
Er spricht mit Ihnen.	He speaks to you (*pol.*).
Er spricht mit ihnen.	He speaks to them.

D. I'M TALKING ABOUT YOU, ETC.

Ich spreche von dir.	I'm talking about you (*fam.*).
Du sprichst von mir.	You're talking about me.
Er spricht von ihm.	He's talking about him.
Sie spricht von ihm.	She's talking about him.
Man spricht von ihr.	People (They) are talking about her.
Wir sprechen von Ihnen.	We're talking about you (*pol.*).
Sie sprechen von uns.	You're talking about us.
Sie sprechen von ihnen.	They're talking about them.

E. I'm Thinking of You, Etc.

Ich denke an dich.	I think of you.
Ich denke an ihn.	I think of him.
Du denkst an sie.	You're thinking of her.
Er denkt an uns.	He is thinking of us.
Wir denken an Sie.	We're thinking of you (*pol.*).

F. He Gives It to Me, You, Etc.

Er gibt es mir.	He gives it to me.
Er gibt es dir.	He gives it to you (*fam.*).
Er gibt es ihm.	He gives it to him.
Er gibt es uns.	He gives it to us.
Er gibt es Ihnen.	He gives it to you (*pol.*).
Er gibt es ihnen.	He gives it to them.

G. Give It to Me, Etc.

Geben Sie es mir!	Give it to me.
Geben Sie es ihm!	Give it to him.
Geben Sie es uns!	Give it to us.
Geben Sie es ihnen!	Give it to them.
Geben Sie das!	Give it! Give this one (that one)!
Geben Sie das mir!	Give it to me.
Geben Sie das ihm!	Give it to him.
Geben Sie das uns!	Give it to us.
Geben Sie das ihnen!	Give it to them.

H. MYSELF, YOURSELF, ETC. (REFLEXIVE PRONOUNS)

Ich wasche mich.	I wash myself.
Du wäschst dich.	You wash yourself.
Er wäscht sich.	He washes himself.
Sie wäscht sich.	She washes herself.
Wir waschen uns.	We wash ourselves.
Ihr wascht euch.	You wash yourselves.
Sie waschen sich.	You wash yourselves.
Sie waschen sich.	They wash themselves.

Notice that myself, yourself, etc., is *mich, dich*, etc. Verbs that take *mich, dich*, etc., are called reflexive verbs. A number of verbs that do not take "myself, yourself," etc., in English, do so in German:

Ich setze mich.	I sit down.
Ich unterhalte mich.	I'm having a conversation.
Ich erinnere mich.	I remember.
Ich freue mich.	I rejoice/I'm glad.
Ich irre mich.	I am mistaken.
Ich langweile mich.	I'm bored.
Ich amüsiere mich.	I'm having a good time/fun.
Ich rasiere mich.	I'm shaving (myself).
Ich ziehe mich an.	I'm getting dressed.

QUIZ 10

1. *Geben Sie ihr das!*　　a. I'm glad to see you again.
2. *Er spricht von ihm.*　　b. I bought myself a hat.

3. *Sie sprechen von ihnen.*

   c. My friends and your friends are having fun.

4. *Er gibt es ihnen.*

   d. He washes himself.

5. *Meine Freunde und Ihre Freunde amüsieren sich.*

   e. I remember.

6. *Ich unterhalte mich.*

   f. He gives it to them.

7. *Ich erinnere mich an sie.*

   g. I'm having a conversation.

8. *Ich habe mir einen Hut gekauft.*

   h. He's talking about him.

9. *Er wäscht sich.*

   i. Give it to her.

10. *Ich freue mich, Sie wiederzusehen.*

    j. They're talking about them.

ANSWERS

1—i; 2—h; 3—j; 4—f; 5—c; 6—g; 7—e; 8—b; 9—d; 10—a.

LESSON 18

A.   HELLO, HOW ARE YOU?

Guten Tag.
Hello. Good afternoon.

Guten Morgen.
Good morning.

Guten Tag, Herr Müller.
Hello, Mr. Müller. Good afternoon, Mr. Müller.

Wie geht es Ihnen?
How are you? How do you do? ("How is it going
with you?")

Danke, gut. Danke, sehr gut.
Very well, thanks.

Nicht besonders.
So, so.

Und Ihnen? (Und wie geht es Ihnen?)
And you? ("And how are you?")

Nicht schlecht.
Not bad.

Nicht schlecht, danke.
Not bad, thanks.

Danke, es geht.
All right, thank you. Fine. ("Thanks, it goes.")

Danke, es geht mir gut.
I am doing fine, thank you. ("Thanks, it goes well
with me.")

B. I'D LIKE YOU TO MEET ...

Ich möchte Sie Frau Müller vorstellen.
I'd like to introduce you to Mrs. Müller.

**Gestatten Sie, dass ich Ihnen Frau Müller vor-
stelle.**
Allow me to present ("to you") Mrs. Müller.

**Gestatten Sie, dass ich Ihnen Herrn Müller vor-
stelle.**
Allow me to present ("to you") Mr. Müller.

Sehr erfreut.
Glad to know you. Glad to meet you. ("Very
pleased.")

Es freut mich.
Glad to meet you.

Sehr erfreut, Sie kennenzulernen.
Glad to meet you ("to make your acquaintance").

Es freut mich, Sie kennenzulernen, gnädige Frau.
Glad to meet you ("gracious lady").

Das ist Herr Müller.
This is Mr. Müller.

Sehr angenehm, Herr Müller.
Glad to know you, Mr. Müller. ("Very agreeable, Mr.
Müller.")

Gleichfalls.
Same here (I'm also glad to meet you).

C.   How Are Things?

Guten Tag.	Hello!
Wie geht's?	How are you? How are things? ("How goes it.")
Es geht gut, danke.	Fine, thanks.
Was gibt es Neues?	What's new?

Nicht viel.	Nothing much.
Rufen Sie mich an!	Phone me!
Vergessen Sie es nicht!	Don't forget.
Ich werde es bestimmt tun.	I'll certainly do so.
Sicher?	You're sure? ("Surely?")
Ganz bestimmt.	Sure! ("Quite certain.")
Bis später.	See you later.
Bis zum nächsten Mal.	Till next time.
Bis gleich.	See you soon. See you in a little while.
Bis Montag.	Till Monday. See you Monday.
Bis morgen.	Till tomorrow. See you tomorrow.
Ich sehe Sie in einer Woche.	I'll see you in a week.
Ich sehe Sie in zwei Wochen.	I'll see you in two weeks.
Ich sehe Sie Freitag abend.	I'll see you Friday evening.
Ich sehe Sie nächsten Donnerstag.	I'll see you next Thursday.
Ich sehe Sie nächsten Donnerstag um acht Uhr abends.	I'll see you next Thursday at eight o'clock (in the evening).
Wir sehen uns heute abend.	We'll see each other this evening (tonight).
Wir treffen uns heute abend.	We'll see each other tonight.

QUIZ 11

1. *Wie geht's?*	a. How are you? How do you do?
2. *Bis morgen.*	b. Very well, thanks.
3. *Sehr erfreut.*	c. Not too bad. ("Not bad.")
4. *Was gibt es Neues?*	d. How are you?
5. *Nun, was gibt es Neues?*	e. Until tomorrow.
6. *Es geht mir gut, danke.*	f. I'm happy to know you.
7. *Nichts Neues.*	g. What's new?
8. *Guten Tag.*	h. Well, what's new?
9. *Nicht schlecht.*	i. Good afternoon. Hello.
10. *Wie geht es Ihnen?*	j. Nothing much. ("Nothing new.")
11. *Bis gleich.*	k. Allow me . . .
12. *Rufen Sie mich!*	l. Phone me!
13. *Bis zum nächsten Mal.*	m. See you Monday. ("Until Monday.")
14. *Gestatten Sie mir . . .*	n. Until the next time.
15. *Bis Montag.*	o. See you soon. See you in a little while.

ANSWERS

1—d; 2—e; 3—f; 4—g; 5—h; 6—b; 7—j; 8—i; 9—c; 10—a; 11—o; 12—l; 13—n; 14—k; 15—m.

D. WORD STUDY

Maus (die)	mouse	*Freund (der)*	friend
Garten (der)	garden	*Busch (der)*	bush

Mann (der)	man	*Fuchs (der)*	fox
Sohn (der)	son	*Fisch (der)*	fish
jung	young	*bringen*	bring

LESSON 19

A. HAVE YOU TWO MET?

Kennen Sie meinen Freund?	Do you know my friend?
Nein, ich glaube nicht.	No, I don't think (believe) so.
Nein, ich habe nicht das Vergnügen.	No, I haven't had the pleasure.
Ich glaube, Sie kennen sich schon?	I believe you already know each other.
Ja, wir haben uns schon kennengelernt.	Yes, we've already met.
Nein, ich glaube nicht, dass wir uns schon kennen gelernt haben.	No, I don't believe we've met before.
Ich hatte bereits das Vergnügen ...	I've already had the pleasure ... (of meeting him)

B. Glad to Have Met You

Ich freue mich, Ihre Bekanntschaft gemacht zu haben.
Glad to have met you.

Ich hoffe, Sie bald wiederzusehen.
Hope to see you soon.

Ganz meinerseits.
The same here.

Lassen Sie uns in den nächsten Tagen wieder zusammenkommen!
Let's get together again one of these days!

Abgemacht!
Fine. ("Agreed.")

Haben Sie meine Adresse und Telefonnummer?
Do you have my address and telephone number?

Nein, geben Sie sie mir!
No, let me have them. ("Give them to me.")

Meine Adresse ist Grosse Friedrichstrasse Nr. 21 (einundzwanzig).
My address is 21 Grosse Friedrichstrasse.

Meine Telefonnummer ist sieben einundachtzig zwölf.
My telephone number is 78112.

Geben Sie mir bitte auch Ihre Geschäftsadresse!
Give me your business address, too, please.

**Ich schreibe es Ihnen auf. Das ist Kurfürstendamm
einhundertzwei.**
I'll write it for you. It's 102 Kurfürstendamm.

**Sie können mich zu Hause vor neun Uhr morgens
erreichen.**
You can get me at home before nine in the morning.

Andernfalls im Büro ab zehn Uhr.
Otherwise ("in the other case") at the office from
10:00 A.M.

Gut, ich werde es nicht versäumen.
Good, I'll do that. ("Good, I won't fail to do so.")

**Auf Wiedersehen und vergessen Sie nicht anzu-
rufen!**
Good-bye, and don't forget to give me a ring.

**Nein, ich werde es nicht vergessen. Auf baldiges
Wiedersehen!**
No, I won't forget.

Auf bald.
See you soon.

QUIZ 12

1. *Nein, ich glaube nicht.*
2. *Ja, wir haben uns schon kennengelernt.*
3. *Nein, geben Sie sie mir!*
4. *Geben Sie mir auch ihre Geschäftsadresse!*
5. *Auf bald.*
6. *Gut, ich werde es nicht versäumen.*
7. *Haben Sie meine Adresse und meine Telefonnummer?*
8. *Nein, ich habe nicht das Vergnügen.*
9. *Ich hoffe, Sie bald wiederzusehen.*

10. *Ich freue mich, Ihre Bekanntschaft gemacht zu haben.*

a. Yes, we've already met.
b. No, I don't have the pleasure.
c. No, I don't think (believe) so.
d. Glad to have met you.
e. I hope to see you soon.
f. Give me your business address too.
g. No, let me have them. ("Give them to me.")
h. Do you have my address and telephone number?
i. Good, I'll do that. ("Good, I won't fail to do so.")
j. See you soon.

ANSWERS
1—c; 2—a; 3—g; 4—f; 5—j; 6—i; 7—h; 8—b; 9—e;
10—d.

REVIEW QUIZ 2

1. *Würden Sie etwas langsamer _____ (speak), bitte.*
   a. *sagen*
   b. *sprechen*
   c. *wiederholen*

2. *Sprechen Sie _____ (slowly), bitte.*
   a. *schnell*
   b. *weniger*
   c. *langsam*

3. *Ich gebe dem Kind _____ (the) Buch.*
   a. *ein*
   b. *das*
   c. *die*

4. *Er gibt seiner Frau _____ (a) Brief.*
   a. *einen*

    b. *die*
    c. *der*

5. *Das ist nicht sehr* _____ (far).
    a. *weit*
    b. *hier*
    c. *dort*

6. *Er gibt* _____ (to the) *Kindern Spielzeuge* (toys).
    a. *die*
    b. *den*
    c. *ich*

7. *Ich* _____ (am) *in dem Zimmer.*
    a. *bist*
    b. *bin*
    c. *nicht*

8. *Er kommt nicht* _____ (late).
    a. *bin*
    b. *bald*
    c. *spät*

9. *Wo* _____ (are) *Ihre Bücher?*
    a. *seine*
    b. *sind*
    c. *ist*

10. _____ (Bring) *Sie mir ein Glas!*
    a. *Möchte*
    b. *Geben*
    c. *Bringen*

11. *Das ist* _____ (less) *schwer.*
    a. *weniger*
    b. *mehr*
    c. *nichts*

12. *Das ist* _____ (for) *die Kinder.*
   a. *ihr*
   b. *für*
   c. *durch*

13. *Ich* _____ (have) *kein Geld.*
   a. *habe*
   b. *haben*
   c. *nichts*

14. _____ (Have) *Sie Zigaretten?*
   a. *Hat*
   b. *Hast*
   c. *Haben*

15. *Ich* _____ (understand) *nicht gut Deutsch.*
   a. *verstehe*
   b. *spreche*
   c. *bitte*

16. *Ich* _____ (thank) *Ihnen vielmals.*
   a. *langsam*
   b. *danke*
   c. *verstehe*

17. *Ist er* _____ (here)?
   a. *wo*
   b. *dass*
   c. *hier*

18. *Sind sie* _____ (ready)?
   a. *wahr*
   b. *bereit*
   c. *spät*

19. *Ist das* _____ (true)?
   a. *langsam*
   b. *wahr*
   c. *dort*

20. *Ich verstehe ein* _____ (little).
   a. *nur*
   b. *sehr*
   c. *wenig*

ANSWERS
1—b; 2—c; 3—b; 4—a; 5—a; 6—b; 7—b; 8—c;
9—b; 10—c; 11—a; 12—b; 13—a; 14—c; 15—a;
16—b; 17—c; 18—b; 19—b; 20—c.

C. WORD STUDY

Mond (der)	moon	*Wetter (das)*	weather
Punkt (der)	point	*Erde (die)*	earth
Onkel (der)	uncle	*Familie (die)*	family
Afrika (das)	Africa	*Kohle (die)*	coal
Ball (der)	ball		

LESSON 20

A. NUMBERS[1]

1. One, Two, Three, etc.

eins   one
zwei   two

---

[1] In Germany, as elsewhere in Europe, numerical punctuation is different than in English. The use of commas and decimal points is reversed, so that 1,000 English style becomes 1.000, and 6.5 is written 6,5 (*sechs* comma *fünf*) in German.

drei	three
vier	four
fünf	five
sechs	six
sieben	seven
acht	eight
neun	nine
zehn	ten
elf	eleven
zwölf	twelve
dreizehn	thirteen
vierzehn	fourteen
fünfzehn	fifteen
sechzehn	sixteen
siebzehn	seventeen
achtzehn	eighteen
neunzehn	nineteen
zwanzig	twenty
einundzwanzig	twenty-one
zweiundzwanzig	twenty-two
dreiundzwanzig	twenty-three
dreissig	thirty
einunddreissig	thrity-one
zweiunddreissig	thirty-two
dreiunddreissig	thirty-three
vierzig	forty
einundvierzig	forty-one
zweiundvierzig	forty-two
dreiundvierzig	forty-three
fünfzig	fifty
einundfünfzig	fifty-one

zweiundfünfzig	fifty-two
dreiundfünfzig	fifty-three
sechzig	sixty
einundsechzig	sixty-one
zweiundsechzig	sixty-two
dreiundsechzig	sixty-three
siebzig	seventy
einundsiebzig	seventy-one
zweiundsiebzig	seventy-two
dreiundsiebzig	seventy-three
achtzig	eighty
einundachtzig	eighty-one
zweiundachtzig	eighty-two
dreiundachtzig	eighty-three
neunzig	ninety
einundneunzig	ninety-one
zweiundneunzig	ninety-two
dreiundneunzig	ninety-three

2. One Hundred, One Thousand, etc.

hundert	hundred
hunderteins	hundred and one
hundertzwei	hundred and two
hundertdrei	hundred and three
hundertzwanzig	hundred and twenty
hundert-zweiundzwanzig	hundred and twenty-two
hundertdreissig	hundred and thirty
hundertvierzig	hundred and forty
hundertfünfzig	hundred and fifty
hunderteinundsiebzig	hundred and seventy-one

hundertachtund-siebzig	hundred and seventy-eight
hundertachtund-neunzig	hundred and ninety-eight
hundertneunund-neunzig	hundred and ninety-nine
zweihundert	two hundred
dreihun-dertvierundzwanzig	three hundred and twenty-four
achthundertfünfund-siebzig	eight hundred and seventy-five
tausend	thousand
tausendeins	thousand and one
tausendzwei	thousand and two
tausenddrei	thousand and three
zehntausenddreihun-dertfünfundsiebzig	ten thousand three hundred and seventy-five
eine Million	one million
eine Milliarde	one billion
eine Billion	one trillion

B. MORE NUMBERS

The numbers are declined as adjectives according to the determiners that precede them. The endings depend on the case they govern. For example:

Ich sehe den dritten Bus. (Acc., Masc., Sing.)	I see the third bus.
Er kauft sich ein drittes hemd. (Acc., Neut., Sing.)	He buys himself a shirt.

1. erster, erste, erstes	first
2. zweiter (-e, -es)	second
3. dritter (-e, -es)	third

4. vierter (-e, -es)	fourth
5. fünfter (-e, -es)	fifth
6. sechster (-e, -es)	sixth
7. siebenter (-e, -es)	seventh
8. achter (-e, -es)	eighth
9. neunter (-e, -es)	ninth
10. zehnter (-e, -es)	tenth

das erste Buch	the first book
die erste Sache	the first thing
der zweite Akt	the second act
die dritte Klasse	the third class
die vierte Etage	the fourth floor
der fünfte Mann	the fifth man
der sechste Tag	the sixth day
die siebente Woche	the seventh week
der achte Monat	the eighth month
das neunte Jahr	the ninth year
der zehnte Brief	the tenth letter
die elfte Person	the eleventh person
das zwölfte Kapitel	the twelfth chapter
der dreizehnte Gast	the thirteenth guest
das vierzehnte Paket	the fourteenth package
die fünfzehnte Tür	the fifteenth door
das sechzehnte Schiff	the sixteenth boat
die siebzehnte Strasse	the seventeenth street
die achtzehnte Ausgabe	the eighteenth edition
das neunzehnte Auto	the nineteenth car
das zwanzigste Haus	the twentieth house
der einundzwanzigste Januar	the twenty-first of January

QUIZ 13

1. *sechs Kilometer*	a. third class
2. *zwei junge Mädchen*	b. the eighth month

3. *zwanzig Minuten*	c. the ninth year
4. *dritter Klasse*	d. six kilometers
5. *neunzehnter*	e. two young girls
6. *die elfte Person*	f. twenty minutes
7. *siebzehnter Stock*	g. the eleventh person
8. *der achte Monat*	h. thirteenth of August
9. *dreizehnter August*	i. seventeenth floor
10. *das neunte Jahr*	j. nineteenth

ANSWERS
1—d; 2—e; 3—f; 4—a; 5—j; 6—g; 7—i; 8—b; 9—h;
10—c.

C. Addition, Subtraction, Multiplication, Division

1. Addition

Zwei und eins macht drei.
Two and one are ("makes") three.

Oder or

Zwei und eins sind drei.
Two and one are three.

Zwei und zwei macht vier.
Two and two are ("makes") four.

Oder or

Zwei und zwei sind vier.
Two and two are four.

Vier und drei macht sieben.
Four and three are ("makes") seven.

2. Subtraction

Dreissig weniger achtzehn sind zwölf.
Thirty minus eighteen is twelve.

Hundert weniger vierundzwanzig sind sechsundsiebzig.
One hundred minus twenty-four is seventy-six.

3. Multiplication

Drei mal fünf ist fünfzehn.
Three times five is fifteen.

Vier mal siebzehn ist achtundsechzig.
Four times seventeen is sixty-eight.

4. Division

Zwanzig durch fünf ist vier.
Twenty divided by five is four.

Achtundneunzig durch zwei ist neunundvierzig.
Ninety-eight divided by two is forty-nine.

LESSON 21

A. IT COSTS . . .

Das kostet . . .
This costs . . .

Das kostet fünf Mark.
This costs five marks.

Dieses Buch kostet zehn Mark fünfzig.
This book costs ten and a half Marks.

**Dieser Hut hat mich vierundfünfzig Mark ge-
kostet.**
This hat cost me fifty-four marks.

**Ich habe zweihundert Mark für dieses Kleid
bezahlt.**
I paid two hundred marks for this dress.

**Ich habe diesen Wagen für dreissigtausend Mark
gekauft.**
I bought this car for thirty thousand marks.

Das ist sechs Mark der Liter.
It's six marks a liter.

Das kostet fünfundzwanzig Mark der Meter.
That costs twenty-five marks a meter.

Der Preis ist zwölfhundert Mark.
The price is twelve hundred marks.

Sie kosten fünfzig Pfennig das Stück.
They cost fifty pfennigs apiece.

B. THE TELEPHONE NUMBER IS . . .

Meine Telefonnummer ist 5 43 13 (*fünf dreiund-
vierzig dreizehn*).
My telephone number is 5 43 13.

Versuchen Sie die Nummer 2 21 12 (*zwei ein-undzwanzig zwölf*).
Try number 2 21 12.

Meine Telefonnummer ist geändert: sie ist jetzt 5 33 89 (*fünf dreiunddreissig neunundachtzig*).
My telephone number has been changed: it's now 5 33 89.

Ihre Telefonnummer ist 4 60 91 (*vier sechzig ein-undneunzig*).
Their telephone number is 4 60 91.

C. My Address Is . . .

Ich wohne Leipzigerstrasse Nummer siebzehn.
I live at 17 Leipziger Street.

Er wohnt Schillerstrasse 4.
He lives at 4 Schiller Street.

Unsere Adresse ist Breitestrasse elf.
Our address is 11 Breitestrasse (Broad Street).

Wir wohnen in der Kaiserstrasse Nummer zweihundertdreiundsechzig.
We live at 263 Kaiserstrasse (Kaiser Street).

Meine Zimmernummer ist zweiundvierzig.
My room number is 42.

D. Some Dates

Amerika wurde vierzehnhundertzweiundneunzig entdeckt.
America was discovered in 1492.

Das geschah achtzehnhunderteinundneunzig.
It happened in 1891.

**Die New Yorker Weltausstellung fand neunzehn-
hundertneunddreissig statt.**
The New York World's Fair took place in 1939.

Ich bin neunzehnhundertsechzig geboren.
I was born in 1960.

Alle das geschah neunzehnhundertachtzig.
All this happened in 1980.

**Die Berliner Mauer fiel neunzehnhundertneun-
undachtzig.**
The Berlin Wall fell in 1989.

Ich war neunzehnhundertneunzig in Frankfurt.
I was in Frankfurt in 1990.

QUIZ 14

1. *Das kostet fünf Mark.*
2. *Ihre Telefonnummer ist drei einundzwanzig
   vierzehn.*
3. *Ich habe diesen gebrauchten Wagen für sechs-
   tausend Mark gekauft.*
4. *Ich war neunzehnhunderteinundfünfzig in Berlin.*
5. *Sie kosten fünfzig Pfennig das Stück.*

a. That costs five marks.
b. I bought this used car for six thousand marks.
c. Their phone number is 3 21 14.
d. They cost fifty pfennigs each (a piece).
e. I was in Berlin in 1951.

ANSWERS
1—a; 2—c; 3—b; 4—e; 5—d.

E. WORD STUDY

mild	mild	*tausend*	thousand
Korn (*das*)	grain	*hundert*	hundred
reich	rich	*Hitze* (*die*)	heat
Weg (*der*)	way	*heiss*	hot
Million (*die*)	million	*Konzert* (*das*)	concert

LESSON 22

A. WHAT TIME IS IT?

When you want to specify whether you mean "seven A.M." or "seven P.M." you say *sieben Uhr morgens* ("seven hours of the morning") or *vormittags sieben Uhr abends* ("seven hours of the evening") or *nachmittags*.

Official time (formal announcements of meetings, timetables, etc.) is on a twenty-four hour basis, like our Army time. Thus, in a formal announcement you may see *siebzehn Uhr dreissig* for 5:30 P.M. Ordinarily, however, you say *fünf Uhr dreissig* or *halb sechs nachmittags*—that is, instead of our "A.M." and "P.M." you add, as necessary, *morgens, nachmittags*, or *abends*.

Wie spät ist es?
What time is it?

Wieviel Uhr ist es, bitte?
What time is it, please?

Es ist ein Uhr.
It's one o'clock.

Es ist zwei Uhr.
It's two o'clock.

Es ist drei Uhr.
It's three o'clock.

Es ist vier Uhr.
It's four o'clock.

Es ist fünf Uhr.
It's five o'clock.

Es ist sechs Uhr.
It's six o'clock.

Es ist sieben Uhr.
It's seven o'clock.

Es ist acht Uhr.
It's eight o'clock.

Es ist neun Uhr.
It's nine o'clock.

Es ist zehn Uhr.
It's ten o'clock.

Es ist elf Uhr.
It's eleven o'clock.

Es ist zwölf Uhr.
It's twelve o'clock.

Es ist Mittag.
It's noon.

Es ist dreizehn Uhr.
It's one P.M. ("thirteen o'clock").

Es ist vierzehn Uhr.
It's two P.M. ("fourteen o'clock").

Es ist fünfzehn Uhr.
It's three P.M. ("fifteen o'clock").

Es ist sechzehn Uhr.
It's four P.M. ("sixteen o'clock").

Es ist siebzehn Uhr.
It's five P.M. ("seventeen o'clock").

Es ist achtzehn Uhr.
It's six P.M. ("eighteen o'clock").

Es ist neunzehn Uhr.
It's seven P.M. ("nineteen o'clock").

Es ist zwanzig Uhr.
It's eight P.M. ("twenty o'clock").

Es ist einundzwanzig Uhr.
It's nine P.M. ("twenty-one o'clock").

Es ist zweiundzwanzig Uhr.
It's ten P.M. ("twenty-two o'clock").

Es ist dreiundzwanzig Uhr.
It's eleven P.M. ("twenty-three o'clock").

Es ist vierundzwanzig Uhr.
It's twelve P.M. ("twenty-four o'clock").

Es ist Mitternacht.
It's midnight.

B. TIME PAST THE HOUR

Die Sekunde   second
Die Minute   minute
Die Stunde   hour

Es ist Viertel nach zwei.
It's a quarter after two.

Es ist zwei Uhr fünfzehn.
It's two-fifteen.

Es ist Viertel drei.
It's two-fifteen.

Es ist Viertel vor vier.
It's a quarter to four.

Es ist Dreiviertel vier.
It's a quarter to (of) four.

Es ist Viertel nach drei.
It's a quarter after three.

Es ist Viertel vier.
It's a quarter after three.

Es ist drei Uhr fünfundvierzig.
It's three forty-five.

Es ist halb drei.
It's half past two.

Es ist zwei Uhr dreissig.
It's two-thirty.

Es ist zwanzig vor fünf.
It's twenty to five.

Es ist neun Uhr fünfunddreissig.
It's nine thirty-five.

Es ist fünf vor zwölf.
It's five to twelve.

Es ist fünf nach zwölf.
It's five past twelve.

Es ist ein Uhr morgens.
It's one o'clock in the morning.

Es ist ungefähr fünf Uhr.
It's about five.

Es ist fast elf Uhr.
It's almost eleven.

Es ist punkt acht Uhr.
It's exactly eight o'clock.

Es ist erst halb sieben.
It's only half past six.

Es ist fünf Uhr durch.
It's after five.

Er kommt gegen sieben *(Uhr).*
He's coming around seven (o'clock).

C.   WHEN CAN YOU COME, ETC.?

Wann kommen Sie?
When will you come?

Um wieviel Uhr kommen Sie?
What time will you come?

Ich werde um drei Uhr dort sein.
I'll be there (at) three o'clock.

Sie ist um zwanzig vor drei gekommen.
She came at twenty to three.

Er wird um zwei Uhr nachmittags kommen.
He'll come at two P.M.

**Wir werden gegen neun Uhr fünfundzwanzig dort
sein.**
We'll be there about nine twenty-five.

**Er wird um zehn Uhr dreissig heute abend zurück-
kommen.**
He'll be back at ten-thirty tonight.

Ich werde Sie dort gegen Viertel nach acht sehen.
I'll see you there about ("toward") eight-fifteen.

Wir treffen uns um sechs.
We'll meet at six.

Ich gehe um vier Uhr aus.
I'm going out at four o'clock.

Kommen Sie zwischen sieben und acht!
Come between seven and eight.

Kommen Sie um zehn Uhr heute abend!
Come at ten o'clock tonight.

Der Zug fährt um neun Uhr vierzig ab.
The train leaves at nine-forty.

D.   IT'S TIME

Es ist Zeit.
It's time.

Es ist Zeit, es zu tun.
It's time to do it.

Es ist Zeit zu gehen.
It's time to leave.

Es ist Zeit, nach Hause zu gehen.
It's time to go home.

Ich habe Zeit.
I have time.

Ich habe genug Zeit.
I have enough time.

Ich habe keine Zeit.
I haven't any time.

Wie lange beabsichtigen Sie, hier zu bleiben?
How long do you intend to stay here?

Seit wann sind Sie hier?
How long have you been here?

Er verliert keine Zeit.
He's wasting no time.

Geben Sie ihm Zeit, es zu tun!
Give him time to do it!

Gib mir Zeit, mich anzuziehen!
Just give me enough time to get dressed!

Er kommt von Zeit zu Zeit.
He comes from time to time.

QUIZ 15

1. *Es ist halb drei.*
2. *Es ist Viertel nach zwei.*
3. *Es ist neun Uhr fünfunddreissig.*
4. *Kommen Sie zwischen sieben und acht!*
5. *Ich werde Sie dort gegen Viertel nach acht sehen.*
6. *Der Zug kommt um sieben Uhr dreiundzwanzig an.*
7. *Kommen Sie gegen zehn Uhr heute abend!*
8. *Es ist ein Uhr morgens.*
9. *Wir werden gegen neun Uhr fünfundzwanzig dort sein.*
10. *Es ist Zeit zu gehen.*

a. I'll see you there about eight-fifteen.
b. The train arrives at seven twenty-three.
c. Come between seven and eight.
d. Come around ten o'clock tonight.
e. It's one o'clock in the morning.
f. It's time to leave.

g. We'll be there about nine twenty-five.
h. It's two-fifteen. (It's a quarter after two.)
i. It's half past two. (It's two-thirty).
j. It's nine thirty-five.

ANSWERS
1—i; 2—h; 3—j; 4—c; 5—a; 6—b; 7—d; 8—e; 9—g;
10—f.

E. WORD STUDY

hoffen	(to) hope	*Krone* (*die*)	crown
Distanz (*die*)	distance	*Pflanze* (*die*)	plant
Seite (*die*)	side	*Kredit* (*der*)	credit
Welt (*die*)	world	*wandern*	(to) wander, hike
Jahr (*das*)	year		

LESSON 23

A. MORNING, NOON, AND NIGHT

der Morgen	morning
der Mittag	noon
der Nachmittag	afternoon
der Abend	evening
die Nacht	night
der Tag	the day
die Woche	the week
acht Tage	a week ("eight days")
vierzehn Tage	two weeks ("fourteen days")
der Monat	the month

das Jahr	the year
gestern	yesterday
heute	today
morgen	tomorrow
vorgestern	the day before yesterday
übermorgen	the day after tomorrow
vor langem	a long time ago
vor kurzem	a while ago
jetzt	now
einen Augenblick, bitte	in a moment, please
lange her	a long time ago
heute morgen	this morning
gestern morgen	yesterday morning
morgen früh	tomorrow morning
heute nachmittag	this afternoon
gestern nachmittag	yesterday afternoon
morgen nachmittag	tomorrow afternoon
heute abend	this evening
gestern abend	last evening
morgen abend	tomorrow evening
heute nacht	tonight
gestern nacht	last night
morgen nacht	tomorrow night

B. This Week, Next Month, One of These Days

diese Woche
this week

{ **letzte Woche**
{ **vorige Woche**
  last week

nächste Woche
next week

in zwei Wochen
in two weeks, the week after next

vor zwei Wochen
two weeks ago, the week before last

dieser Monat
this month

der vorige Monat
last month

der nächste Monat
next month

in zwei Monaten
in two months, the month after next

vor zwei Monaten
two months ago, the month before last

dieses Jahr
this year

voriges Jahr
last year

nächstes Jahr
next year

in zwei Jahren
in two years, the year after next

vor zwei Jahren
two years ago, the year before last

am Morgen
in the morning

am Abend
in the evening

gegen Mittag
towards noon

nach dem Abendessen
after dinner

am Ende der Woche
at the end of the week

gegen Wochenende
toward the end of the week

vor einer Stunde
an hour ago

in einer Viertelstunde
in a quarter of an hour

eines Tages
one of these days

alle Tage
every day

den ganzen Tag
all day (long)

die ganze Nacht
all night (long)

Er arbeitet von morgens bis abends.
He works from morning to night.

Was für ein Datum ist heute?
What's the date? (''today'')

Der wievielte ist heute?
What's today's date?

C. EXPRESSIONS OF PAST, PRESENT, AND FUTURE

Vergangenheit	*Gegenwart*	*Zukunft*
Past	Present	Future
Vor einem Augenblick	*In diesem Augenblick*	*im nächsten Augenblick*
a moment ago	now	in a moment, soon
gestern morgen	*heute morgen*	*morgen früh*
yesterday morning	this morning	tomorrow morning
gestern nachmittag	*heute nachmittag*	*morgen nachmittag*
yesterday afternoon	this afternoon	tomorrow afternoon
gestern abend	*heute abend*	*morgen abend*
last evening, last night	this evening, tonight	tomorrow evening, tomorrow night
vorige Woche	*diese Woche*	*nächste Woche*
last week	this week	next week

vorigen[1] Monat	diesen Monat	nächsten Monat
last month	this month	next month
voriges[1] Jahr	dieses Jahr	nächstes Jahr
last year	this year	next year
		nächstes Wochenende
		next weekend

LESSON 24

A. DAYS OF THE WEEK

Montag	Monday
Dienstag	Tuesday
Mittwoch	Wednesday
Donnerstag	Thursday
Freitag	Friday
Samstag or **Sonnabend**	Saturday
Sonntag	Sunday

B. WHAT DAY IS TODAY?

The following expressions are all used for "What's the date today?"

Der wievielte ist heute?
What is today's date?
"The how many is it?"

Welches Datum ist heute?
"What date is today?"

---

[1]*letze, letzter, letztes* also may be used to say "last."

Den wievielten haben wir heute?
"The how many do we have today?"

Der wievielte ist Sonntag?
What's the date Sunday?

Heute ist der zehnte.
Today's the tenth.

Heute haben wir den zwanzigsten.
Today is ("we have") the twentieth.

Welchen Tag haben wir heute?
What day is it today?

Ist heute Dienstag oder Mittwoch?
Is today Tuesday or Wednesday?

Heute ist Mittwoch.
Today is Wednesday.

Kommen Sie nächsten Samstag zurück!
Come back next Saturday.

Er fährt nächsten Sonntag fort.
He's leaving next Sunday.

Er ist letzten Montag angekommen.
He arrived last Monday.

Er kommt nächsten Donnerstag an.
He's arriving next Thursday.

QUIZ 16

1. *vorgestern*	a. afternoon
2. *heute*	b. day before yesterday
3. *nachmittag*	c. today
4. *vor kurzem*	d. day after tomorrow
5. *morgen nachmittag*	e. a while ago
6. *heute nachmittag*	f. tomorrow afternoon
7. *übermorgen*	g. this evening
8. *Er verliert seine Zeit.*	h. He's wasting his time.
9. *heute nacht*	i. this afternoon
10. *Seit wann sind Sie hier?*	j. How long have you been here?
11. *nächste Woche*	k. in two months, the month after next
12. *vorige Woche*	l. two weeks ago, the week before last
13. *vor zwei Wochen*	m. next week
14. *in zwei Monaten*	n. two years ago, the year before last
15. *vor zwei Jahren*	o. last week
16. *Es ist Zeit*	p. It's time to go home.
17. *Ich habe Zeit.*	q. tomorrow night
18. *Es ist Zeit, nach Hause zu gehen.*	r. tonight
19. *morgen abend*	s. It's time.
20. *heute abend*	t. I have time.

ANSWERS

1—b; 2—c; 3—a; 4—e; 5—f; 6—i; 7—d; 8—h; 9—r;
10—j; 11—m; 12—o; 13—l; 14—k; 15—n; 16—s;
17—t; 18—p; 19—q; 20—g.

C. MONTHS AND DATES

Januar	January
Februar	February
März	March
April	April
Mai	May
Juni	June
Juli	July
August	August
September	September
Oktober	October
November	November
Dezember	December

Heute ist der erste Juni.
Today is the first of June.

Ich wurde am zwölften April geboren.
I was born (on) April 12.

Mein Geburtstag ist am zweiten Februar.
My birthday is (on) February 2.

Ich komme am vierzehnten Juli.
I'll come (on) the fourteenth of July.

Die Schule beginnt am zwanzigsten September.
School begins (on) the twentieth of September.

Ich bin am zweiundzwanzigsten März zurück.
I'll be back (on) March 22.

Der erste Januar ist ein Feiertag.
January 1 is a holiday.

Er fährt am sechsten Juli ab.
He's leaving (on) July 6.

Der Brief ist vom neunten Juni.
The letter is dated June 9.

Wir besuchen Sie am elften Mai.
We'll come to see you (on) May 11.

**Heute ist der zweite Mai, neunzehnhunderteinund-
neunzig.**
Today is May 2, 1991.

D.   SEASONS

der Frühling	spring
der Sommer	summer
der Herbst	autumn
der Winter	winter

im Winter	in winter
im Sommer	in summer
im Herbst	in autumn, in the fall
im Frühling	in spring

Ich lieber den Sommer.
I love summer.

Ich ziehe den Frühling vor.
I prefer the spring.

QUIZ 17

1. *Welches Datum ist heute?*
2. *Eines Tages werden wir zusammenkommen.*
3. *Den ganzen Tag muss ich arbeiten.*

4. *Im Sommer gehen wir schwimmen.*
5. *In einer Viertelstunde.*
6. *Er kommt nächsten Montag an.*
7. *Heute ist Montag.*
8. *Kommen Sie nächsten Samstag!*
9. *Der Winter ist schon hier.*
10. *Sonntage sind immer schön.*
11. *Wir haben heute den zwanzigsten.*
12. *Der wievielte ist Dienstag?*
13. *Ich komme am vierzehnten Juli.*
14. *Heute ist der erste Juni.*
15. *Der Brief ist vom sechsten Juni.*

a. Sundays are always nice.
b. in a quarter of an hour
c. One of these days we'll get together.
d. All day I have to work.
e. What's today's date?
f. In the summer we go swimming.
g. Winter is already here.
h. What's the date Tuesday?
i. Today's the twentieth.
j. Today's Monday.
k. Come next Saturday.
l. He'll arrive next Monday.
m. The letter is dated June 6.
n. I'll come (on) the fourteenth of July.
o. Today is the first of June.

ANSWERS
1—e; 2—c; 3—d; 4—f; 5—b; 6—l; 7—j; 8—k;
9—g; 10—a; 11—i; 12—h; 13—n; 14—o; 15—m.

E. VOR DEM ZEITUNGSSTAND[1]
   (At the Newsstand)

1. *Kunde: Guten Morgen, Fräulein! Geben Sie mir bitte „Die Welt" und auch die Illustrierte, „Der Stern". Könnten Sie mir einen Hundertmarkschein wechseln? Ich habe leider kein Kleingeld dabei.*

   Customer: Good morning, Miss. Please give me *Die Welt* and also the magazine *Der Stern*. Could you change a hundred-mark bill? I'm sorry, I have no change on me.

2. *Verkäuferin: Ich kenne Sie doch, Herr Mergl. Die drei Mark funfzig bleiben Sie mir schuldig. Sie können mir morgen zahlen.*

   Saleslady: I know you, Mr. Mergl. You'll owe me the three and a half marks. You can pay me tomorrow.

3. *Kunde: Ich danke Ihnen recht schön. Übrigens, gehen die Busse heute oder muss ich wieder mit der Untergrundbahn fahren?*

   Customer: I thank you very much. By the way, are the buses running today or do I have to take the subway again?

4. *Verkäuferin: Während der letzten Viertelstunde sind schon drei Busse vorbeigefahren. Sie waren voll. Heute wäre es besser mit der Unteregrundbahn zu fahren.*

   Saleslady: During the last fifteen minutes three buses went by. They were full. It would be better to go by subway today.

[1] Another word for "newsstand" is *Zeitungskiosk*.

5. *Kunde: Also, dann muss ich mich beeilen. Es ist schon Viertel nach acht, und ich muss punkt neun Uhr im Büro sein. Auf Wiedersehen, bis morgen!*
   Customer: Well, then, I really have to hurry up. It's already a quarter past eight, and I have to be at the office at nine on the dot. So long, see you tomorrow (Until tomorrow).

6. *Verkäuferin: Auf Wiedersehen, Herr Mergl!*
   Saleslady: Good-bye, Mr. Mergl.

NOTES

1. *der Kunde*—the customer
2. *die Verkäuferin*—the saleslady
3. *die Illustrierte*—the magazine
4. *Könnten Sie . . . ?*—Could you . . . ? Would you be able to . . . ?
5. *wechseln*—to (ex)change
6. *schuldig sein*—to owe: (from *schulden,* dative verb) to owe: *Er schuldet mir, ihm (ihr, uns, ihnen) zwanzig Mark.* He owes me (him, her, us, them) twenty Marks.
7. *apropo*—by the way
8. *die Untergrundbahn*—the subway
9. *vorbeifahren*—to drive by: *Der Bus ist einfach vorbeigefahren, ohne anzuhalten.* The bus simply drove past without stopping.
10. *sich beeilen*—to hurry: *ich beeile mich, du beeilst dich, er, sie, es beeilt sich, wir beeilen uns, ihr beeilt euch, sie (Sie) beeilen sich*
11. *also*—well then
12. *das Büro*—the office
13. *Es wäre* (Subjunctive form of *sein*)—it would be

14. *Er geht ins Büro.*—He's going to the office (acc.).

15. *Er arbeit et im Büro.*—He's working in the office (dat.).

LESSON 25

A. To Go, to Walk: *GEHEN*

1. I go

ich gehe	I go, I'm going
du gehst	you go
er geht (*sie, es*)	he goes
wir gehen	we go
ihr geht	you go
Sie gehen	you go
sie gehen	they go

2. I don't go

ich gehe nicht	I don't go; I'm not going
du gehst nicht	you don't go
er geht nicht	he doesn't go
wir gehen nicht	we don't go
ihr geht nicht	you don't go
Sie gehen nicht	you don't go
sie gehen nicht	they don't go

3. Some Common Expressions with *gehen*:

Geh!
Go (*fam.*)!

Gehen Sie!
Go!

Gehen Sie langsam!
Go slowly.

Gehen Sie weiter!
Go on! Keep going!

Gehen Sie es suchen!
Go look for it! Go get it!

Wo gehen Sie hin?
Where are you going?

Gehen Sie nicht dorthin!
Don't go there.

Gehen Sie nicht dort hinüber!
Don't go over there.

Wir müssen dorthin gehen.
We have to go there. (We must go there.)

Ich gehe zum Bannhof.
I'm going to the station.

Ich gehe zur Bank.
I'm going to the bank.

Ich gehe ins Theater.
I'm going to the theater.

Er geht aufs Land.
He's going to the countryside.

Ich gehe Hans besuchen.
I'm going to John's place (home). ("I'm going to visit Hans.")

Sie geht nachmittags einkaufen.
She is going shopping in the afternoon.

Wie geht es Ihnen?
How are you? ("How goes it with you?")

Es geht mir gut.
Well, thanks. Fine, thanks.

Wie geht's?
How are you? How are things?

Gut. Danke.
Fine. All right. O.K.

B. To Go, to Ride, to Drive: *Fahren*

When speaking of a trip, you may also use the verb *fahren*.

1. I go

ich fahre	I go
du fährst	you go
er fährt	he goes
wir fahren	we go
ihr fahrt	you go
Sie fahren	you go
sie fahren	they go

2. Study these examples:

Wo fahren wir hin?
Where are we going?

Wohin fährst du?
Where are you going?

Wohin fährt er?
Where is he going?

Sie fährt nach Berlin.
She is going to Berlin.

Wohin fahren wir?
Where are we going?

Wohin fahren Sie?
Where are you going?

Fahrt ihr nach Berlin?
Are you going to Berlin?

Nein, wir fahren nach Frankfurt.
No, we are going to Frankfurt.

Wohin fahren sie?
Where are they going?

Wie fährst du in die Stadt?
How are you going to the city?

Ich fahre mit der Bahn.
I'm going by train.

C. A FEW ACTION PHRASES

Achtung!
Watch out! Pay
  attention!

Vorsichtig sein!
  Vorsicht!
Be careful! Watch out!

Schnell.
Fast.

Schneller.
Faster.

**Sprechen Sie nicht so
  schnell!**
Don't speak so fast!

Nicht zu schnell.
Not too fast.

Langsamer.
More slowly.

Langsamer fahren!
Drive more slowly!

Früher.
Sooner.

Später.
Later.

Ich komme.
I'm coming.

Bis später.
See you later.

Beeilen Sie sich!
Hurry up!

Beeilen Sie sich nicht!
Don't hurry up!

Ich habe es eilig.
I'm in a hurry.

Ich habe es nicht eilig.
I'm not in a hurry.

Lassen Sie sich Zeit.
Take your time.

Einen Moment!
Just a minute!

Sofort.
Right away.

Ich rufe ihn sofort an.
I'll telephone him right
away.

Bald.
Soon.

Es wird bald regnen.
It's going to rain soon.

Ich komme sofort.
I'm coming right away.

D. WORD STUDY

Feuer (das)	fire
Grammatik (die)	grammar
Suppe (die)	soup
füllen	(to) fill
Argument (das)	argument

Monument (das)	monument
flach	flat
dick	thick
Stein (der)	stone

LESSON 26

A. ONE, THEY, PEOPLE

man
one; they; people; we.

Man sagt, dass ...
They say that ... It's said that ... People say that ...

Man hat mir gesagt, dass ...
I've been told that ...

Man sagt es.
They say it.

Man sagt, dass es wahr ist.
They say it's true.

Man hat es mir gesagt.
I've been told that.

Man weiss es nicht.
Nobody knows.

Man spricht hier Deutsch.
German is spoken here.

Hier spricht man Englisch.
English is spoken here.

Man spricht hier Spanisch.
We speak Spanish here.

Spricht man Englisch hier?
Do they speak English here?

Wie sagt man das auf Deutsch?
How do you say that in German?

Wie sagt man "Good morning" auf Deutsch?
How do you say "Good morning" in German?

Wie schreibt man dieses Wort auf Deutsch?
How is this word written (spelled) in German?

Man läutet.
Someone's ringing.

Man schliesst um acht.
They're closing at eight.

Was spielt man heute abend im Theater?
What's playing at the theater tonight?

Notice that *man* can often be translated by the English passive:

Man sagt, dass . . .
It's said that . . .

Man hat mir gesagt, dass . . .
I've been told that . . .

Wie schreibt man dieses Wort?
How is this word written?
(How does one write this word?)

QUIZ 18

1. *Ich habe es eilig.*	a. Right away.
2. *Ich komme sofort.*	b. In a minute.
3. *Einen Moment.*	c. I'm in a hurry.
4. *Sofort.*	d. I'm coming right away.
5. *Lassen Sie sich Zeit.*	e. Someone's ringing.
6. *Man läutet.*	f. Take your time.
7. *Man hat mir gesagt.*	g. Nobody knows.
8. *Man weiss es nicht.*	h. I've been told.
9. *Hier spricht man Englisch.*	i. How do you say that in German?
10. *Wie sagt man das auf deutsch?*	j. English spoken here.

ANSWERS

1—c; 2—d; 3—b; 4—a; 5—f; 6—e; 7—h; 8—g;
9—j; 10—i.

B. WORD STUDY

Logik (die)	logic	*Szene (die)*	scene
tanzen	(to) dance	*frei*	free
privat	private	*modern*	modern
Preis (der)	price	*Name (der)*	name

C. A LITTLE AND A LOT

wenig
a little

viel oder wenig
a lot or a little

ein wenig
a little

sehr wenig
very little

ein klein wenig
a very little

ein ganz klein wenig
a very little bit

allmählich
little by little

Das ist zu wenig.
It's not enough.

noch ein wenig
a little bit more

Er spricht wenig
He doesn't talk much.

Wollen Sie viel oder wenig davon?
Do you want a lot of it or a little?

Bleiben wir noch ein wenig hier!
Let's stay here a little longer.

Geben Sie mir ein wenig davon!
Give me a little of it.

Geben Sie mir ein wenig Wasser!
Give me a little water.

Ich spreche sehr wenig Deutsch.
I speak very little German.

viel
much, a lot, very

Ich habe nicht viel Geld.
I haven't much money.

Ich habe nicht viel Zeit.
I haven't much time.

Ich mag ihn sehr.
I like him (her, it) a lot.

Ich habe viel zu tun.
I have a lot to do.

D. Too Much

Zu viel.
Too. Too much.

Das ist zu viel.
It's too much.

Das ist nicht zu viel.
That is not too much.

zu wenig
too little

zu heiss
too hot

zu kalt
too cold

zu viel Wasser
too much water

E. More or Less

mehr oder weniger
more or less

höchstens
at the most

wenigstens
at the least

immer und mehr
more and more

immer weniger
less and less

sechs mal mehr
six times more

Es gibt nichts mehr davon.
There's no more of it.

Es ist mehr als das.
It's more than that.

Das ist das meist gelesene Buch, das ich kenne.
This is the most popular book I know.
("This is the most read book I know.")

F. ENOUGH AND SOME MORE

genug
enough

Ist es genug?
Is it enough?

Das ist genug.
It's enough.

Das ist nicht genug.
That is not enough.

Das ist mehr als genug.
It's more than enough.

Das ist gross genug.
That's large enough.
That's rather large.

gut genug
fairly well, rather well

Haben Sie genug Geld?
Do you have enough money?

Sagen Sie es noch einmal!
Say it again.

Wiederholen Sie, bitte, noch einmal.
Please repeat it again.

noch
some more

Noch mehr? Noch etwas?
Some more?

noch ein wenig
a little more, another little bit

noch mehr Brot
some more bread

noch ein Glas Wasser
another glass of water

noch etwas Fleisch
some more meat

noch viel mehr
much more, lots more

Kommen Sie noch einmal.
Come again.

LESSON 27

A. GOOD

Gut!
Good!

Das ist gut.
That's good.

Das ist sehr gut.
That's very good. It's very good.

Das ist nicht gut.
That's not good. It's not good.

Das ist nett.
That's nice. That's lovely.

Das ist grossartig!
That's great! That's neat!

Das ist prima!
That's super! That's cool!

Das ist ausgezeichnet.
That's excellent.

Das ist hervorragend!
That's outstanding!

Das ist bewundernswert.
That's admirable. It's wonderful.

Das ist wunderbar. Das ist wundervoll.
That's wonderful.

Das ist perfekt.
That's perfect.

Der Wein ist gut.
This wine is good.

Das Fleisch ist gut.
This meat is good.

Sie sind gut.
They're good.

Guten Tag!
Hello! Good afternoon. Good day.

Guten Abend!
Good evening!

Gute Nacht!
Good night!

B. GOOD, WELL

gut
good, well

nicht zu gut
not too good

Sehr gut, mein Herr.
Very well, sir.

Ist es gut?
Is it good?

Das ist gut gemacht.
That's well done.

Alles geht gut.
Everything's going well. Everything's all right.

Es geht viel besser.
It's going much better.

Ich fühle mich nicht wohl.
I don't feel well.

Gute Besserung!
I hope you get well soon!

Es passt sehr gut.
It fits well.

C. BEAUTIFUL, NICE, FINE

schön
beautiful

Es ist sehr schön.
It's very beautiful.

Das ist schön.
That's beautiful.

nicht sehr schön
not very beautiful (nice)

schönes Wetter
nice weather

ein schönes Land
a beautiful country

ein schöner Tag
a nice day

Es ist schön draussen.
It's nice out.

die schönen Künste
the fine arts

schön und gut
well and good

QUIZ 19

1. *Alles geht gut.*
2. *Das ist sehr gut.*
3. *Ist es gut?*
4. *Es ist sehr schön.*
5. *Haben Sie genug davon?*
6. *Sagen Sie es noch einmal.*
7. *Wiederholen Sie, bitte, noch einmal!*
8. *Kommen Sie noch einmal!*
9. *Das ist prima!*
10. *Schön und gut.*

a. That's very good.
b. Do you have enough of it?
c. Say it again.
d. well and good
e. That's super!
f. It's very beautiful.
g. Everything is going well. Everything's all right.

h. Is it good?
i. Please repeat it.
j. Come again.

ANSWERS
1—g; 2—a; 3—h; 4—f; 5—b; 6—c; 7—i; 8—j; 9—e;
10—d.

D. WORD STUDY

nervös	nervous
Episode (*die*)	episode
Summe (*die*)	sum
meinen	(to) mean, think (believe)
natürlich	natural
Nagel (*der*)	nail
elektrisch	electrical
Braut (*die*)	bride
Zeremonie (*die*)	ceremony

LESSON 28

A. LIKE, AS

wie
like, as

wie ich
like me

wie das
like this (that)

wie die andern
like the others

wie dieses
like this

nicht so wie das
not like this (that)

wie Sie wünschen
as you wish

Wie früh es ist!
How early (it is)!

Wie spät es ist!
How late (it is)!

Wie teuer das ist!
How expensive this is!

B. ALL, EACH, EVERY, ETC.

all, alle, alles
all

jeder, jede, jedes
every, each

jeder Mensch
every human being

jeder Mann
every man, each man

jede Frau
every woman, each woman

jedes Kind
every child, each child

alle Menschen
all human beings

alle Männer
all men

alle Frauen
all women

jeder, jederman
everybody, everyone

jeden Tag
every day

Alles ist hier.
Everything's here.

den ganzen Tag
all day long ("the whole day")

Alles ist fertig.
Everything's ready.

Alle sind fertig.
All are ready.

Nehmen Sie sie alle!
Take all of them!

Wir sind alle da.
We're all here.

Der Kaffee ist alle.
The coffee is all gone (used up).

Das ist alles.
That's all. That's the whole lot. That'll do.

Ist das alles?
Is that all? Is that everything? Is that the whole lot?

alle
everybody (all of them)

Jeder weiss es.
Everybody knows it.

ganz
entire, entirely; complete, completely; whole, wholly

Er hat die ganze Torte aufgegessen.
He ate up the whole cake.

ganz schlecht
completely bad

Ganz und gar nicht.
Not at all.

Überhaupt nicht.
Not at all.

C. SOME, ANY, NOTHING, ETC. (COMBINATIONS WITH DA-)

a. *Da-* is often combined with a preposition to form the following expressions:

davon: of it, of that
darin: in it, in them
daran: at it, at them
darüber: about/over it, about/over them
darunter: among/under it, among/under them
dadurch: through it, through them
dazu: to it, to them
dafür: for it, for them
daraus: from/out of it, from/out of them

**Hier ist die Tafel Schokolade. Geben Sie jedem
    Kind ein Stück davon.**
Here is the chocolate bar. Give each child a piece
    of it.

**Sie gab mir eine Pfeife. Was soll ich damit
    tun?**
She gave me a pipe. What should I do with it?

**Bitte nehmen Sie dieses Buch! Wir haben schon
    darüber gesprochen.**
Please take this book. We have already spoken about
    it.

Ich habe genug davon.
I have enough of it.

Geben Sie uns etwas davon!
Give us some of it!

Geben Sie ihnen nichts mehr davon.
Don't give them any more of it.

Ich habe mit ihr darüber gesprochen.
I spoke to her about it.

**Ich habe mit ihr über Politik und Sport ge-
   sprochen.**
I spoke with her about politics and sports.

Kommt er aus Deutschland?
Does he come from Germany?
Is he coming from Germany?

Ja, er kommt direkt daher.
Yes, he is coming directly from there.

Was halten Sie davon?
What do you think of (about) it?

Was halten Sie von ihm (*ihr*)**?**
What do you think of him (her)?

   b. *etwas*
      some, any

Hat er (etwas) Geld?
Does he have any money?

Ja, er hat etwas.
Yes, he has some.

Haben Sie (etwas) Geld?
Do you have any money?

Nein, ich habe keins.
No, I don't have any.

Ich noch etwas von dem guten Wein übrig?
Is there (still) anything left of the good wine?

Nein, es ist nichts mehr davon übrig.
No, there is nothing (more) left of it.

Hier ist etwas Geld.
Here's some money.

Geben Sie Hans etwas davon!
Give some of it to John.

Geben Sie mir etwas!
Give me something!

Geben Sie ihm etwas!
Give him something!

Ich habe ihm etwas davon gegeben.
I gave him some of it.

Geben Sie ihr nichts!
Don't give her anything! (Give her nothing!)

Es gibt etwas.
There is something.

Gibt es noch etwas davon?
Is (are) there any more of it?

D. PREPOSITIONAL COMPOUNDS REFERRING TO PEOPLE

When the prepositional phrase refers to a person, the *da-* compounds are not used. Instead, the preposition and a pronoun is used. The preposition governs the case.

EXAMPLES

Er hält nicht viel von meinem Bruder.
He doesn't think much of my brother.

Er hält nicht viel von ihm.
He doesn't think much of him.

NOTE

Halten von is an expression meaning "to consider someone to be." The preposition *von* governs the dative case.

Er denkt immer an seinen Vater.
He always thinks of his father.

Er denkt immer an ihn.
He always thinks of him.

NOTE

The preposition *an* is a two-way preposition, governing the accusative or dative case. Here it is used in the accusative case because the expression *denken an* governs the accusative case.

E. IDIOMATIC EXPRESSIONS WITH PREPOSITIONS

Below is a list of useful idiomatic expressions. The case each governs is in parentheses:

AN

sich erinnen an (acc.)	to remember
glauben an (acc.)	to think of
leiden an (dat.)	to suffer from
schreiben an (acc.)	to write to

sich wenden an (acc.)	to turn to
teilnehmen an (dat.)	to take part in

AUF

achten auf (acc.)	to pay attention to
bestehen auf (acc.)	to insist upon
böse sein auf (acc.)	to be angry with
sich freuen auf (acc.)	to look forward to
hoffen auf (acc.)	to hope for
stolz sein auf (acc.)	to be proud of
sich verlassen auf (acc.)	to reply upon
warten auf (acc.)	to wait for

ÜBER

denken über (acc.)	to think about
sich freuen über (acc.)	to be happy about
sich beschweren über (acc.)	to complain about
lachen über (acc.)	to laugh about
sich unterhalten über (acc.)	to converse about (something)

OTHER EXPRESSIONS

bitten um (acc.)	to ask for something
sich bewerben um (acc.)	to apply for
sich kümmern um (acc.)	to be concerned about
sich interessieren für (acc.)	to be interested in
Angst haben vor (dat.)	to be afraid of
warnen vor (dat.)	to warn against
gehen in (acc.)	to go (in)to
bleiben in (dat.)	to remain

QUIZ 20

1. *Gibt es noch etwas davon?*
2. *Es gibt etwas.*
3. *Haben Sie etwas Geld?*
4. *Haben Sie etwas davon?*
5. *Geben Sie ihm etwas mehr davon!*
6. *Geben Sie mir etwas!*
7. *Nein, sie haben nichts.*
8. *Was halten Sie davon?*
9. *Ich habe ihm etwas gegeben.*
10. *Das ist gut.*
11. *Ein schönes Land ist Amerika.*
12. *Wir haben heute schönes Wetter.*
13. *Das ist sehr schön.*
14. *Das Wetter ist schön.*
15. *Ein schöner Tag ist endlich hier.*

a. It's very beautiful today.
b. Nice weather.
c. A nice day is finally here.
d. It's nice out. The weather's nice.
e. America is a beautiful country.
f. I gave him something.
g. It's good.
h. Do you have any?
i. Do you have any money?
j. Give me something.
k. Give him some more of it.
l. There is something.
m. Is (are) there more of it?
n. No, they haven't any.
o. What do you think of it?

ANSWERS

1—m; 2—l; 3—i; 4—h; 5—k; 6—j; 7—n; 8—0; 9—j; 10—g; 11—e; 12—b; 13—a; 14—d; 15—c.

LESSON 29

A.   OF COURSE, I SUPPOSE SO, ETC.

Aber sicher!
Of course! Certainly!

Natürlich!
Of course! Naturally!

Einverstanden!
Of course! Agreed!

In Ordnung.
Agreed!

Ich bin damit einverstanden.
I agree with that (to it).

Das versteht sich.
Of course. Naturally. Certainly.

Tatsächlich?
Indeed? In fact? Really?

Wirklich?
Really?

Um so schlimmer.
So much the worse.

Um so besser.
So much the better.

Ich denke ja!
I think so.

Ich nehme es an.
I suppose so.

Ich nehme es nicht an.
I suppose not.

{ **Ich hoffe.**
{ **Hoffentlich.**
  I hope so.

{ **Ich hoffe nicht.**
{ **Hoffentlich nicht.**
  I hope not.

Vielleicht doch.
Perhaps so.

Das hängt davon ab.
That all depends.

Sicher, Sicherlich.
Certainly.

Sicher nicht.
Certainly not.

B.   IT'S A PITY, IT DOESN'T MATTER, ETC.

Das ist schade!
It's a pity! It's a shame! Too bad!

Schade!
Too bad!

Das macht nichts.
That's not important. That doesn't matter.

Das macht gar nichts.
That doesn't matter at all.

Das macht mir nichts aus.
It doesn't matter to me. I don't care.

Wenn es Ihnen nichts ausmacht
If you have no objection;
If it doesn't inconvenience you.

Das ist mir völlig gleich.
I don't care. It's all the same to me.

Das kümmert mich nicht im geringsten.
That doesn't bother me at all.

{ **Ich mache mir nicht das geringste daraus.**
Das ist mir total schnuppe (*coll.*).[1]
Es ist mir wurst (*coll.*).[2]
I couldn't care less.

C. HE'S A GREAT GUY, SHE'S A GREAT GAL

{ **Er ist ein famoser Kerl.**
Er ist ein grossartiger Kerl.
He's a great guy.

Er ist klasse (*coll.*).
He's a great guy.

[1] *Coll.* stands for "colloquial."
[2] Literally, "It's a sausage (to me)." Note that this expression and the one above are *highly* colloquial.

Er ist sehr nett.
He's very nice.

Sie ist eine fabelhafte Frau.
She's a fabulous woman.

Sie ist klasse (*coll.*).
She's a great gal.

Sie ist sehr liebenswürdig.
She's very kind (amiable).

Sie sind sehr liebenswürdig.
You're very kind. That's very kind of you.

QUIZ 21

1. *Das ist schade!*	a. Of course, certainly.
2. *Das macht nichts.*	b. I agree to it.
3. *Das macht mir nichts aus.*	c. Of course.
4. *Das hängt davon ab.*	d. He's a great guy.
5. *Einverstanden.*	e. I suppose so.
6. *Ich bin damit einverstanden.*	f. I hope so.
7. *Ich hoffe.*	g. It's a pity (shame). Too bad!
8. *Aber sicher.*	h. That all depends.
9. *Er ist ein grossartiger Kerl.*	i. That's nothing. That's not important. That doesn't matter.
10. *Ich nehme es an.*	j. I don't care. It doesn't matter to me.

ANSWERS
1—g; 2—i; 3—j; 4—h; 5—c; 6—b; 7—f; 8—a; 9—d;
10—e.

D. THE SAME, MYSELF

dasselbe (*derselbe, dieselbe*)
the same

Das ist dasselbe.
That's the same thing.

Das sind nicht dieselben.
These aren't the same.

zur selben Zeit
at the same time

im (*in dem*) **selben Augenblick**
at the same moment

in derselben Stadt
in the same town

selbst/selber
myself, yourself, etc.

{ **Ich mache es selbst.**
{ **Ich mache es selber.**
   I'm doing it myself.

{ **Du machst es selbst.**
{ *Du machst es selber.*
   You're doing it yourself.

{ **Er macht es selbst.**
{ *Er macht es selber.*
He's doing it himself.

{ **Wir machen es selbst.**
{ *Wir machen es selber.*
We're doing it ourselves.

{ **Ihr macht es selbst.**
{ *Ihr macht es selber.*
You're doing it yourselves.

Sie machen es selbst.
You're doing it yourself.

Sie machen es selbst.
They are doing it themselves.

E. ALREADY

Schon.
Already.

Er ist schon da.
He's already here.

Er ist noch nicht da.
He is not here yet.

Er hat es schon getan.
He's already done that.

Ist er schon fort?
Has he left already?

Nein, er ist noch da (hier).
No, he is still here.

Er ist noch nicht fort.
He hasn't left yet.

Sind Sie schon fertig?
Have you finished already?

F. WORD STUDY

Milch (die)	milk	*Öl (das)*	oil
Stahl (der)	steel	*Sand (der)*	sand
Zinn (das)	tin	*Eis (das)*	ice
Sturm (der)	storm	*Amerika (das)*	America
Wolle (die)	wool	*Finger (der)*	finger

LESSON 30

A. I LIKE IT, IT'S GOOD

Mir gefällt es.
I like it. (It's pleasing to me.)

Das gefällt mir.
I like that.

Das habe ich gern.
I like that.

Ich mag es.
I like it.

Das ist gut.
It's good.

Ich mag es.
I like it (food).

Das ist sehr gut.
It's very good.

Das gefällt mir sehr.
I like that very much.

Es gefällt mir grossartig.
It's grand. I like it a great deal.

Ich bin begeistert davon.
I'm enthusiastic about it.

Magst du ihn gern?
Do you like it?

Ihr gefällt er.
She likes him.

Ihm gefällt sie.
He likes her.

Das ist komisch.
That's strange, comical.

B. I DON'T LIKE IT, IT'S BAD

Ich mag es nicht.
I don't like it.

Das gefällt mir nicht.
I don't like that. ("It doesn't please me.")

Ich mag ihn nicht.
I don't like him.

Ich mag sie nicht.
I don't like her.

Das ist nicht gut.
That's not good.

Das ist schlecht.
It's bad. That's bad.

Es ist nicht schön.
It's not nice (beautiful).

Das ist nicht schön von Ihnen.
That's not nice of you.

Das ist wertlos.
It's worthless.

Es ist langweilig.
It's boring.

Es ist blöd!
It's stupid!

Es ist nervtötend (*coll.*).
It's boring! It's a drag!

QUIZ 22

1. *Ich mag es nicht.*	a. It's strange.
2. *Das ist wertlos.*	b. It's boring.
3. *Das ist schön.*	c. Do you like it?
4. *Es ist langweilig.*	d. She likes him.
5. *Magst du ihn gern?*	e. I like it.
6. *Ihr gefällt er.*	f. That's bad.
7. *Das gefällt mir nicht.*	g. That's beautiful.
8. *Das ist schlecht.*	h. I don't like that.
9. *Mir gefällt es.*	i. I don't like it.
10. *Das ist komisch.*	j. It's worthless.

ANSWERS
1—i; 2—j; 3—g; 4—b; 5—c; 6—d; 7—h; 8—f;
9—e; 10—a.

C. EIN WITZ

Zwei Freunde gehen in ein Restaurant und jeder bestellt ein Beefsteak. Ein paar Minuten später kommt der Kellner zurück und bringt ein grosses und ein kleines Stück Fleisch. Der eine Freund nimmt sich sofort das grosse Stück. Der andere wird wütend und sagt zu ihm:

"Was für schlechte Manieren du hast! Weisst du nicht, dass du als erster das kleinere Stück hättest nehmen sollen?"

Der andere Freund antwortet:
"Welches Stück hättest du denn genommen, wenn du an meiner Stelle gewesen wärest."

"Das kleinere, natürlich," sagt der eine.

"Nun gut," antwortet der andere, "Worüber beschwerst du dich denn? Du hast es doch, nicht wahr?"

A JOKE

Two friends go to a restaurant and each orders a steak. A few minutes later the waiter comes back with a large piece of meat and a small one. One of the two immediately takes the larger piece. The other is furious and says to him:

"What bad manners you have! Don't you know that since you were the first to help yourself you should have taken the smaller piece?"

The other answers:

"If you had been in my place, which piece would you have taken?"

"The smaller one, of course," says the first one.

"Well, then," the other answers, "what are you complaining about? You have it, don't you?"

NOTES

1. *ein paar*—a few
   ein Paar—a pair
2. *Später kommt der Kellner zurück:* example of inverted word order (verb–subject).

3. *Werden* here is not used as an auxiliary but as the equivalent of "to become" in English.

4. *Ich hätte nehmen sollen:* pluperfect subjunctive. There is no *zu* before *nehmen,* because the auxiliary *sollen* rules the phrase.

5. *Du hättest genommen:* pluperfect subjunctive of *nehmen*

   wärest: Pluperfect of *sein* to be. Note the use of the pluperfect subjunctive in the contrary-to-fact statement referring to past tense.

   If the contrary-to-fact statement were in reference to present time, it would read:

   Welches Stück nähmest du (or: *würdest du nehmen), wenn du an meiner Stelle wärest?* Which piece would you take, if you were in my place?

6. *Worüber:* contraction of *über was.*

REVIEW QUIZ 3

1. *Er hat es _____ (in) seine Tasche getan.*
   a. *auf*
   b. *in*
   c. *im*

2. *Es ist _____ (under) dem Stuhl.*
   a. *darin*
   b. *unter*
   c. *unten*

3. *Sie können es _____ (without) Schwierigkeit tun.*
   a. *ohne*
   b. *durch*
   c. *mit*

4. *Ich habe es* _____ (under) *einem Haufen Papier gefunden.*
   a. *über*
   b. *unter*
   c. *oben*

5. *Man sagt, es sei* _____ (true).
   a. *spricht*
   b. *wahr*
   c. *das*

6. *Ich* _____ (am going) *zur Bank.*
   a. *gehen*
   b. *geht*
   c. *gehe*

7. *Er* _____ (is going) *aufs Land.*
   a. *geht*
   b. *muss*
   c. *gehen*

8. *Geben Sie mir ein* _____ (little) *Wasser!*
   a. *wenig*
   b. *viel*
   c. *hier*

9. *Ich habe nicht* _____ (much) *Geld.*
   a. *wenig*
   b. *viel*
   c. *zu viel*

10. *Das ist* _____ (more) *als das.*
    a. *weniger*
    b. *mehr*
    c. *früh*

11. *Das ist nicht* _____ (enough).
    a. *noch*
    b. *gut*
    c. *genug*

12. *Sie ist* _____ (beautiful).
    a. *gut*
    b. *schön*
    c. *nett*

13. _____ (as) *Sie wünschen.*
    a. *Nicht*
    b. *Wie*
    c. *Sehr*

14. *Wir sind* _____ (all) *da.*
    a. *wie*
    b. *genug*
    c. *alle*

15. _____ (Everyone) *weiss es.*
    a. *Alle*
    b. *Jeder*
    c. *Ganz*

16. *Ich* _____ (think) *nie daran.*
    a. *halte*
    b. *denke*
    c. *bin*

17. *Ich* _____ (hope) *nicht.*
    a. *helfe*
    b. *hoffe*
    c. *nehme an*

18. *Das macht* _____ (nothing).
    a. *nicht*
    b. *nichts*
    c. *schon*

19. *Das ist* _____ (the same).
    a. *dasselbe*
    b. *schon*
    c. *natürlich*

20. *Sind Sie* _____ (already) *fertig?*
    a. *selbst*
    b. *schöner*
    c. *schon*

ANSWERS
1—b; 2—b; 3—a; 4—b; 5—b; 6—c; 7—a; 8—a;
9—b; 10—b; 11—c; 12—b; 13—b; 14—c; 15—b;
16—b; 17—b; 18—b; 19—a; 20—c.

D. WORD STUDY

studieren	(to) study	*Bündel (das)*	bundle
hart	hard	*Karton (der)*	carton
Wagen (der)	wagon	*Farm (die)*	farm
Mitte (die)	middle		

LESSON 31

A. WHO? WHAT? HOW? ETC.

Wer?	Who?	
Was?	What?	Example: *Was hat er gesagt?*
		What did he say?

Wer is declined as follows:

wer	who	Example: *Wer hat das gesagt?*
		Who said that?
wessen	whose	*Wessen Geld ist das?*
		Whose money is that?
wem	to whom	*Wem haben Sie das gesagt?*
		To whom did you say that?
wen	whom	*Wen lieben Sie?*
		Whom do you love?

1. *Wer?* Who?

Wer ist da?
Who is it?

Wer sind Sie?
Who are you?

Wer weiss das?
Who knows that?

Wer kommt mit uns?
Who's coming with us?

Wem gehört das?
Whose is it? (To whom does it belong?)

Für wen ist das?
Who's that for?

Mit wem sprechen Sie?
With whom are you talking?

Über wen sprechen Sie?
Whom are you speaking about?

Mit wem kommen Sie?
With whom are you coming?

Wen möchten Sie sehen?
Whom do you want to see?

Wen suchen Sie?
For whom are you looking?

2. *Was?* What

Mit was? or **Womit?**
With what?

Über was? or **Worüber?**
About what?

Wozu?
To what?

Was gibt es Neues?
What's new?

An wen denken Sie?
Whom are you thinking about?

Was brauchen Sie?
What do you need?

Was sagen Sie?
What are you saying?

Was sagen Sie dazu?
What do you say about that?

Was tun Sie?
What are you doing?

Was möchten Sie?
What do you want?
What would you like?

Was wollten Sie jetzt tun?
What did you want to do now?

Was möchten Sie sagen?
What do you mean?
What would you like to say?

Was suchen Sie?
What are you looking for?

Was haben Sie?
What do you have? What's the matter with you?
What's wrong with you?

Was hat er?
What does he have? What's the matter with him?

NOTES

These forms are used like nouns.

The masculine and feminine forms *Wer*, etc., refer only to persons.

The neuter form *Was* refers to things.

The masculine and feminine forms in the dative and accusative, *wem* and *wen*, do not change when preceded by a preposition.

Mit wem kommt er?	*Mit seinem Vater/seiner Mutter*
With whom is he coming?	With his father/his mother.
Für wen kauft sie den Mantel?	*Für ihren Sohn/ihr Kind.*
For whom is she buying the coat?	For her son/her child.

However, the neuter form *Was* changes to *Wo* whenever connected with a preposition and it is contracted with that preposition.

Mit was	becomes	*womit*	With what?
Für was	becomes	*wofür*	For what?
Zu was	becomes	*wozu*	To what?
Über was	becomes	*worüber*	About what?
Durch was	becomes	*wodurch*	By what?

Womit (Mit was) sehen wir?—Mit den Augen.
With what do we see?—With our (the) eyes.

Wofür (Für was) kämpfen sie?—Für die Freiheit.
What are they fighting for?—For (the) liberty.

3. *Welcher? Welche? Welches?* Which (one)?

These forms are used as adjectives or as nouns. They follow the same declension as the article *der, die, das.*

Welcher Garten ist der schönste?
Which garden is the most beautiful?

Welcher ist Ihr Garten?
Which one is your garden?

Welcher, welche, welches?
Which (one)?

Welcher Mann?
What man? (Which man?)

Welche Männer?
What men? (Which men?)

Welches Buch?
What book? Which book?

Welcher Tag ist heute?
What's today?

In welchem Monat sind wir?
What month is it? ("In which month are we?")

Welche Frau?
What woman?

Welche Frauen?
What women?

Welch ein Unterschied!
What a difference!

**Welcher Unterschied besteht zwischen den beiden
    Dingen?**
What's the difference between the two things?

4. *Was für ein, eine, ein?* What kind of?
Was für remains unchanged. *Ein, eine, ein* follows
the declension of the indefinite article. In the plural
was für stands without an article.

Was für ein Schuh ist das? Das ist ein schwarzer Schuh.
What kind of shoe is that? That is a black shoe.

Was für Schuhe sind das? Das sind schwarze Schuhe.
What kind of shoes are these? These are black shoes.

Das sind schwarze.
These are black ones.

Was für ein Mann ist das?
What kind of man is that?

Was für einen Film sehen Sie?
What kind of movie are you seeing?

Was für Menschen?
What kind of people?

5. *Wie?* How?

Wie?
How?

Aber wie?
But how?

Wie meinen Sie das?
How's that? What do you mean?

Wie heissen Sie?
What's your name?

Wie heisst diese Stadt?
What is the name of this town?

Wie geht's?
How are you?

Wie schreibt man das Wort auf Deutsch?
How do you write this word in German? How's this
    word written in German?

Wie sagen Sie das auf Englisch?
How do you say that in English?

Wie sagen Sie "Thanks" auf Deutsch?
How do you say "Thanks" in German?

Wie ist das geschehen?
How did that happen?

Wie macht man das?
How do you do that?

Wie haben Sie das gemacht?
How did you do (accomplish) it?

Wie geht man dorthin?
How do you go there?

Wieviel Uhr ist es?
What's the time? ("What hour is it?")

Um wieviel Uhr?
What time? ("At what hour?")

6. *Wann?* When?

Wann ist das?
When is it?

Wann kommen Sie?
When are you coming?

Bis wann bleiben Sie?
Until when are you staying?

Wann gehen Sie?
When are you going?

Wann fahren Sie ab?
When are you leaving?

Wann kommt er?
When will he come? When is he coming?

Seit wann sind Sie hier?
How long have you been here?

7. *Warum?* Why?

Und warum nicht?
And why not?

Warum sagen Sie das?
Why do you say that?

Warum hat er das getan?
Why did he do it?

QUIZ 23

1. *Was tun Sie?*	a. What's new?
2. *Was wünschen Sie?*	b. What do you need?
3. *Was gibt es?*	c. And why not?

4. *Was möchten Sie
   sagen?*

d. Why do you say
   that?

5. *Was suchen Sie?*

e. Why did he do it?

6. *Wie heisst diese
   Strasse?*

f. What's your name?

7. *Was macht das
   aus?*

g. How are you?

8. *Welch ein Unter-
   schied?*

h. But how?

9. *Welcher ist besser?*

i. When are you leav-
   ing?

10. *Wann fahren Sie
    ab?*

j. Who are you?

11. *Wer sind Sie?*

k. Whom do you want
   to see?

12. *Wen möchten Sie
    sehen?*

l. What a difference?

13. *Was brauchen Sie?*

m. Which is the better?

14. *Warum hat er es
    getan?*

n. What do you mean?

15. *Aber wie?*

n. What are you look-
   ing for?

16. *Wie geht's?*

p. What's the matter?

17. *Warum sagen Sie
    das?*

q. What difference
   does it make? What
   does it matter?

18. *Und warum nicht?*

r. What's the name of
   this street?

19. *Was gibt es Neues?*

s. What are you do-
   ing?

20. *Wie heissen Sie?*

t. What do you want?

ANSWERS
1—s; 2—t; 3—p; 4—n; 5—o; 6—r; 7—q; 8—l;
9—m; 10—i; 11—j; 12—k; 13—b; 14—e; 15—h;
16—g; 17—d; 18—c; 19—a; 20—f.

B. WORD STUDY

komisch	comical	*Land (das)*	land
Muskel (der)	muscle	*Juni (der)*	June
Fuss (der)	foot	*Boot (das)*	boat
Haar (das)	hair	*Offizier (der)*	officer
Hand (die)	hand		

C. HOW MUCH?

Der Preis?
The price?

Was ist der Preis?
What's the price? (How is the price?)

Wieviel?
How much?

Wieviel macht es?
How much is it?

Wieviel für alles?
How much for everything? How much does it all cost?

Wieviel für jedes?
How much each?

Wieviel pro Dutzend?
How much a dozen?

Wieviel wollen Sie dafür haben?
How much do you want for it?

D. HOW MANY?

Wie viele?
How many?

Wieviel Geld?
How much (money)?

Wie viele Menschen?
How many people?

Wieviel Zeit?
How much time?

Wieviel Zeit braucht man, um dorthin zu kommen?
How long ("how much time") does it take to get there?

Wie viele sind dort?
How many are there?

Wie viele bleiben davon übrig?
How many of them are left?

Wie viele haben Sie davon?
How many of them ("of it") do you have?

Den wievielten haben wir heute?
What's (the date) today? ("How many have we today?")

Der wievielte ist Montag?
What's the date Monday? ("The how many will Monday be?")

QUIZ 24

1. *Wieviel gibt es davon?*
2. *Wieviel macht es?*
3. *Wieviel möchten Sie davon?*

4. *Welcher Preis?*
5. *Wieviel Zeit? Wie lange?*
6. *Den wievielten haben wir?*
7. *Wieviel bleibt davon übrig?*
8. *Wie viele haben Sie davon?*
9. *Welcher Preis ist das?*
10. *Der wievielte ist Montag?*

a. How much remains?
b. What's the date today? ("The how many?")
c. What's the date Monday?
d. What's the price?
e. What price?
f. How much is it?
g. How many do you want?
h. How much time? How long?
i. How many of them do you have?
j. How many are there?

ANSWERS
1—j; 2—f; 3—g; 4—e; 5—h; 6—b; 7—a; 8—i;
9—d; 10—c.

LESSON 32

A. SOME, SOMEONE, SOMETHING,
SOMETIMES

etwas
some, something

etwas Geld
some money

etwas Neues
Something new

einige Menschen, einige Leute
some people

einige Wörter
some words, a few words

jemand
someone, somebody

Ist jemand hier, der das kann?
Is there anyone here who can do it?

manchmal
sometimes

Ich sehe ihn manchmal.
I see him sometimes.

B. ONCE, TWICE

einmal
once, one time

zweimal
twice, two times

das erste Mal
the first time

das nächste Mal
the next time

das letzte Mal
the last time

noch einmal
another time; again; once more

jedes Mal, *jedesmal*
every time, each time

dieses Mal, diesmal
this time

C.   UP TO

bis
up to

bis jetzt
up to now

Bis jetzt hat er keine Arbeit gefunden.
Up to now he hasn't found any work.

bis dort
up to there

Wir fahren bis dorthin.
We are going (driving) up to that point.

Bis zu Ende
(up) to the end

Ich bleibe bis Ende August.
I'm staying until the end of August.

bis zum Bahnhof
up to (as far as) the station

Er fährt uns nur bis München.
He's driving us only as far as Munich.

Er fährt uns bis zum Bahnhof.
He's driving us up to the train station.

bis heute abend
up to this evening; See you this evening.

Also, bis heute abend!
Well then, see you this evening.

Der Film spielt bis heute abend.
The movie is playing until tonight.

bis morgen
up to tomorrow; See you tomorrow.

bis Montag
up to Monday; See you Monday.

D.   I NEED IT, IT'S NECESSARY

Ich brauche es.
I need it (that).

Das braucht er nicht.
He doesn't need it (that).

Brauchen Sie etwas?
Do you need anything?

Ich brauche nichts.
I don't need anything.

Ich brauche es überhaupt nicht.
I don't need it at all.

Sie brauchen es nicht zu kaufen.[1]
You do not need to (have to) buy it.

Es ist unbedingt notwendig, dass ich Sie spreche.
It's absolutely necessary that I speak to you.

Sie müssen es ihm sagen.
You have to (must) tell him.

Sie müssen früh nach Hause kommen.
You must come home early.

Sie müssen die Wahrheit sagen.
You must tell the truth.

NOTE

After the modal verb *müssen,* the main verb is placed at the end of the sentence in its infinitive form without *zu.* The following are modal verbs: *dürfen* (to be allowed, ''may''), *mögen* (to like), *müssen* (to have to, ''must''), *sollen* (ought to, is supposed to, ''should''), *können* (to be able to, ''can''), and *wollen* (to want).

E.   I FEEL LIKE . . .

Ich möchte es haben.
I'd like to have it. I feel like having it.

Ich möchte nicht dorthin gehen.
I don't feel like going there.

[1]Note that the infinitive construction includes *zu.*

Ich möchte gern einen Apfel essen.
I feel like having an apple.

Möchten Sie gern den Film sehen?
Would you like to see this movie?

F. AT THE HOME OF

zu Hause
at home

bei
at the home of

Fühlen Sie sich wie zu Hause!
Make yourself at home.

Wir waren bei Freunden.
We were at some friends' house.

Ich werde Sie bei Müllers sehen.
I'll see you at the Müllers'.

Er war beim (*bei dem*) **Arzt.**
He was at the doctor's.

Kommen Sie zu uns!
Come over to our place.

**Ich wohnte bei meinen Eltern, als ich die Stellung
bekam.**
I was living with my parents when I got the job.

Ist Herr Müller zu Hause?
Is Mr. Müller at home?

Ich muss zum Arzt gehen.
I have to go to the doctor's.

G. HERE IT IS, THERE IT IS

Hier ist es!
Here it is!

Hier bin ich.
Here I am.

Hier ist er.
Here he is.

Hier ist sie.
Here she is.

Hier sind sie.
Here they are.

Hier ist das Buch.
Here's the book.

Dort ist es!
There it is!

Dort ist er.
There he is.

Dort ist sie.
There she is.

Dort sind sie.
There they are.

QUIZ 25

1. *Ich brauche etwas Geld.*	a. to the end of May.
2. *einmal*	b. I need that.
3. *bis Ende Mai*	c. Here's the book.
4. *Ich brauche das*	d. I need some money.
5. *Hier ist das Buch.*	e. Once

ANSWERS
1—d; 2—e; 3—a; 4—b; 5—c.

REVIEW QUIZ 4

1. _____ (What) *ist der Name dieser Stadt?*
   a. *Was*
   b. *Welches*
   c. *Wann*

2. _____ (Who) *sind Sie?*
   a. *Wer*
   b. *Welcher*
   c. *Wo*

3. _____ (When) *wird er kommen?*
   a. *Wenn*
   b. *Wann*
   c. *Welcher*

4. _____ (Why) *sagen Sie das?*
   a. *Wo*
   b. *Wann*
   c. *Warum*

5. *Das* _____ (twelfth) *Kapitel ist sehr lang.*
    a. *zwölfte*
    b. *siebzehnte*
    c. *sechste*

6. *Der Hut hat mich* _____ (fifty-four) *Mark gekostet.*
    a. *fünfundfünfzig*
    b. *fünfundvierzig*
    c. *vierundfünfzig*

7. *Ich wohne Nummer* _____ (seventeen) *Friedrichstrasse.*
    a. *dreiunddreissig*
    b. *siebzehn*
    c. *siebzig*

8. *Es ist* _____ (noon).
    a. *Mittag*
    b. *Mitternacht*
    c. *elf Uhr*

9. *Wir sehen uns um* _____ (six) *Uhr.*
    a. *fünf*
    b. *sieben*
    c. *sechs*

10. *Es ist* _____ (time), *es zu tun.*
    a. *Uhr*
    b. *Zeit*
    c. *Stunde*

11. *Wir haben heute* _____ (Wednesday).
    a. *Dienstag*
    b. *Mittwoch*
    c. *Montag*

12. *Er fährt* _____ (Tuesday) *ab.*
    a. *Dienstag*
    b. *Donnerstag*
    c. *Mittwoch*

13. *Heute ist der erste* _____ (June).
    a. *Juni*
    b. *Juli*
    c. *August*

14. *Er* _____ (need) *das nicht.*
    a. *macht*
    b. *braucht*
    c. *müssen*

15. _____ (how) *schreibt man das Wort auf Deutsch?*
    a. *Warum*
    b. *Wie*
    c. *Wann*

16. *Ich bin am* _____ (twelve) *April geboren.*
    a. *zwanzigsten*
    b. *elften*
    c. *zwölften*

17. _____ (Here's) *das Buch.*
    a. *Hier ist*
    b. *Dort ist*
    c. *Wo*

18. *Ich habe mein* _____ (money) *verloren.*
    a. *Tasche*
    b. *Geld*
    c. *Hof*

19. *Er arbeitet von* _____ (morning) *bis abends.*
    a. *morgens*
    b. *nachts*
    c. *nachmittags*

20. *An welcher Station muss ich* _____ (get off)*?*
    a. *gehen*
    b. *aussteigen*
    c. *anrufen*

ANSWERS
1—a; 2—a; 3—b; 4—c; 5—a; 6—c; 7—b; 8—a;
9—c; 10—b; 11—b; 12—a; 13—a; 14—b; 15—b;
16—c; 17—a; 18—b; 19—a; 20—b.

LESSON 33

A. ON THE ROAD

Verzeihung!
Pardon me.

Entschuldigen Sie!
Excuse me.

Wie heisst diese Stadt?
What is the name of this town (city)?

Wie weit sind wir von Berlin?
How far are we from Berlin?

Wieviel Kilometer sind es von hier bis Linz?
How many kilometers from here to Linz?

Von hier sind es zehn Kilometer.
It's ten kilometers from here.

Das ist zwanzig Kilometer von hier.
That's twenty kilometers from here.

Wie komme ich von hier nach Salzburg?
How do I get to Salzburg from here?

Fahren Sie diese Strasse entlang!
Follow this road.

Wo soll ich abbiegen?
Where should I turn?

Darf ich hier parken?
May I park here?

B. WALKING AROUND

Wie komme ich zu dieser Adresse?
How do I get to this address?

**Können Sie mir sagen, wie ich zu dieser Adresse
komme?**
Can you tell me how I can get to this address?

Können Sie mir sagen, wie ich dorthin komme?
Can you tell me how I can get to this place?

Haben Sie einen Stadtplan?
Do you have a map of the city?

Ich glaube, ich habe mich verlaufen.
I think I'm lost.

Wie heisst diese Strasse?
What is the name of this street?

Können Sie mir sagen, wo sich diese Strasse befindet?
Can you tell me where this street is?

Wo ist die Kaiserstrasse?
Where is Kaiser Street?

Ist es weit von hier?
Is it far from here?

Wie weit ist es?
How far is it?

Kann ich zu Fuss dahin?
Can I get there by foot?

Ist es in der Nähe?
Is it near here?

Es ist die dritte Strasse rechts.
It's the third street to the right.

Gehen Sie diesen Weg!
Go this way.

Gehen Sie geradeaus!
Go straight ahead.

Gehen Sie bis zur Ecke und dann links!
Go to the corner and turn left.

Nehmen Sie die erste Seitenstrasse rechts!
Turn right ("Take the first side street to the right").

Wo befindet sich die Garage?
Where is the garage?

Wo befindet sich das Polizeiamt?
Where is the police station?

Wo befindet sich das Museum?
Where is the museum?

C. Bus, Train, Subway

Wo ist die Bushaltestelle?
Where is the bus stop?

Wievel kostet eine Fahrt?
How much is the fare?

Sagen Sie mir bitte, wann ich austeigen muss.
Please tell me when to get off.

An welcher Station muss ich aussteigen?
What station do I get off at?

Wo muss ich aussteigen?
Where do I get off?

Wo ist der Bahnhof?
Where is the train station?

Wohin fährt dieser Zug?
Where does this train go?

Wo bekomme ich den Zug nach Berlin?
Where do I get the train for Berlin?

Auf Gleis zwei.
On track two.

Der Zug ist gerade abgefahren.
The train just left.

Um wieviel Uhr fährt der nächste Zug ab?
What time does the next train leave?

**Könnte (*Kann*) ich eine Rückfahrkarte nach Berlin
 haben?**
Could (May) I have a round-trip ticket for Berlin?

Wieviel macht das?
How much is that?

Siebzig Mark fünfundzwanzig.
Seventy marks and twenty-five pfennigs.

Wie lange dauert die Reise?
How long does it take to get there (''does the trip
 last'')?

Etwas über eine Stunde.
A little over an hour.

Gibt es einen Taxistand in der Nähe?
Is there a taxi stand nearby?

Wo ist die nächste U-Bahn-Station?
Where is the nearest subway station?

D.   WORD STUDY

Parfüm (*das*)	perfume	*neu*	new
falsch	false	*Australien*	Australia
		(*das*)	

freundlich	friendly	*rund*	round
frisch	fresh	*März*	March
grün	green	*brechen*	(to) break

LESSON 34

A. WRITING AND MAILING LETTERS

Ich möchte einen Brief schreiben.
I'd like to write a letter.

Haben Sie einen Bleistift?
Do you have a pencil?

Haben Sie einen Kugelschreiber?
Do you have a ballpoint pen?

Haben Sie eine Feder?
Do you have a pen?

Haben Sie Schreibpapier?
Do you have writing paper?

Haben Sie einen Briefumschlag?
Do you have an envelope?

Haben Sie eine Briefmarke?
Do you have a stamp?

Wo kann ich eine Briefmarke kaufen?
Where can I buy a stamp?

Haben Sie eine Luftpostmarke?
Do you have an air-mail stamp?

Wo befindet sich das Postamt?
Where is the post office?

Wie viele Briefmarken brauche ich für diesen Brief?
How many stamps do I need on this letter?

Ich möchte diesen Brief aufgeben.
I'd like to mail this letter.

Wo ist der Briefkasten?
Where is the mailbox?

An der Ecke.
At the corner.

B. FAXES AND TELEGRAMS

Ich möchte ein Telefax senden.
I'd like to send a facsimile.

Ich möchte etwas faxen.
I'd like to fax (something).

Wo kann ich ein Telefax aufgeben?
Where can I send a fax?

Wieviel kostet ein Telefax nach Berlin?
How much is a fax to Berlin?

Ich möchte ein Telegramm senden.
I'd like to send a telegram.

Wo befindet sich das Telegrafenamt?
Where is the telegraph office?

Es ist im Postamt.
It's in the post office.

Wieviel kostet ein Telegramm nach Berlin?
How much is a telegram to Berlin?

Wie lange dauert es bis dorthin?
How long will it take to get there?

C.   TELEPHONES

Gibt es ein Telefon hier?
Is there a phone here?

Wo kann ich telefonieren?
Where can I phone?

Wo befindet sich das Telefon?
Where is the telephone?

Wo ist ein öffentlicher Fernsprecher?
Where is the phone booth?

Im Zigarrengeschäft.
In the tobacco shop.

Darf ich (Dürfte ich) Ihr Telefon benutzen?
May I (Might I) use your phone?

Selbstverständlich! Bitte sehr!
Of course! Go ahead!

Ein Ferngespräch, bitte.
May I have long distance, please?

Was kostet ein Gespräch nach Hamburg?
How much is a (telephone) call to Hamburg?

Bitte sieben elf einundzwanzig.
7 11 21, please.

Einen Augenblick, bitte.
One moment, please.

Die Leitung ist besetzt.
The line's busy.

Sie haben mich falsch verbunden.
You gave me the wrong number.

Niemand antwortet.
There is no answer.

Kann ich bitte Herrn Wagner sprechen?
May I speak to Mr. Wagner, please?

Am Apparat.
Speaking.

Hier Lorenz.
This is Mr. Lorenz speaking.

LESSON 35

A. WHAT IS YOUR NAME?

Wie heissen Sie?
What is your name?

Ich heisse Hans Bauer.
My name is Hans Bauer.

Wie heisst er?
What is his name?

Er heisst Fritz Müller.
His name is Fritz Müller.

Wie heisst sie?
What is her name?

Sie heisst Lotte Schneider.
Her name is Lotte Schneider.

Wie heissen sie?
What are their names?

Er heisst Ludwig Schmitz und sie heisst Grete Meier.
His name is Ludwig Schmitz and hers is Grete Meier.

Was ist sein Vorname?
What's his first name?

Sein Vorname ist Mark.
His first name is Mark.

Was ist sein Familienname?
What is his last name?

Sein Familienname ist Pulver.
His last name is Pulver.

B. WHERE ARE YOU FROM?

Woher sind Sie?
Where are you from?

Woher kommen Sie?
Where do you come from?

Ich bin aus den Vereinigten Staaten.
I'm from the United States.

Ich komme aus Berlin.
I'm from Berlin.

Wo sind Sie geboren?
Where were you born?

Ich bin in Hamburg geboren.
I was born in Hamburg.

Ich wohne in England.
I live in England.

C. HOW OLD ARE YOU?

Wie alt sind Sie?
How old are you?

Ich bin zwanzig Jahre alt.
I'm twenty (years old).

Ich werde einundzwanzig im September.
I'll be twenty-one in September.

Ich wurde am neunzehnten August neunzehnhundertfünfundfünfzig geboren.
I was born August 19, 1955.

Wann ist Ihr Geburtstag?
When is your birthday?

Mein Geburtstag ist in zwei Wochen, am drei-undzwanzigsten Januar.
My birthday is in two weeks, January 23rd.

Wieviele Geschwister haben Sie?
How many brothers and sisters do you have?

Ich habe zwei Brüder.
I have two brothers.

Der älteste ist zweiundzwanzig (Jahre alt).
The oldest is twenty-two (years old).

Er besucht die Universität.
He attends the university.

Der jüngste ist siebzehn.
The youngest is seventeen.

Er ist das letzte Jahr auf dem Gymnasium.
He's in the last year of the "Gymnasium" (college prep school).

Wie viele Schwestern haben Sie?
How many sisters do you have?

Ich habe eine Schwester.
I have one sister.

Sie ist fünfzehn.
She's fifteen.

D. PROFESSIONS

Was machen Sie beruflich?
What's your occupation?

Was sind Sie von Beruf?
What's your profession?

Ich bin Arzt.
I'm a doctor.

Ich bin Ärztin.
I'm a doctor.

Was tut Ihr Vater?
What does your father do?

Was tut Ihre Mutter?
What does your mother do?

Was tut Ihr Mann?
What does your husband do?

Was tut Ihre Frau?
What does your wife do?

Sie ist Rechtsanwältin.
She's a lawyer.

Er ist Rechtsanwalt.
He's a lawyer.

Er ist Architekt.
He's an architect.

Sie ist Lehrerin.
She's a teacher.

Er ist Universitätsprofessor.
He's a university professor.

Sie ist Zahnärztin.
She's a dentist.

Sie ist Krankenpflegerin.
She's a nurse.

Er ist Geschäftsmann.
He's in business.

Er ist im Textilhandel.
He's in the textile business.

Er ist Landwirt.
He's a farmer.

Sie ist Beamtin.
She's a government employee.

Er ist Techniker.
He's a technician.

Er arbeitet in einer Automobilfabrik.
He works in an automobile factory.

NOTES

1. German does not use indefinite articles when
   speaking of professions: *Sie ist Verkäuferin.* She
   is a salesperson.
2. The feminine forms are derived in most cases
   by adding the suffix -*in* and placing an umlaut
   over the main vowel.

E.   FAMILY MATTERS

Haben Sie Verwandte hier?
Do you have any relatives here?

Wohnt Ihre ganze Familie hier?
Does your whole family live here?

Meine ganze Familie ausser meinen Grosseltern.
All my family except my grandparents.

Sie wohnen auf einem Gut, in Westfalen.
They live in a country home, in Westphalia.

Sind Sie mit Herrn Schneider verwandt?
Are you related to Mr. Schneider?

Er ist mein Onkel.
He's my uncle.

Er ist mein Vetter.
He's my cousin.

Sind Sie mit Frau Müller verwandt?
Are you related to Mrs. Müller?

Sie ist meine Tante.
She's my aunt.

Sie ist meine Kusine.
She's my cousin.

REVIEW QUIZ 5

1. *Wie heisst* _____ (this) *Stadt?*
   a. *dieser*
   b. *dieses*
   c. *diese*

2. _____ (How) *komme ich von hier nach Berlin?*
    a. *Wieviel*
    b. *Wie*
    c. *Welcher*

3. _____ (How) *heisst diese Strasse?*
    a. *Was*
    b. *Wann*
    c. *Wie*

4. _____ (Where) *ist die Friedrichstrasse?*
    a. *Wo*
    b. *Wann*
    c. *Dass*

5. _____ (go) *diesen Weg?*
    a. *Gehen Sie*
    b. *Gehen wir*
    c. *Gehen sie*

6. *Gehen Sie zur Ecke und nehmen Sie die erste Strasse nach* _____ (left).
    a. *links*
    b. *rechts*
    c. *weit*

7. _____ (How much) *macht es?*
    a. *Wie*
    b. *Wieviel*
    c. *Dass*

8. *Ich möchte einen Brief* _____ (to write).
    a. *zu schreiben*
    b. *schreiben*
    c. *schreibe*

9. *Wo kann ich eine* _____ (stamp) *kaufen?*
   - a. *Briefmarke*
   - b. *Post*
   - c. *Stempel*

10. *An der Ecke von dieser* _____ (street) *gibt es einen Briefkasten.*
    - a. *Strasse*
    - b. *Bahnhof*
    - c. *Allee*

11. _____ (Is there) *ein Telefon hier?*
    - a. *Gibt es*
    - b. *Es gibt*
    - c. *Haben*

12. *Fräulein, Sie haben mich* _____ (wrong) *verbunden.*
    - a. *falsch*
    - b. *viel*
    - c. *nicht*

13. *Was ist sein* _____ (first name)?
    - a. *Vorname*
    - b. *Familie*
    - c. *nennt sich*

14. *Wo sind Sie* _____ (born)?
    - a. *gewesen*
    - b. *geboren*
    - c. *gekommen*

15. *Der jüngste ist siebzehn* _____ (years) *alt.*
    - a. *Jahre*
    - b. *Jahr*
    - c. *jährlich*

16. *Er ist* _____ (lawyer).
   a. *Professor*
   b. *Rechtsanwalt*
   c. *Beamter*

17. *Er ist* _____ (worker).
   a. *Arbeiter*
   b. *Geschäftsmann*
   c. *Fabrik*

18. *Sie wohnen auf einem Gut,* _____ (near) *von Westfalen.*
   a. *in der Nähe*
   b. *in*
   c. *weit*

19. _____ (Follow) *dieser Strassenbahn!*
   a. *Gehen Sie*
   b. *Folgen Sie*
   c. *Nehmen Sie*

20. *Ist es* _____ (far) *von hier?*
   a. *weit*
   b. *geradeaus*
   c. *nahe*

21. *Auf* _____ (track) *zwei.*
   a. *Gleis*
   b. *Rückkehr*
   c. *Zug*

22. *Das bin* _____ (I).
   a. *mir*
   b. *mich*
   c. *ich*

23. *Das ist nicht* _____ (free).
   a. *früh*
   b. *falsch*
   c. *frei*

24. *Sind Sie mit Herrn Schneider* _____ (related)?
   a. *gekommen*
   b. *verwandt*
   c. *gefahren*

25. *Meine ganze Familie,* _____ (except) *meinen Grosseltern, kommen aus Frankfurt am Main.*
   a. *ausser*
   b. *aus*
   c. *davon*

ANSWERS
1—c; 2—b; 3—c; 4—a; 5—a; 6—a; 7—b; 8—b; 9—a; 10—a; 11—a; 12—a; 13—a; 14—b; 15—a; 16—b; 17—a; 18—a; 19—b; 20—a; 21—a; 22—a; 23—a; 24—b; 25—a.

LESSON 36

A. SHOPPING

Einkäufe
Purchases
 1. Wieviel kostet das?
   How much is this?

 2. Zehn Mark.
   Ten marks.

3. **Das ist zu teuer. Haben Sie nichts anderes?**
That's too expensive. Haven't you anything else?

4. **Von derselben Sorte?**
Of the same kind?

5. **Ja, dasselbe oder etwas Ähnliches.**
Yes, the same kind or something similar.

6. **Wir haben so etwas.**
We have this.

7. **Können Sie mir nichts anderes zeigen?**
Don't you have anything else to show me?

8. **Etwas Billigeres?**
Something cheaper?

9. **Wenn möglich.**
If possible.

10. **Möchten Sie so etwas?**
Would you like this?

11. **Das kommt auf den Preis an.**
That depends on the price.

12. **Das kostet acht Mark.**
This is eight marks.

13. **Und das hier? Ist es billiger oder teurer?**
How about this? Is it cheaper or more expensive?

14. **Teurer.**
More expensive.

15. Haben Sie nichts anderes?
Haven't you anything else?

**16. Im Moment nicht, aber ich erwarte einige Neu-
heiten.**
Not at the moment, but I'm expecting some new
styles.

17. Wann?
When?

**18. Jeden Tag. Kommen Sie gegen Ende der
Woche.**
Any day now. Drop in toward the end of the
week.

19. Ganz bestimmt. Übrigens, wieviel kostet es?
I'll do that. By the way, how much is this?

20. Fünfzehn Mark das Paar.
Fifteen marks a pair.

21. Geben Sie mir ein Dutzend (davon)!
Let me have a dozen (of them).

22. Möchten Sie sie mitnehmen?
Will you take them with you?

23. Nein, bitte lassen Sie sie mir zuschicken!
No, please have them delivered.

24. Immer noch an dieselbe Adresse?
Still at the same address?

25. Ja, es ist immer noch dieselbe.
Yes, it's still the same.

26. Danke schön. Auf Wiedersehen!
Thank you very much. Good-bye.

27. Auf Wiedersehen!
Good-bye.

NOTES

1. *Wieviel kostet es?* How much does it cost?
   Was macht es? How much does that make?
4. *Von:* always with the dative case.
5. *Ähnliches* has neuter declension, because it refers to *etwas* which is always neuter.
6. *So etwas:* Something like this.
8. *Etwas billigeres:* Something cheaper; neuter declension.
10. *Möchten Sie:* Would you like to?; polite form to express a want or wish; (conditional of *mögen*).
11. *ankommen* (*an-kommen*): separable prefix idiomatically, to depend on.
12. *Mark:* always singular.
13. Comparative: two examples of the comparative. Note that the second *e* in *teuer* is dropped in the comparative form.
16. *Im:* contraction of *in dem* (dative). *Einige:* Use for *etwas* to express something precise.
18. *Jeden Tag:* accusative as generally used for expressions of time. *Gegen Ende* (idiomatic) toward the end; requires no article.
19. *Ganz bestimmt:* "Quite definite, certainly."
21. *mir:* Dative of the personal pronoun.
22. *mitnehmen* (*mit-nehmen*): separable prefix. *Ich nahm es mit.* I took it along.
23. *schicken lassen:* to have something sent. *machen lassen:* to have something done or

made; *bauen lassen:* to have something built; etc.

24. *an* plus accusative (motion toward a destination): *Er schickt es an mich.*

B. GENERAL SHOPPING EXPRESSIONS

Wo finde ich . . .
Where can I find . . .

Können Sie mir helfen?
Can you help me?

Ich schaue mich nur um.
I'm just browsing.

Ich suche eine Armbanduhr.
I'm looking for a wristwatch.

Zeigen Sie mir bitte einen Pullover.
Please show me a sweater.

Ich möchte etwas Billigeres.
I'd like something less expensive.

Ich möchte etwas Grösseres.
I'd like something bigger.

Ich möchte etwas Kleineres.
I'd like something smaller.

Können Sie es mir bitte bestellen?
Can you please order it for me?

Ich nehme es.
I'll take it.

Wo ist die Kasse?
Where do I pay?

Kann ich das umtauschen?
Can I exchange this?

Kann ich mit Reiseschecks bezahlen?
Can I pay with traveler's checks?

QUIZ 26

1. _____ (How much) *macht das?*
   a. *Wieviel*
   b. *Wie*
   c. *Wann*

2. *Von derselben* _____ (kind).
   a. *Sorte*
   b. *Sache*
   c. *Abteilung*

3. *Ja, von derselben Sorte* _____ (or) *etwas ähnliches.*
   a. *wann*
   b. *oder*
   c. *und*

4. *Es gibt* _____ (this).
   a. *den*
   b. *das*
   c. *dieser*

5. *Etwas* _____ (less).
   a. *aber*
   b. *weniger*
   c. *nichts*

6. _____ (That) *kommt auf den Preis an.*
   a. *Das*
   b. *Dieses*
   c. *Dem*

7. *Ich möchte etwas* _____ (less expensive).
   a. *Kleineres*
   b. *Billigeres*
   c. *Grösseres*

8. _____ (When) *denn?*
   a. *Wie*
   b. *Wieviel*
   c. *Wann*

9. *Geben Sie mir ein Dutzend* _____ (of them)!
   a. *dort*
   b. *davon*
   c. *dann*

10. *Nein, schicken Sie* _____ (them) *mir, bitte!*
    a. *sie*
    b. *ihnen*
    c. *es*

ANSWERS
1—a; 2—a; 3—b; 4—c; 5—b; 6—a; 7—b; 8—c;
9—b; 10—a.

LESSON 37

A. ORDERING BREAKFAST

1. *Es ist Viertel nach sieben morgens. Herr und Frau Kleinmann möchten im Frühstückszimmer des Hotels frühstücken.*

It's a quarter past seven in the morning. Mr. and Mrs. Kleinmann would like to have breakfast in the breakfast room of the hotel.

2. *Herr K.:* **Du bist sicher hungrig, nicht wahr?**
Mr. K.: You're probably hungry, right?

3. *Frau K.:* **Ja, ich möchte ein gutes Frühstück essen.**
Mrs. K.: Yes, I would like to eat a good breakfast.

4. *Herr K.:* **Das Frühstückszimmer im Hotel soll sehr gut sein. Die Auswahl und die Bedienung sind erstklassig. Gehen wir dorthin und bestellen wir Frühstück!**
Mr. K.: They say the breakfast room in the hotel is very good. The selection (of foods) and the service are outstanding. Let's go there and order some breakfast.

5. *Frau K.:* **Das ist eine gute Idee.**
Mrs. K.: That's a good idea.

6. *Herr und Frau Kleinmann gehen ins Cafe. Die Hostess begrüsst sie und setzt das Ehepaar an einen Tisch. Dann kommt der Kellner mit der Speisekarte an.*
Mr. and Mrs. Kleinmann go into the breakfast room. The hostess greets them and seats the couple at a table. Then the waiter arrives with the menu.

7. *Herr K.:* **Guten Morgen. Herr Ober, wir möchten gleich bestellen.**

Mr. K.: Good morning. We would like to order right away.

8. *Kellner:* **Bitte sehr.**
   Waiter: Yes?

9. *Herr K.:* **Wir möchten mit Apfelsaft anfangen.**
   Mr. K.: We'd like to start with some apple juice.

10. *Frau K.:* **Ich ziehe ein Gläschen Orangensaft vor.**
    Mrs. K.: I prefer a small glass of orange juice.

11. *Kellner:* **Also, einmal Apfelsaft und einmal Orangensaft. Heute gibt es auch Spiegeleier mit Speck oder Schinken, Rühreier, weichgekochte Eier, Pfannkuchen und gekochte Haferflocken.**
    Waiter: Okay, one apple juice and one orange juice. Today we also have eggs sunny side up with bacon or ham, scrambled eggs, soft boiled eggs, pancakes, and cooked oats.

12. *Herr K.:* **Ich nehme eine Portion Pfannkuchen, zwei Spigelgeleier mit Toast und ein Kännchen Bohnenkaffee.**
    Mr. K.: I'll have an order of pancakes, two eggs sunny side up, and a pot of regular coffee.

13. *Kellner:* **Und Sie, gnädige Frau?**
    Waiter: And you, madam?

14. *Frau K.:* **Ich möchte lieber ein Kännchen Tee mit Zitrone, ein Kaiserbrötchen mit Butter und Marmelade.**

Mrs. K.: I prefer a pot of tea with lemon, a large roll with butter and marmalade.

15. *Kellner:* **Wir haben Erdbeeren- und Aprikosenmarmelade.**
Waiter: We have strawberry and apricot marmalade.

16. *Frau K.:* **Ich möchte beides versuchen. Und bringen Sie mir bitte auch ein weichgekochtes Ei und zwei Scheiben Toast.**
Mrs. K.: I'd like to try both. And would you also please bring me a soft-boiled egg and two slices of toast.

17. *Kellner:* **Ich bringe Ihnen gleich den Kaffee und den Tee. Noch etwas?**
Waiter: I'll bring you the coffee and the tea right away. Will that be all?

18. *Herr K.:* **Nein, es fehlt mir eine Serviette.**
Mr. K.: No, I'm missing a napkin.

19. *Frau K.:* **Und noch etwas mehr Zucker, bitte.**
Mrs. K.: And a little more sugar, please.

20. *Keller:* **Verzeihung! Ich bringe Ihnen alles sofort.**
Waiter: Pardon me. I'll bring you everything right away.

21. *Der Kellner kommt sofort mit einer frischen Serviette, dem Zucker, einem Kännchen Kaffee und Tee zurück.*
The waiter returns immediately with a fresh napkin, the sugar, and a pot of coffee and tea.

22. *Kellner:* **Bitte sehr.**
Waiter: Here you are.

23. *Nach fünf Minuten bringt der Kellner die Pfannkuchen, die Brötchen, ein weichgekochtes Ei und die Marmelade zum Tisch.*
After five minutes the waiter brings the pancakes, the rolls, a soft-boiled egg, and marmalade to the table.

24. *Herr K.:* **Herr Ober, der Kaffee ist kalt geworden. Möchten Sie so gut sein und mir frischen Kaffee auf den Tisch stellen?**
Mr. K.: Waiter, the coffee has gotten cold. Would you be so kind and put some fresh coffee on the table?

25. *Kellner:* **Gerne.**
Waiter: Gladly (Of course).

26. *Nach etwa zwanzig Minuten . . .*
After some twenty minutes . . .

27. *Herr K.:* **Herr Ober, die Rechnung, bitte.**
Mr. K.: Waiter, the check, please.

28. *Kellner:* **Bitte schön!**
Waiter: Here you are, sir.

29. *Herr Kleinmann zahlt die Rechnung, legt ein extra Trinkgeld auf den Tisch und verlässt die Kaffeestube mit seiner Frau.*
Mr. Kleinmann pays the bill, puts an extra tip on the table, and leaves the coffee shop with his wife.

30. *Kellner:* **Danke schön, mein Herr! Auf Wiedersehen, gnädige Frau.**
Waiter: Thank you very much, sir. Good-bye, madam.

31. *Herr und Frau K.:* **Auf Wiedersehen!**
Mr. and Mrs. K.: Good-bye.

NOTES

1. *das Frühstückszimmer,* the breakfast room (of a hotel). Sometimes it is known as a *Kaffeestube*, equivalent to a coffee shop.
2. *hungrig sein,* "to be hungry." One can also express "to be hungry" by *Hunger haben: Ich habe grossen Hunger,* "I'm very hungry."
4. *die Auswahl,* the selection, from the verb *auswählen,* "to choose, select." *die Bedienung*, the service, from *bedienen* "to serve."
6. *das Ehepaar,* the married couple. *die Speisekarte,* the menu, from *speisen,* "to have a meal," and *Karte,* "card."
7. *Herr Ober:* abbreviation for *Oberkellner,* "headwaiter."
8. *Bitte sehr:* Yes, may I help you? When the waiter or waitress brings you your order, he/she might say *"bitte schön."* Ordinarily this expression means "Thank you"; it has the idiomatic meaning of "It's a pleasure to serve you, now enjoy your meal."
9. *anfangen:* a separable prefix verb. *Ich fange . . . an; du fängst . . . an; er, sie es fängt . . . an; wir fangen . . . an; ihr fangt . . . an; sie (Sie) fangen . . . an.* It is used in its infinitive form because it is used in conjunction with the conditional form of *mögen.*

10. *ein Gläschen:* the diminutive form of *Glas.*

12. *ein Kännchen Bohnenkaffee:* a pot of coffee, tea, or chocolate is usually ordered. The pot holds about two and a half cups. *Bohnenkaffee* means the person wished to order 100 percent coffee, and no substitutes.

13. *gnädige Frau:* a polite form used in addressing a married woman.

14. *ich möchte lieber* is equivalent to *ich ziehe . . . vor:* "I prefer." The verb *vorziehen* is a separable prefix verb.

17. *Noch etwas:* May I bring you anything else?

18. *Es fehlt mir:* the verb *(fehlen)* is a dative verb. *Es fehlt ihnen das Auto.* They miss the car.

24. *auf den Tisch stellen:* the phrase governs the accusative case because the verb describes motion toward a goal and change of position. Contrast: *Er hat den Regenschirm in die Ecke gestellt.* He placed the umbrella in(to) the corner. *Jetzt steht der Regenschirm in der Ecke.* The umbrella is now standing in the corner. Note the change of verb and case. *In der Ecke* is dative, feminine, after the two-way preposition *in.*

27. *die Rechnung,* from the verb *rechnen,* to count, add up.

29. *das Trinkgeld,* the waiter's tip. Most food establishments include a 15 percent to 20 percent service charge in the price of a meal. It is customary to leave some small change as an additional tip for the waiter/waitress to show the service was very good. *verlassen:* to leave a place. *Verlassen* is an inseparable prefix verb: *ich verlasse; du verlässt; er, sie, es verlässt; wir verlassen; ihr verlasst; sie (Sie) verlassen.*

B. A SAMPLE MENU

SPEISEKARTE

VORSPEISEN

APPETIZERS

Geräucherte Forelle	Smoked Trout
Dänischer Lachs	Danish Smoked Salmon
Hering in Weinsosse	Herring in Wine Sauce
Hühnerleber mit Zwiebeln	Chicken Livers with Onions

SUPPEN

SOUPS

Frühlingssuppe	Vegetable Soup
Kartoffelsuppe	Potato Soup
Erbsensuppe mit Schinken	Green Pea Soup with Ham
Hühnerbrühe	Clear Broth (Chicken Soup)

HAUPTGERICHTE

MAIN DISHES

Gebackenes Hünchen	Baked Chicken
Brathendl	Broiled Chicken
Rostbraten mit Pilzen	Pot Roast with Mushrooms
Kalbschnitzel	Veal Cutlet
Schweinekotelett	Breaded Pork Chop
Schinkenomelett	Ham Omelet
Rinderbraten	Roast Beef

SALATE

SALADS

Tomatensalat	Tomato Salad
Kartoffelsalat mit Ei	Potato Salad with Egg
Gurkensalat mit Zwiebeln	Cucumber Salad with Onions
Salat (zwei Sorten)	Salad (two kinds)

GEMÜSE	VEGETABLES
Grüne Bohnen	String Beans
Spargel	Asparagus
Karotten (Mohrrüben)	Carrots
Spinat	Spinach
Salzkartoffeln	Boiled Potatoes
Rostkartoffeln	Roasted Potatoes
Käseplatte	Assorted Cheeses
Wurstplatte	Assorted Cold Cuts

GEBÄCK	PASTRY
Apfelkuchen mit Schlagsahne	Apple Pie with Whipped Cream
Schwarzwälder Torte	Black Forest Cake
Hörnchen mit Honig	Horns with Honey

GETRÄNKE	DRINKS
Bier	Beer
Mineralwasser	Mineral Water
Sodawasser (Sprudel)	Soda (water)
Weisswein	White Wine
Rotwein	Red Wine
Kaffee	Coffee
Tee	Tea

ZUM NACHTISCH	FOR DESSERT
Kompott	Stewed Fruit
Speiseeis:	Ice Cream:
Schokolade	Chocolate
Pfirsich	Peach
Vanillie	Vanilla
Kirsch	Cherry
Kaffee	Coffee

REVIEW QUIZ 6

1. *Du musst Hunger* _____ (have).
   a. *sein*
   b. *haben*
   c. *machen*

2. *Wir haben heute keine* _____ (butter).
   a. *Bier*
   b. *Butter*
   c. *Brot*

3. _____ (There is) *ein gutes Restaurant im Hotel.*
   a. *Es gibt*
   b. *Gibt es*
   c. *Das ist*

4. *Mein Kaffee ist* _____ (cold).
   a. *kalt*
   b. *warm*
   c. *mild*

5. *Geben Sie mir* _____ (the same)!
   a. *auch*
   b. *dasselbe*
   c. *viel mehr*

6. *Herr Ober, eine* _____ (napkin) *bitte!*
   a. *Gabel*
   b. *Messer*
   c. *Serviette*

7. *Würden Sie so gut sein und mir* _____ (also)
   eine Gabel geben?
   a. *sehr*
   b. *nicht*
   c. *auch*

8. *Herr Ober,* _____ (the check).
   a. *der Tisch*
   b. *die Splisekarte*
   c. *die Rechnung*

9. *Etwas* _____ (more) *Zucker, bitte.*
   a. *gefällt*
   b. *mir*
   c. *mehr*

10. *Behalten Sie das* _____ (change)!
    a. *Rechnung*
    b. *Kleingeld*
    c. *Ordnung*

ANSWERS
1—b; 2—b; 3—a; 4—a; 5—b; 6—c; 7—c; 8—c;
9—c; 10—b.

LESSON 38

A. APARTMENT HUNTING

1. **Ich komme wegen der Wohnung.**
   I've come about the apartment.

2. **Welche, bitte?**
   Which one, please?

3. **Die zu vermieten ist.**
   The one for rent.

4. **Aber es gibt zwei.**
But there are two.

5. **Können Sie mir eine Beschreibung geben?**
Can you describe them?

6. **Die im fünften Stock ist unmöbliert.**
The one on the fifth floor is unfurnished.

7. **Und die andere?**
And the other?

8. **Die auf der zweiten Etage ist möbliert.**
The one on the second floor is furnished.

9. **Wieviele Zimmer hat jede?**
How many rooms does each one have?

10. **Die auf der fünften Etage hat vier Zimmer, Küche, und Bad.**
The one on the fifth floor has four rooms, a kitchen, and bath.

11. **Die Wohnung hat auch eine gute Aussicht auf den Hof.**
The apartment also has a good view of the courtyard.

12. **Und die im zweiten Stock?**
And how about the one on the second floor?

13. **Sie hat fünf Zimmer, drei Schlafzimmer, ein Esszimmer, und ein Wohnzimmer.**
It has five rooms, three bedrooms, a dining room, and a parlor.

14. Liegt sie auch nach dem Hof hinaus?
Is it also on the court?

15. Nein, sie liegt nach der Strasse zu.
No, it faces the street.

16. Wie hoch ist die Miete?
What's the rent?

17. Die grössere kostet zwölfhundert Mark ohne Gas, Wasser, und Strom.
The larger one is twelve hundred marks without gas, water, and electricity.

18. Und die möblierte Wohnung?
And the furnished apartment?

19. Vierzehnhundert Mark (Tausendvierhundert Mark). Gas, Wasser, und Strom sind miteingeschlossen.
Fourteen hundred Marks. Gas, water, and electricity are included (in the price).

20. Was für Möbel hat sie? Und in welchem Zustand sind sie?
What kind of furniture does it have? And is it in good condition?

21. Es sind antike Möbel in bestem Zustand.
It's antique furniture (and) in excellent condition.

22. Sind Wäsche und Silber einbegriffen?
Are linens and silverware included?

23. Sie finden alles, was man braucht, sogar eine vollständige Kücheneinrichtung.

You'll find everything you need, even a complete
set of kitchen utensils.

24. **Würde der Besitzer einen Mietvertrag mit mir machen? Und auf wie lange?**
Would the owner give me a lease? And for how
long?

25. **Deswegen müssen Sich sich an den Hausverwalter wenden.**
You'd have to see the renting agent for that.

26. **Wie sind die Bedingungen?**
What are the terms?

27. **Sie zahlen drei Monate im voraus.**
You pay three months' rent in advance.

28. **Sonst nichts?**
Nothing else?

29. **Referenzen, selbstverständlich.**
References, of course.

30. **Übrigens, ist ein Fahrstuhl vorhanden?**
By the way, is there an elevator?

31. **Nein, es ist keiner da.**
No, there isn't.

32. **Das ist schade.**
That's too bad.

33. **Davon abgesehen, ist das Haus aber ganz modern.**

Apart from that, though, the house is quite modern.

34. Wie meinen Sie das?
What do you mean?

35. Es hat neue Zentralheizung, drei Klimaanlagen und einen Geschirrspüler.
It has a new central heating system, three air conditioners, and a dishwasher.

36. Natürlich. Die Badezimmer wurden vor Kurzem renoviert.
Of course. The bathrooms were remodeled recently.

37. Sind eingebaute Schränke vorhanden?
Are there any closets?

38. Ja, einige grosse.
Yes, several large ones.

39. Wann kann man die Wohnungen sehen?
When can one see the apartments?

40. Nur am Morgen.
Only in the morning.

41. Sehr gut. Ich werde morgen früh kommen. Besten Dank.
Very well, I'll come tomorrow morning. Thanks a lot.

42. Keine Ursache, gern zu Ihren Diensten.
Not at all, glad to be of service.

NOTES

1. *Wegen:* because of (another preposition with the genitive.)
3. *Die, welche:* "The one which" Observe the comma after the relative pronoun *die.*
5. *Können Sie mir eine Beschreibung geben?*— Can you give me a description?
6. *Die:* "the one"
   Auf der: (Dative)
   In Germany the first floor is *das Erdgeschoss* ("Ground floor").
   Therefore the first floor, *erster Stock,* is really the second floor for us.
9. *Jede* (standing alone) is "each one" and can also be used with a noun:
   jeder Mann—"each or every man"
   Here *jede* is feminine because it refers to the apartment: *die Wohnung.*
11. *Liegt sie nach dem Hof?*—Does it lie toward the court?
    nach is always followed by the dative.
13. *Schlafzimmer:* bedroom ("sleeping room")
    Esszimmer: dining room ("eating room")
    Wohnzimmer: living room or parlor.
16. *Wie hoch ist die Miete?*—How high is the rent?
    Die Miete: the rent
    mieten: to rent
20. *Die Möbel:* furniture
    Das Möbel: a piece of furniture
22. *Die Wäsche:* linen; *also* laundry (underwear, etc.)
    Die Wäscherei: laundry (a place)
23. *Was man braucht:* "What one needs" *man* is used much more frequently than the English "one"

41. *Ich werde kommen:* Future of *kommen,* to come
42. *Keine Ursache*—("no cause, no reason") *Gern zu Ihren Diensten.*—("Gladly at your service.")

B. AT HOME

Wir haben eine Wohnung.
We have an apartment.

Wir haben eine Eigentumswohnung.
We have a condominium.

Wir haben ein Haus.
We have a house.

Fühlen Sie sich wie zu Hause.
Make yourself at home.

Machen Sie es sich bequem.
Make yourself comfortable.

Was für ein schönes Haus haben Sie!
What a lovely house you have!

QUIZ 27

1. _____ (How many) *Zimmer haben Sie?*
   a. *Anderes*
   b. *Wieviele*
   c. *Jede*

2. *Die Wohnung hat eine Aussicht auf die* (street)?
   a. *Hof*
   b. *Wohnzimmer*
   c. *Strasse*

3. *Was ist der* _____ (price)?
   a. *Preis*
   b. *Miete*
   c. *Art*

4. *Man* _____ (pays) *drei Monate im voraus.*
   a. *sind*
   b. *kauft*
   c. *zahlt*

5. *Das* _____ (house) *ist sehr modern.*
   a. *Halle*
   b. *Hause*
   c. *Bad*

6. *Sind die* _____ (furniture) *modern.*
   a. *Möbel*
   b. *Teppiche*
   c. *Heizung*

7. *Ist eine* _____ (air conditioner) *auch vorhand-en?*
   a. *Klimaanlage*
   b. *Zimmer*
   c. *Geschirrspüler*

8. _____ (Only) *morgens.*
   a. *Besuchen Sie*
   b. *Nur*
   c. *Auch*

9. *Ich komme* _____ (tomorrow) *früh.*
   a. *morgen*
   b. *gestern*
   c. *heute*

10. _____ (Thank you) *vielmals.*
   a. *Morgen*
   b. *Dienst*
   c. *Danke*

ANSWERS
1—b; 2—c; 3—a; 4—c; 5—b; 6—a; 7—b; 8—b;
9—a; 10—c.

REVIEW QUIZ 7

1. *Ich ziehe* _____ (this) *vor.*
   a. *das*
   b. *dieses*
   c. *die*

2. *Was soll* _____ (this) *heissen?*
   a. *das*
   b. *dort*
   c. *dieser*

3. *Ich weiss nicht* _____ (how).
   a. *noch*
   b. *wo*
   c. *wie*

4. *Er kommt* _____ (never).
   a. *auch*
   b. *niemals*
   c. *wie*

5. *Er hat* _____ (nothing) *gesagt.*
   a. *kein*
   b. *nicht*
   c. *nichts*

6. *Ihr Buch ist besser als* _____ (his) *Buch.*
   a. *Ihr*
   b. *sein*
   c. *mein*

7. *Ich bin* _____ (happy), *Sie kennenzulernen.*
   a. *erfreut*
   b. *vorstellen*
   c. *Bekanntschaft*

8. *Bis nächste* _____ (week)!
   a. *Monat*
   b. *Woche*
   c. *Jahr*

9. *Bis zum* _____ (next) *Mal!*
   a. *neulich*
   b. *nächsten*
   c. *heute*

10. *Es geht gut,* _____ (thanks).
    a. *denke*
    b. *danke*
    c. *sage*

11. *Rufen Sie mich diese* _____ (week) *an!*
    a. *Woche*
    b. *Tage*
    c. *Monat*

12. _____ (Know) *Sie meinen Freund?*
    a. *Kennen*
    b. *Treffen*
    c. *Wissen*

13. *Nein, ich* _____ (think) *nicht.*
    a. *will*
    b. *denke*
    c. *kenne*

14. *Ich* _____ (hope), *Sie bald wiederzusehen.*
    a. *erfreut*
    b. *gemacht*
    c. *hoffe*

15. *Ich werde es Ihnen* _____ (write).
    a. *haben*
    b. *schreiben*
    c. *sehen*

16. *Sie können mich* _____ (in the morning) *an-rufen.*
    a. *nachmittags*
    b. *abends*
    c. *morgens*

17. *Ich habe ihn* _____ (met).
    a. *erfreut*
    b. *getroffen*
    c. *angerufen*

18. _____ (give) *Sie mir Ihre Adresse!*
    a. *Gehen*
    b. *Geben*
    c. *Rufen*

19. *Das ist sehr* _____ (good).
    a. *gut*
    b. *bald*
    c. *ganz*

20. *Auf* _____ (soon).
    a. *bald*
    b. *morgen*
    c. *auch*

ANSWERS
1—b; 2—a; 3—c; 4—b; 5—c; 6—b; 7—a; 8—b;
9—b; 10—b; 11—a; 12—a; 13—b; 14—c; 15—b;
16—c; 17—b; 18—b; 19—a; 20—a.

LESSON 39

A. To Come: *KOMMEN*

ich komme	I come	*wir kommen*	we come
du kommst	you come	*ihr kommt*	you come
er kommt	he comes	*Sie kommen*	you come
sie kommt	she comes	*sie kommen*	they come
es kommt	it comes		

Komm!	Come! (*fam.*)
Kommen Sie!	Come! (*pol.*)
Kommen Sie hierher!	Come (over) here!
Kommen Sie mit mir!	Come with me!
Kommen Sie wieder!	Come again!
Kommen Sie nach Hause!	Come home!
Kommen Sie mal einen Abend!	Come some evening!
Kommen Sie nicht!	Don't come!

Woher kommen Sie?	Where do you come from? Where are you coming from?
Ich komme aus Berlin.	I come from Berlin. I'm coming from Berlin.
Ich komme aus dem Theater.	I'm coming from the theater.
Ich komme sofort.	I'm coming right away.

B. TO SAY: *SAGEN*

ich sage	I say	*wir sagen*	we say
du sagst	you say	*ihr sagt*	you say
er sagt	he says	*sie sagen*	they say
sie sagt	she says	*Sie sagen*	you say
es sagt	it says		

Man sagt, dass . . .	It's said that . . . People say that . . . They say that . . .
Man hat es mir gesagt.	I've been told (it).
Das ist schwer zu sagen.	That's hard to say.
Sagen Sie!	Say (it)!
Sagen Sie es!	Say it!
Sagen Sie es noch einmal!	Say it again!
Sagen Sie es auf Deutsch!	Say it in German!
Sagen Sie es langsam!	Say it slowly!
Sagen Sie es nicht!	Don't say it!
Sagen Sie das nicht!	Don't say that!
Sagen Sie mir . . .	Tell me. Well, tell me. Say, . . .

Sagen Sie, ist das Ihr Ernst?	Say, you're not serious, are you?
Sagen Sie mir.	Tell me.
Sagen Sie es mir.	Say it to me. Tell me it.
Sagen Sie ihm.	Tell him.
Sagen Sie es ihm.	Tell it to him.
Sagen Sie ihm, er soll kommen!	Tell him to come!
Sagen Sie es ihm nicht.	Don't tell it to him. Don't tell him.
Sagen Sie ihm nichts.	Don't tell him anything. Tell him nothing.
Sagen Sie es niemand.	Don't tell it to anybody.
Was sagen Sie?	What did you say? ("What say you?")
sozusagen	so to say, so to speak
Können Sie mir sagen, wo ein Hotel ist?	Can you tell me where there's a hotel?
Was möchten Sie sagen?	What do you mean? ("What do you want [would you like] to say?")
Er hat nichts gesagt.	He hasn't said anything.

QUIZ 28

1. *Ich komme aus dem Theater.*	a. Come with me.
2. *Ich komme sofort*	b. Where are you coming from?
3. *Ich komme später.*	c. Come some evening.

4. Woher kommen Sie?	d. I'm coming right away.
5. *Sagen Sie mir!*	e. I'm coming from the theater.
6. *Sagen Sie es auf Deutsch!*	f. Say it in German.
7. *Das ist schwer zu sagen.*	g. So to say, so to speak.
8. *Kommen Sie mit mir!*	h. That's hard to say.
9. *Kommen Sie einen Abend!*	i. I'll come later.
10. *Sozusagen.*	j. Tell me.

ANSWERS
1—e; 2—d; 3—i; 4—b; 5—j; 6—f; 7—h; 8—a; 9—c; 10—g.

C. TO DO: *TUN*

Ich tue	I do	*wir tun*	we do
du tust	you do	*ihr tut*	you do
er tut	he does	*Sie tun*	you do
sie tut	she does	*sie tun*	they do
es tut	it does		

Ich tue es.	I do it. I'm doing it.
Ich tue es nicht.	I don't do it. I'm not doing it.
Was tun Sie?	What are you doing?
Wie tun Sie das?	How do you do it?
Was haben Sie getan?	What have you done?
Tun Sie es nicht.	Don't do it.
Tun Sie es nicht mehr.	Don't do it anymore.
Das ist getan.	It's done. It's over.

Das tut mir weh.	That hurts me.
Das tut mir leid.	I'm sorry.
Ich tue nichts.	I'm not doing anything. I'm doing nothing.
Tun Sie das nicht!	Don't do that!
Tun Sie es noch einmal.	Do it again.
Tun Sie es schnell!	Do it quickly!
Tun Sie nichts!	Don't do anything!
Sie dürfen das nicht tun.	You may not do that.
Ich habe es gerade getan.	I've just done it.
Was ist zu tun?	What's to be done? (What should one do?)
Was kann man tun?	What can one do? (''What to do?'')
Wie sollen wir es tun?	How shall we do it?
Wer hat das getan?	Who did that?
Ich weiss nicht, was ich tun soll.	I don't know what to do.
So etwas tut man nicht.	That isn't done. (''One doesn't do that.'')

QUIZ 29

1. *Was haben Sie getan?*   a. I'm sorry.
2. *Tun Sie es nicht!*   b. Do it quickly.
3. *Das ist getan.*   c. What are you doing?
4. *Ich habe es getan.*   d. What have you done?
5. *Was ist zu tun?*   e. Don't do it!
6. *Tun Sie es noch einmal!*   f. That's done. It's over.

7. *Wer hat das geo getan?*   g. Do me a favor.

8. *Ich habe es gerade getan.*   h. You are hurting me!

9. *Tun Sie mir einen Gefallen.*   i. That isn't done. You don't do that. ("One does not do that.")

10. *Du tust mir weh!*   j. I have done it.

11. *Das tut mir leid.*   k. What are we doing tomorrow?

12. *Was tun Sie?*   l. What's to be done?

13. *Tun Sie es schnell.*   m. I've just done it.

14. *So etwas tut man nicht.*   n. Do it again.

15. *Was tun wir morgen?*   o. Who has done that?

ANSWERS

1—d; 2—e; 3—f; 4—j; 5—l; 6—n; 7—o; 8—m; 9—g; 10—h; 11—a; 12—c; 13—b; 14—i; 15—k.

REVIEW QUIZ 8

1. *Ich* _____ (am coming) *sofort.*
   a. *kenne*
   b. *komme*
   c. *sehe*

2. *Das ist schwer zu* _____ (say).
   a. *kommen*
   b. *antworten*
   c. *sagen*

3. *Was* _____ (do) *Sie?*
   a. *sagen*
   b. *tun*
   c. *macht*

4. *Ich weiss nicht, was ich* _____ (do) *soll.*
   a. *sagen*
   b. *kommen*
   c. *tun*

5. _____ (Take) *Sie es nicht!*
   a. *Nehmen*
   b. *Schicken*
   c. *Versuchen*

6. _____ (Stop) *Sie sofort* _____ !
   a. *Halten . . . an*
   b. *Hören . . . an*
   c. *Helfen . . . mit*

7. *Ich* _____ (hope), *bald von Ihnen zu hören.*
   a. *komme*
   b. *hoffe*
   c. *helfe*

8. *Ich* _____ (see) *nicht gut ohne Brille.*
   a. *spreche*
   b. *weiss*
   c. *sehe*

9. *Ich werde Sie heute abend* _____ (see).
   a. *sehen*
   b. *können*
   c. *gesehen*

10. *Er* _____ (holds, is holding) *seinen Hut in der Hand.*
    a. *haltet*
    b. *kann*
    c. *hält*

11. *Ich sehe nicht, wie wir das machen* _____
    (can).
    a. *könnt*
    b. *können*
    c. *mögen*

12. *Er* _____ (understand) *einfach nicht.*
    a. *besucht*
    b. *versteht*
    c. *stellt*

13. _____ (Take) *Sie Ihr Buch.*
    a. *Stellen*
    b. *Nehmen*
    c. *Geben*

14. *Sie* _____ (owe) *mir nichts.*
    a. *schulden*
    b. *fragen*
    c. *brauchen*

15. *Er* _____ (ask) *mich, wo der Laden ist.*
    a. *fährt*
    b. *fragt*
    c. *darf*

ANSWERS
1—b; 2—c; 3—b; 4—c; 5—a; 6—a; 7—b; 8—c;
9—a; 10—c; 11—b; 12—b; 13—b; 14—a; 15—b.

D. COULD YOU GIVE ME SOME INFORMATION?

1. Verzeihung, mein Herr.
I beg your pardon, sir.

2. Bitte sehr.
Not at all.

3. Können Sie mir eine Auskunft geben?
Could you give me some information?

4. Gewiss, mit Vergnügen.
Certainly, I'd be glad to.

5. Ich kenne die Stadt nicht. Ich finde mich nicht zurecht.
I don't know the town. I can't find my way around.

6. Das ist doch ganz einfach.
It's quite simple.

7. Sehen Sie, ich bin fremd hier.
You see, I'm a stranger here.

8. Das macht nichts.
That's nothing.

9. Könnten Sie mir erklären, wo die wichtigsten Gebäude sind?
Could you tell me (explain to me) where the most important buildings are (located)?

10. Natürlich. Passen Sie gut auf!
Surely. Pay careful attention!

11. Ich passe gut auf und schreibe alles auf.
I'll pay careful attention, and write everything down.

12. Fangen wir mit der Post an!
Let's begin with the post office.

13. Schön. Das ist eine gute Idee.
Fine! That's a good idea.

14. Sehen Sie das Gebäude an der Ecke?
Do you see the building at the corner?

15. Das mit der blauen Laterne?
The one with the blue lantern?

16. Ja, das ist es. Das Postamt ist im Erdgeschoss.
Yes, that's the one. The post office is on the ground floor.

17. Der Laden mit der Fahne—was ist das?
The store with the flag—what's that?

18. Das ist unser Polizeiamt.
That's our police station.

19. Dort ist ein anderes Gebäude mit einer Fahne.
There's another building with a flag.

20. Das ist das Rathaus.
That's the City Hall.

21. Wie heisst diese Strasse?
What's the name of this street?

22. Das ist die Marktstrasse. Sehen Sie das Geschäft?
This is Market Street. Do you see that store?

23. Welches? Das auf der rechten Seite?
Which one? The one on the right?

24. Ja. Das mit der grossen grünen Kugel im Fenster.
Yes. The one with a large green globe in the window.

25. Und einer roten in dem andern?
And a red one in the other?

26. Richtig. Das ist die Apotheke.
That's right. That's the pharmacy.

27. Ah, ich verstehe.
Oh, I see.

28. Der Arzt wohnt nebenan.
The doctor lives right next door.

29. Ist er ein guter Arzt?
Is he a good doctor?

30. Er ist auch Herzspezialist und ist jeden Morgen im Krankenhaus.
He's also a heart specialist and is at the hospital every morning.

31. Wo befindet sich das Krankenhaus?
Where's the hospital?

32. Zwei Strassen von hier, links, gerade bevor Sie auf die Landstrasse kommen.
Two streets from here, to your left, just before you come to the main highway.

33. Gibt es ein Schreibwarengeschäft hier in der Nähe?
Is there a stationery store around here?

34. Natürlich. Das ist nicht weit von hier, auf der Hauptstrasse, gegenüber Ihrem Hotel.
Of course. It's not far from here, on Main Street, across from your hotel.

35. Jetzt bin ich ganz im Bilde.
Now I've got my bearings.

36. Kaufen Sie sich doch einen Stadtplan!
Why don't you go and buy yourself a map of the city?

37. Das ist eine gute Idee! Wo bekomme ich einen?
That's a good idea. Where can I get one?

38. Entweder am Bahnhof oder am Zeitungsstand.
Either at the station or at the newspaper stand.

39. Wo ist der Bahnhof?
Where is the station?

40. Der Bahnhof ist am andern Ende der Marktstrasse.
The station is at the other end of Market Street.

41. Und wo ist ein Zeitungsstand?
And where's there a newspaper stand?

42. An der nächsten Ecke.
At the next corner.

43. Ich hatte Glück, Sie zu treffen. Sie scheinen die Stadt sehr gut zu kennen.

I was lucky to meet you. You seem to know the town very well.

44. Das ist selbstverständlich. Ich bin der Bürgermeister der Stadt.

It's quite natural. ("It is obvious.") I'm the mayor of the town.

45. Besten Dank.

Thank you very much.

46. Ich hoffe, dass Sie in unserer Stadt einen guten Aufenthalt haben.

I hope you have an enjoyable stay in our city.

NOTES

1. *Verzeihung, Entschuldigen Sie, Entschuldigung:* I beg your pardon, Excuse me, I am sorry.
6. *Doch* gives emphasis to the sentence.
8. *Das macht nichts:* "That's nothing." *Das ist unwichtig:* "That's unimportant."
10. *Aufpassen:* "to listen to" or "to watch out" (separable prefix)
12. *Die Post or Das Postamt:* the post office.
14. *An der Ecke:* (dative) (no motion toward anything).
20. *Das Rathaus:* "the council house" (city hall) *Der Bürgermeister:* "the mayor"
25. *Einer roten:* (feminine, dative) because of *mit* in sentence 24.
28. Physicians are called *Doktor* or *Arzt* and are addressed as *Herr Doktor.*
31. *Befindet sich:* is located ("Where does it find itself?") *finden:* to find

32. Note verb transposition. *Bevor* is a subordinating conjunction.
33. *Das Schreibwarengeschäft:* another example of compound nouns; "store for merchandise to write."
34. Another case of transposition: *wo ihr Hotel ist.*
35. *Jetzt bin ich* . . . (inverted word order)
38. *Entweder* . . . *oder* either . . . or *weder* . . . *noch* neither . . . nor
44. *Selbstverständlich:* "That understands itself"; "That is self-evident." (Another polite expression: *Gern geschehen:* "It happened with pleasure.")
45. *Besten Dank* ("best thanks").

QUIZ 30

1. _____ (Not at all).
   a. *Ich bitte Sie* . . .
   b. *Das macht nichts.*
   c. *Keine Ursache.*

2. *Können Sie mir einige Auskünfte* _____ (give)?
   a. *besorgen*
   b. *sprechen*
   c. *geben*

3. *Sie müssen mir alles* _____ (explain).
   a. *hören*
   b. *erklären*
   c. *anfangen*

4. *Sehen Sie das* _____ (house) *an der Ecke?*
   a. *Büro*
   b. *Gebäude*
   c. *Laterne*

5. *Wie heisst diese* _____ (Street)?
    a. *Geschäft*
    b. *Strasse*
    c. *Ecke*

6. *Der Arzt* _____ (lives) *nebenan.*
    a. *wohnt*
    b. *singt*
    c. *macht*

7. *Bei* _____ (green) *Licht dürfen Sie über-queren.*
    a. *roten*
    b. *grünem*
    c. *gelbes*

8. *Er ist jeden* _____ (morning) *im Krenkenhaus.*
    a. *Nachmittag*
    b. *Morgen*
    c. *Abend*

9. *Ich hatte* _____ (luck), *Sie zu treffen.*
    a. *Pech*
    b. *Spass*
    c. *Glück*

10. *Wo befindet sich* _____ (the train station)?
    a. *das Postamt*
    b. *der Bahnhof*
    c. *das Rathaus*

ANSWERS
1—c; 2—c; 3—b; 4—b; 5—b; 6—a; 7—b; 8—b;
9—c; 10—b.

LESSON 40

A.   THE MOST COMMON VERB FORMS

1. Verbs are divided into two classes:
   Class I weak verbs (regular verbs)
   Class II strong verbs (irregular verbs)

INFINITIVE

PRESENT

fragen   to ask   *sprechen*   to speak

PAST

gefragt haben   *gesprochen haben*
to have asked   to have spoken

PARTICIPLES

PRESENT

fragend   asking   *sprechend*   speaking

PAST

gefragt   asked   *gesprochen*   spoken

INDICATIVE

PRESENT

frage   *spreche*
fragst   *sprichst*
fragt   *spricht*

fragen	*sprechen*
fragt	*sprecht*
fragen	*sprechen*

IMPERFECT

fragte	*sprach*
fragtest	*sprachst*
fragte	*sprach*

fragten	*sprachen*
fragtet	*spracht*
fragten	*sprachen*

FUTURE

werde fragen	*werde sprechen*
wirst fragen	*wirst sprechen*
wird fragen	*wird sprechen*

werden fragen	*werden sprechen*
werdet fragen	*werdet sprechen*
werden fragen	*werden sprechen*

CONDITIONAL

würde fragen	*würde sprechen*
würdest fragen	*würdest sprechen*
würde fragen	*würde sprechen*

würden fragen	*würden sprechen*
würdet fragen	*würdet sprechen*
würden fragen	*würden sprechen*

PRESENT PERFECT
(CONVERSATIONAL PAST)

habe gefragt	*habe gesprochen*
hast gefragt	*hast gesprochen*
hat gefragt	*hat gesprochen*
haben gefragt	*haben gesprochen*
habt gefragt	*habt gesprochen*
haben gefragt	*haben gesprochen*

PAST PERFECT
(PLUPERFECT)

hatte gefragt	*hatte gesprochen*
hattest gefragt	*hattest gesprochen*
hatte gefragt	*hatte gesprochen*
hatten gefragt	*hatten gesprochen*
hattet gefragt	*hattet gesprochen*
hatten gefragt	*hatten gesprochen*

FUTURE PERFECT

werde gefragt haben	*werde gesprochen haben*
wirst gefragt haben	*wirst gesprochen haben*
wird gefragt haben	*wird gesprochen haben*
werden gefragt haben	*werden gesprochen haben*
werdet gefragt haben	*werdet gesprochen haben*
werden gefragt haben	*werden gesprochen haben*

PAST CONDITIONAL

würde gefragt haben	würde gesprochen haben
würdest gefragt haben	würdest gesprochen haben
würde gefragt haben	würde gesprochen haben
würden gefragt haben	würden gesprochen haben
würdet gefragt haben	würdet gesprochen haben
würden gefragt haben	würden gesprochen haben

IMPERATIVE

frage!	sprich!
fragt!	sprecht!
fragen wir!	sprechen wir!
fragen Sie!	sprechen Sie!

SUBJUNCTIVE

PRESENT

dass ich frage	dass ich spreche
dass du fragest	dass du sprechest
dass er frage	dass er spreche
dass wir fragen	dass wir sprechen
dass ihr fraget	dass ihr sprechet
dass sie fragen	dass sie sprechen

IMPERFECT

dass ich fragte	*dass ich spräche*
dass du fragtest	*dass du sprächest*
dass er fragte	*dass er spräche*
dass wir fragten	*dass wir sprächen*
dass ihr fragtet	*dass ihr sprächet*
dass sie fragten	*dass sie sprächen*

PRESENT PERFECT

dass ich gefragt hätte	*dass ich gesprochen hätte*
dass du gefragt habest	*dass du gesprochen habest*
dass er gefragt hätte	*dass er gesprochen hätte*
dass wir gefragt hätten	*dass wir gesprochen hätten*
dass ihr gefragt habet	*dass ihr gesprochen habet*
dass sie gefragt hätten	*dass sie gesprochen hätten*

PAST PERFECT

dass ich gefragt hätte	*dass ich gesprochen hätte*
dass du gefragt hättest	*dass du gesprochen hättest*
dass er gefragt hätte	*dass er gesprochen hätte*
dass wir gefragt hätten	*dass wir gesprochen hätten*

| *dass ihr gefragt hättet* | *dass ihr gesprochen hättet* |
| *dass sie gefragt hätten* | *dass sie gesprochen hätten* |

2. Some common forms of common verbs:

a) I have gone, etc.

I have gone

ich bin gegangen	*wir sind gegangen*
du bist gegangen	*ihr seid gegangen*
er ist gegangen	*sie (Sie) sind gegangen*

Compare: *Ich habe gegeben* ("I have given") and *ich bin gegangen* ("I have gone").

Notice that most verbs use *ich habe, du hast, er hat,* etc., but that a few (chiefly verbs of motion) have *ich bin, du bist, er ist,* as a helping verb.

The commonest verbs which have the latter form are:

ich bin eingetreten	I have entered, I entered
ich bin ausgegangen	I have gone out, I went out
ich bin angekommen	I have arrived, I arrived
ich bin abgereist	I have left, I left
ich bin hinaufgegangen	I have gone up, I went up
ich bin hinunterge-gangen	I have gone down, I went down
ich bin geblieben	I have remained, I remained
ich bin zurückgekommen	I have returned, I returned

ich bin gefallen	I have fallen, I fell
ich bin geboren	I was born
ich bin geworden	I have become, I became
ich bin hingefahren	I went (traveled) there

b) I had given, had gone, etc.

I had given

ich hatte gegeben	*wir hatten gegeben*
du hattest gegeben	*ihr hattet gegeben*
er hatte gegeben	*Sie (sie) hatten gegeben*

Other examples:

ich hatte gesprochen	I had spoken
ich hatte gefragt	I had asked
ich hatte gebracht	I had brought

I had gone

ich war gegangen	*wir waren gegangen*
du warst gegangen	*ihr wart gegangen*
er war gegangen	*Sie (sie) waren gegangen*

Other examples:

ich war angekommen	I had arrived
ich war gekommen	I had gone
ich war eingetreten	I had entered
ich war ausgegangen	I had gone out
ich war abgereist	I had left
ich war hinaufgegangen	I had gone up
ich war gefallen	I had fallen
ich war gewesen	I had been

c) Help! Bring!

Helfen Sie mir!	Help me!
Bringen Sie mir noch mehr . . . !	Bring me some more . . . !
Bringen Sie es mir!	Bring it to me.
Halten Sie an!	Stop!
Halten Sie sofortan!	Stop right away!
Halten Sie dort!	Stop there!
Halten Sie ihn!	Stop him!
Setzen Sie sich!	Sit down! Have a seat!
Glauben Sie mir!	Believe me!
Hören Sie!	Listen!
Hören Sie mir zu!	Listen to me!
Hören Sie mir gut zu!	Listen to me carefully!
Hören Sie sich das an!	Listen to this (that)!
Hören Sie gut zu!	Listen carefully!

The *Sie* form corresponds to the polite, that is, the formal form.

The familiar form, that is, the *du* form, is as follows:

To give: *geben*

du gibst	you give
Gib!	Give!

To speak: *sprechen*

du sprichst	you speak
Sprich!	Speak!

To take: *nehmen*

du nimmst	you take
Nimm!	Take!

d) Giving, Speaking

gebend	giving
sprechend	speaking

kommend	coming
sehend	seeing
fliessendes Wasser	running water
den Sitten folgend (dative plural)	following the custom

Notice that the *-end* form corresponds to our "-ing" form in English.

e) Let's

Gehen wir dorthin!	Let's go over there.
Sehen wir einmal!	Let's see.
Gehen wir!	Let's leave!
Versuchen wir!	Let's try!
Warten wir!	Let's wait!
Nehmen wir etwas!	Let's take some!
Hören Sie ihm zu!	Listen to him.
Hören Sie ihm nicht zu!	Don't listen to him.
Nehmen Sie das fort!	Take that away.
Herein!	Come in!
Treten Sie ein!	Go in! Come in! Enter!
Schicken Sie es ihm!	Send it to him.
Schicken Sie sie mir!	Send them to me.
Schicken Sie ihm einige!	Send him some!
Schicken Sie mir einige!	Send me some!
Versuchen Sie!	Try!
Versuchen Sie nicht!	Don't try!
Versuchen Sie nicht, das zu tun!	Don't try to do that!
Waschen Sie sich!	Wash yourself!
Stehen Sie auf!	Get up! Stand up!

Lesen Sie das!	Read that!
Führen Sie mich dorthin!	Take me there!
Gehen Sie dort hinauf!	Go up there!
Zeigen Sie mir!	Show me!
Zeigen Sie mir das!	Show me it (that)!
Zeigen Sie ihm!	Show him!
Zeigen Sie es ihm nicht!	Don't show it to him!
Vergessen Sie nicht!	Don't forget!
Gehen Sie fort!	Leave!
Gehen Sie schnell fort!	Leave quickly! Go right away!
Gehen Sie hinein!	Go in!
Denken Sie daran!	Think of it!
Tragen Sie das dorthin!	Carry this over there!
Nehmen Sie!	Take!
Nehmen Sie es!	Take it!
Nehmen Sie es nicht!	Don't take it!
Nehmen Sie noch eins!	Take another one!
Nehmen Sie den Zug!	Take the train!
Nehmen Sie ein Taxi!	Take a taxi!
Sehen Sie!	Look!
Sehen Sie noch einmal!	Look again!
Sehen Sie hierher!	Look (over) here!
Sehen Sie mich an!	Look at me!
Sehen Sie das an!	Look at this (that)!
Sehen Sie nicht hierher!	Don't look [over here].
Geben Sie es mir wieder!	Return it to me!
Gehen Sie nach Hause!	Go home!
Gehen Sie früher nach Hause!	Go home earlier!
Wiederholen Sie!	Repeat! Say it again!

Wiederholen Sie das!	Repeat it (this, that). Say it (this, that) again.
Bleiben Sie!	Stay!
Bleiben Sie hier!	Stay here!
Bleiben Sie ruhig!	Be still! (quiet, calm)
Gehen Sie hinaus!	Go out!
Folgen Sie!	Follow!
Folgen Sie mir!	Follow me!
Folgen Sie ihm!	Follow him!
Berühren Sie es nicht!	Don't touch it!
Schenken Sie mir Kaffee ein.	Pour me some coffee.

QUIZ 31

1. *Zeigen Sie mir!*	a. Look at (that).
2. *Treten Sie ein!*	b. Look here.
3. *Darf ich mal?*	c. Take a taxi.
4. *Denken Sie daran.*	d. Take another one.
5. *Zeig mir das Buch!*	e. Show me the book!
6. *Führen Sie mich dorthin.*	f. Take me there.
7. *Nehmen Sie ein Taxi.*	g. May I?
8. *Nehmen Sie noch eins.*	h. Think of it.
9. *Sehen Sie her.*	i. Go in!
10. *Sehen Sie das an.*	j. Show me.

ANSWERS

1—j; 2—i; 3—g; 4—h; 5—f; 6—e; 7—c; 8—d;
9—b; 10—a.

B. MEETING AN OLD FRIEND

Zwei alte Freunde treffen sich auf der Strasse.
Two old friends meet on the street.

1. *M.:* **Na, unglaublich! Du bist es. Was für eine Überraschung! Wie geht's dir denn?**
M.: This is unbelievable! It's you. What a surprise! Well, how are you?

2. *W.:* **Prima! Mensch, wir haben uns schon seit drei Jahren nicht gesehen.**
W.: Great! You know, we haven't seen each other in three years.

3. *M.:* **Du hättest mich doch auch mal anrufen können. Aber das macht nichts. Wir werden doch immer Freunde bleiben. Arbeitest du noch immer als Ingenieur?**
M.: You, too, could have telephoned me. But that doesn't matter. We will always remain friends. Are you still working as an engineer?

4. *W.:* **Ja. Seit fünf Jahren.**
W.: Yes. For five years.

5. *M.:* **Darf ich dir meine Frau vorstellen?**
M.: May I introduce my wife to you?

6. *W.:* **Mit Vergnügen.**
W.: With pleasure.

7. *M.:* **Liebes, das ist Max Wagner.**
M.: This is Max Wagner, dear.

8. *W.:* **Sehr erfreut, Sie kennenzulernen.**
W.: I'm very happy to know you.

9. *Frau M.:* **Ganz meinerseits. Wir können uns duzen, nicht?**
Mrs. M.: The pleasure is mine. We don't have to be formal, right?

10. *W.:* **Ich freue mich wirklich, dich wiederzusehen.**
W.: It's really good to see you again.

11. *M.:* **Ich auch. Du hast dich überhaupt nicht verändert.**
M.: I'm certainly glad, too. You haven't changed a bit.

12. *W.:* **Du aber auch nicht.**
W.: Neither have you.

13. *Frau M.:* **Gefällt es deiner Frau in den Vereinigten Staaten?**
Mrs. M.: Does Mrs. Wagner like the United States?

14. *W.:* **Sehr gut.**
W.: She likes it a lot.

15. *Frau M.:* **Es ist sicher ganz anders als in Berlin?**
Mrs. M.: It must be quite different from Berlin?

16. *W.:* **Es gibt bestimmt eine Menge merkwürdiger Dinge in den Vereinigten Staaten.**
W.: There certainly are lots of very curious things in the United States!

17. *Frau M.:* **Zum Beispiel?**
Mrs. M.: For example?

18. *W.:* **Zum Beispiel, du wirst bestimmt nicht auf den Gedanken kommen, in einer Apotheke Mittag zu essen.**
W.: For example, it certainly wouldn't occur to you to have lunch in a pharmacy.

19. *M.:* **Das ist wohl ein Scherz.**
M.: You're joking!

20. *W.:* **Gar nicht, ich meine es sehr ernst.**
W.: Not at all, I'm very serious.

21. *Frau M.:* **Wie bitte? Erzähle uns das. Du sagst . . . man isst zu Mittag in einer Apotheke?**
Mrs. M.: Come, tell us about it! You say . . . one has lunch in a pharmacy?

22. *W.:* **Ja, sogar ein Beefsteak. . . .**
W.: Yes, you can even have a steak. . . .

23. *M.:* **In einer Apotheke?**
M.: In a pharmacy?

24. *W.:* **Ja, in einer Apotheke, und als Nachtisch kann man ausgezeichnetes Eis haben.**
W.: Yes, in a pharmacy—and you can have excellent ice cream for dessert.

25. *Frau M.:* **Aber der Geruch der Apotheke stört dich nicht?**
Mrs. M.: But the smell of the pharmacy—doesn't it bother you?

26. *W.:* **Es gibt keinen Geruch in unsern ...**
    W.: There isn't any smell in our ...

27. *M.:* **Apotheken?**
    M.: ... pharmacies?

28. *W.:* **Übrigens nennen wir sie nicht Apotheken
    sondern "drug stores."**
    W.: No, ("Moreover") we don't call them phar-
    macies but "drug stores."

29. *M.:* **Ah! Deshalb! Du gibst ihnen einen andern
    Namen!**
    M.: Oh! That's the trick! They give them a dif-
    ferent name!

30. *Frau M.:* **Aber was ändert das?**
    Mrs. M.: But how does that change things?

31. *M:* **Dann ist es eben keine Apotheke mehr!**
    M.: Then it's no longer a pharmacy!

32. *W.:* **Man findet auch eine Menge anderer Dinge
    in einem "drug store." Spielsachen, Brief-
    marken, Zigaretten, Bonbons, Armbanduhren
    ...**
    W.: One also finds many other things in a drug
    store: toys, stamps, cigarettes, candy, wrist-
    watches, ...

33. *M.:* **Das ist wirklich komisch!**
    M.: That's really very funny.

34. *W.:* **Bücher, Schreibpapier, Küchengeräte, Toi-
    lettenartikel und wer weiss noch ...**

W.: Books, stationery, cooking utensils, toilet articles and what-have-you.

35. *M.:* **Dann ist es also ein Kaufhaus!**
M.: It's a department store, then!

36. *W.:* **Nein, es ist eben ein "drug store"!**
W.: No, it's just a drugstore!

NOTES

1. *Du bist es.* It's you. There you are! *die Überraschung:* the surprise. The verb *überraschen* means "to surprise." *Was für ein . . . :* idiomatic for "What a . . ."
2. *Mensch!:* colloquial for "boy," as in "Boy (Man), I don't believe this."
3. *Du hättest mich anrufen können:* you could have called me. Note the pluperfect subjunctive form with a modal verb (*können*). When a main verb is used with a modal in one of the perfect tenses, the double infinitive construction is employed. Note that the past participle of *anrufen* is normally expressed by *angerufen.*
4. *seit fünf Jahren:* for five years; dative, plural.
5. Also: *Gestatten Sie, dass ich Sie bekannt mache.* "Allow me to introduce you."
8. *Kennenzulernen:* to get acquainted ("to learn to know").
9. *Ganz meinerseits:* "completely on my part (behalf)" *sich duzen:* to use the *du* or *du-* form in addressing someone; to be informal.
10. *Sich freuen:* to rejoice. *wiedersehen*—to see again (separable prefix)
13. *Gefällt es deiner Frau . . .?:* Does your wife

like . . .? The verb *gefallen* is dative. Therefore, the ending of *dein* is *-er* (dative, feminine, singular).

18. Conditional of *kommen.* (*würden . . . kommen*)

19. *Sie machen einen Scherz:* "You are making a
joke." *scherzen:* to joke, to kid.

28. *sondern:* is used instead of *aber* after a negation.

31. Inverted word order is used after *dann.*

34. *Wer weiss was noch:* "Who knows what else"
infinitive: *wissen* (*see table, page 338*)

QUIZ 32

1. *Wie lange waren Sie* _____ (there)?
   a. *dessen*
   b. *hier*
   c. *dort*

2. _____ (How) *geht's, mein lieber Freund?*
   a. *Dort*
   b. *Wie*
   c. *Ihr*

3. *Nicht zu* _____ (tiring) *diese Reise?*
   a. *erfrischend*
   b. *erfindend*
   c. *ermüdend*

4. *Ich werde Sie meiner* _____ (wife) *vorstellen.*
   a. *Frau*
   b. *Freude*
   c. *Freund*

5. *Es* _____ (pleases) *mich sehr, Sie wiederzu-sehen.*
   a. *wechselt*
   b. *freut*
   c. *selbst*

6. *Es gibt wirklich komische* _____ (things).
   a. *sehr*
   b. *dieser*
   c. *Dinge*

7. *Ich meine es* _____ (very) *ernst.*
   a. *sehr*
   b. *aber*
   c. *viel*

8. *Wir* _____ (call) *sie nicht Apotheken.*
   a. *nennen*
   b. *nehmen*
   c. *heissen*

9. *Sehr erfreut, Sie* _____ ("to learn to know").
   a. *zu lernen*
   b. *kennenzulernen*
   c. *Bekanntschaft machen*

10. *Das ist ganz* _____ (different) *hier als in Deutschland.*
    a. *anders*
    b. *anderen*
    c. *ändert*

ANSWERS
1—c; 2—b; 3—c; 4—a; 5—b; 6—c; 7—a; 8—a; 9—b; 10—a.

C. COMMONLY USED VERBS

1. To see, to look: *sehen*

ich sehe	*wir sehen*
du siehst	*ihr seht*
er sieht	*Sie (sie) sehen*
sie sieht	
es sieht	

Sehen wir einmal nach!
Let's see. (Let's go take a look.)

Ich sehe nicht.
I don't see.

Er sieht alles.
He sees everything.

Haben Sie ihn gesehen?
Have you seen him? Did you see him?

Ich habe sie gerade gesehen.
I've just seen her.

Wen sehen Sie?
Whom do you see?

Können Sie mich jetzt sehen?
Can you see me now?

2. To know: *wissen*

ich weiss	*wir wissen*
du weisst	*ihr wisst*

er weiss   *Sie (sie) wissen*
sie weiss
es weiss

Ich weiss es.
I know it.

Ich weiss es nicht.
I don't know it.

Ich weiss es sehr gut.
I know it very well.

Er weiss nichts.
He doesn't know anything.

Ich weiss nichts darüber.
I don't know anything about it.

Ich weiss, dass er hier ist.
I know that he is here.

Wissen Sie das?
Do you know that?

Wissen Sie, wo er ist?
Do you know where he is?

Wer weiss?
Who knows?

Wir wissen nicht, ob er kommt.
We don't know whether he is coming.

3. To hold: *halten*

ich halte	*wir halten*
du hältst	*ihr haltet*
er hält	*Sie (sie) halten*
sie hält	
es hält	

Halten Sie mir das einen Moment!
Hold this for me a minute.

Er hält seinen Hut in der Hand.
He's holding his hat in his hand.

Halten Sie sich fest!
Hold on firmly!

Bleiben Sie am Apparat!
Hold the phone a minute.

Halten Sie still!
Keep still! Don't move!

Er hält es für selbstverständlich.
He takes it for granted.

Was halten Sie davon?
What do you think about it?

Ich halte nicht viel davon.
I don't think much of it.

Halten Sie sich rechts!
Keep to your right.

Halten Sie Ihr Versprechen!
Keep your promise!

4. To be able, can: *können*

ich kann	*wir können*
du kannst	*ihr könnt*
er, sie, es kann	*Sie (sie) können*

Ich kann nicht.
I can't.

Ich kann es tun.
I can do it.

Können Sie mir sagen, ob . . .
Can you tell me whether . . .

Können Sie kommen?
Can you come?

Ich verstehe nicht, wie er das kann.
I don't see how he can do that.

Ich kann nicht auf die Frage antworten.
I can't answer the question.

Sie können es ohne Schwierigkeit tun.
You can do it without any difficulty.

Ich kann nicht dorthin gehen.
I can't go there.

Wann können wir gehen?
When can we leave?

Sie können dorthin gehen.
You can go there.

Können Sie mir helfen?
Can you help me?

5. To understand: *verstehen*

ich verstehe	*wir verstehen*
du verstehst	*ihr versteht*
er, sie, es versteht	*Sie (sie) verstehen*

Er versteht nicht.
He doesn't understand.

Ich verstehe sehr gut.
I understand very well.

Ich verstehe Sie nicht.
I don't understand you.

Verstehen Sie mich nicht?
Don't you understand me?

Verstehen Sie?
Do you understand?

Verstehen Sie Deutsch?
Do you understand German?

Verstehen Sie Englisch?
Do you understand English?

Verstehen Sie alles, was er Ihnen sagt?
Do you understand everything he's saying to you?

Ich habe nicht verstanden.
I don't understand, ("I haven't understood. I didn't
    understand.")

Haben Sie verstanden?
Did you understand? ("Have you understood?")

Er versteht nichts vom Geschäft.
He doesn't understand anything about business.

Verstanden?
Did you understand? Do you understand? ("Is that understood?")

Ich verstehe es überhaupt nichts.
I don't understand it at all.

6. *legen*   to put in a prone position
   stellen   to put in a standing position
   hinstellen   to put down

Stellen Sie es dorthin!
Put it there (in an upright position).

Wo haben Sie es hingestellt?
Where did you put it?

Legen Sie es hin!
Lay it down.

Er weiss nie, wo er seine Sachen hinlegt.
He never knows where he puts his things.

Stellen Sie den Schirm in die Ecke!
Put the umbrella in the corner.

Legen Sie das Buch auf den Tisch hin!
Put the book (down) on the table.

7. To know, to be acquainted with: *kennen*

ich kenne   *wir kennen*
du kennst   *ihr kennt*
er, sie, es kennt   *Sie (sie) kennen*

Ich kenne ihn.
I know him.

Ich kenne es nicht.
I don't know it.

Kennen Sie dieses Wort?
Do you know this word?

Ich kenne seine Familie.
I know his family.

Jeder kennt es.
Everybody knows it.

Ich kenne ihn dem Aussehen nach.
I know him by sight (according to the way he looks).

Ich kenne ihn dem Namen nach.
I know him by name.

Das ist sehr bekannt.
It's very well known.

Das ist nicht sehr bekannt in Deutschland.
That's not very well known in Germany.

Das ist unbekannt.
It's unknown.

8. To want: *wollen*

ich will	*wir wollen*
du willst	*ihr wollt*
er, sie, es will	*Sie* (*sie*) *wollen*

Ich will es.
I want it.

Ich will es nicht.
I don't want it.

Ich will nichts.
I don't want anything.

Ich will etwas.
I want some (''something'').

Er will nichts davon.
He doesn't want any of it.

Er kann es tun, aber er will nicht.
He can do it but he doesn't want to.

Wollen Sie?
Do you want to?

Was wollen Sie?
What do you want? (not very polite)

Was möchten Sie?
What do you want (wish)? What would you like?

Wollen Sie kommen?
Do you want to come?

Wollen Sie mit uns kommen?
Do you want to come with us?

Wollen Sie Samstag kommen?
Do you want to come Saturday?

Wollen Sie mit uns zu Mittag essen?
Will you have lunch with us?

Wer will das?
Who wants that?

Was wollen Sie sagen?
What do you want to say?

Wollen Sie mir folgen?
Will you follow me?

Wie Sie wollen.
As you wish.

Wenn Sie wollen, kann ich es Ihnen bringen.
If you wish, (If you want to) I'll bring it to you.

9. To have to, to be obliged to, must: *müssen*

ich muss	*wir müssen*
du musst	*ihr müsst*
er, sie, es muss	*Sie (sie) müssen*

Ich muss jetzt gehen.
I must (have to) go now.

Er muss kommen.
He must (has to) come.

Er muss hier sein.
He must (has to) be here.

Sie müssen dort sein.
They have to (should, ought to) be there.

Müssen Sie dort hingehen?
Do you have to go (there)?

Was muss ich tun?
What do I have to do?

    10. To wait: *warten*

Warten Sie hier!
Wait here.

Warten Sie dort!
Wait there.

Warten Sie auf mich!
Wait for me!

Warten Sie ein wenig!
Wait a little!

Warten Sie einen Moment!
Wait a minute!

Warten Sie nicht auf ihn!
Don't wait for him!

Ich warte auf ihn.
I'm waiting for him.

Sie wartet auf die andern.
She's waiting for the others.

Auf wen warten Sie?
Whom are you waiting for?

Warum warten Sie?
Why are you waiting?

Es tut mir leid, dass ich Sie habe warten lassen.
I'm sorry I kept you waiting.

    11. To ask: *fragen*

Fragen Sie dort drüben!
Ask over there.

Was fragt er?
What's he asking? What does he want?

Fragen Sie nach dem Weg, wenn Sie sich verlaufen.
Ask your way if you get lost.

Fragen Sie ihn, wie spät es ist!
Ask him the time (what time it is).

Gehen Sie und fragen Sie ihn!
Go and ask him!

Ich komme gleich zurück, falls jemand nach mir fragt.
I'll be right back if someone asks for me.

Er hat gefragt, wo es ist.
He asked where it is.

Was man weiss, soll man nicht fragen.
What one knows, one should not ask.

Stellen Sie nicht so viele Fragen!
Don't ask so many questions.

Jemand fragt nach Ihnen.
Someone is asking for you. You're wanted.

Ich frage mich, ob das wahr ist.
I wonder if it's true. ("I ask myself if . . .")

Ich frage mich, warum er nicht kommt.
I wonder why he doesn't come.

Das frage ich mich selbst.
I wonder about that. ("That's what I am asking myself.")

12. To love: *lieben*

gern haben	to like
lieber haben	to prefer

Er liebt sie.
He loves her.

Er ist in sie verliebt.
He's in love with her.

Haben Sie ihn gern?
Do you like him?

Das habe ich nicht gern.
I don't like that.

Ich habe das andere lieber.
I like the other better. (I prefer the other.)

Ich gehe lieber heute abend dorthin.
I'd rather go there this evening.

13. To be worth: *wert sein*

Wieviel ist das wert?
How much is that worth?

Das ist keinen Pfennig wert.
That's not worth a cent.

Das ist nichts wert.
That's not worth anything. That's no good.

Das ist es nicht wert.
It's not worth that.

Das ist nicht viel wert.
That's not worth much.

Das ist preiswert.
That's reasonable. ("It's worth its price.")

Das ist viel Geld wert.
That's worth a lot of money.

Das ist nicht der Mühe wert.
That's not worth the effort.

D.   COMMON NOTICES AND SIGNS

Bekanntmachung	Public Notice
Herren	Gentlemen
Damen	Ladies
Herrentoilette	Men's Room

Damentoilette	Ladies' Room
W.C.	Toilet
Nichtraucher	Nonsmokers
Rauchen verboten!	No smoking
Geöffnet	Open
Geschlossen	Closed
Eingang	Entrance
Ausgang	Exit
Notausgang	Emergency Exit
Fahrstuhl	Elevator
Erdgeschoss	Ground Floor
Drücken	Push
Ziehen	Pull
Drehen	Turn
Bitte klingeln	Please Ring
Durchgang verboten!	Keep Out! No Thoroughfare!
Flugplatz	Airport
Herein!	Come In!
Herein ohne zu klopfen	Come In Without Knocking
Vor Eintritt klopfen	Knock Before Entering
Wegen Umbau geschlossen	Closed For Repairs
Unter neuer Leitung	Under New Management
Eintritt verboten!	No Admittance!
Eröffnung in Kürze	Will Open Shortly
Ganze Nacht geöffnet	Open All Night
Es ist verboten, auf den Boden zu spucken!	No Spitting!
Füsse abputzen	Wipe your feet
Hunde an der Leine	Keep your Dogs On Leash
Für Fussgänger verboten!	Pedestrians Keep Out!

Betreten des Geländes verboten	No Trespassing
Beschwerdebüro	Complaint Department
Am Schalter fragen	Apply at the Window
Geldwechsel	Money Exchanged (at a bank)
Zu verkaufen	For Sale
Zu vermieten	For Rent
Wohnung zu vermieten	Apartment to Let
Möblierte Wohnung zu vermieten	Furnished Apartment to Let
Preisnachlass	Reductions
Ausverkauf	Sale
Garderobe	Check Room (in a hotel, restaurant, or cafe)
Passkontrolle	Passport Checkpoint
Portier	Janitor
Abstellraum	Cloakroom
Umleitung	Detour
Strassenarbeiten	Road under Repair
Achtung: Kurve	Attention: Curve
Parken verboten	No Parking
Einbahnstrasse	One-Way Street
Überschreiten der Gleise verboten!	Do not Cross the Tracks!
Eisenbahnkreuzung	Railroad Crossing
Eisenbahnstrecke	Railroad (Rail Route)
Unterführung	Underpass
Halt!	Stop!
Vorsicht!	Caution!
Fussgänger	Pedestrian Crossing
Kreuzung	Crossroads
Omnibushaltestelle	Bus Stop
Plakate ankleben verboten!	Post No Bills!

Höchstgeschwindigkeit 30 Stundenkilometer	Maximum Speed 30 Kilometers Per Hour
Langsam fahren!	Go Slow!
Schule	School—Go Slow
Gefahr!	Danger!
Frisch gestrichen	Wet Paint
Haltestelle	Stops Here (Stop)
Nicht aus dem Fenster lehnen!	Don't Lean Out of the Window!
Alarmsignal	Alarm Signal
Hochspannung	High Voltage
Untergrundbahn	Subway
Gepäckaufbewahrung	Baggage Room, Check Room (in a railroad station)
Garderobe	Coat Room
Wartesaal	Waiting Room
Erster Klasse	First Class
Zweiter Klasse	Second Class
Dritter Klasse	Third Class
Gaststätte	Restaurant
Altstadt	Old Part of the City
Ankunft	Arrival
Abfahrt	Departure
Bahnsteig	Platform
Auskunft	Information
Auskunftsschalter	Information Booth
Theaterkasse	Box Office
Postamt	Post Office
Briefkasten	Mail Box
Kartenschalter	Ticket Office
Feuerlöscher	Fire Box
Bibliothek	Public Library
Polizeiwache	Police Station
Tankstelle/Benzin	Gas Station

Buchhandlung	Bookstore
Rathaus	City Hall
Herren-und Damen Frisör	Barber Shop and Hair Dresser
Friseuse	Ladies' Hairdresser
Arzt	Physician
Zahnarzt	Dentist
Schuhmacher	Shoe Repairing
Matinee	Matinee
Abendvorstellung um 8:30	Evening Performance at 8:30
Abendkleidung	Formal Dress
Laufende Vorstellung	Continuous Performance
Programmwechsel	Change of Program
Erfrischungen	Refreshments

FINAL QUIZ

1. _____ (How) *geht es Ihnen?*
   a. *Wann*
   b. *Wie*
   c. *Wenn*

2. _____ (Speak) *Sie langsam!*
   a. *Sprechen*
   b. *Sprecht*
   c. *Sprich*

3. _____ (Have) *Sie Zigaretten?*
   a. *Habe*
   b. *Hast*
   c. *Haben*

4. *Bringen Sie* _____ (me) *die Speisekarte, bitte.*
   a. *mir*
   b. *mich*
   c. *es*

5. _____ (I'd like) *eine Tasse Kaffee.*
   a. *Ich will*
   b. *Ich möchte*
   c. *Ich gehe*

6. *Wir möchten für drei Personen* _____ (breakfast).
   a. *Mittagessen*
   b. *Frühstück*
   c. *Abendessen*

7. _____ (Bring) *Sie mir einen Teelöffel!*
   a. *Geben*
   b. *Bringen*
   c. *Können*

8. *Wo befindet sich* _____ (the train station)?
   a. *der Weg*
   b. *der Bahnhof*
   c. *das Büro*

9. _____ (Are you) *sicher?*
   a. *Machen Sie*
   b. *Sagen Sie*
   c. *Sind Sie*

10. _____ (I have) *genug Zeit.*
    a. *Ich bin*
    b. *Ich habe*
    c. *Ich hatte*

11. _____ (Does he have) *Geld?*
    a. *Gibt es*
    b. *Ist er*
    c. *Hat er*

12. _____ (Are there) *welche Briefe für mich?*
　　a. *Es gibt*
　　b. *Gibt es*
　　c. *Hat er*

13. _____ (Understand) *Sie gut deutsch?*
　　a. *Verstehe*
　　b. *Verstehen*
　　c. *Hören*

14. *Es* _____ (I'm glad) *Sie kennenzulernen.*
　　a. *glücklich*
　　b. *freut mich*
　　c. *geehrt*

15. *Wollen Sie davon wenig oder* _____ (a lot)?
　　a. *noch*
　　b. *viel*
　　c. *mehr*

16. *Was* _____ (say) *Sie?*
　　a. *machen*
　　b. *sagen*
　　c. *gesagt*

17. *Wie* _____ (does one say) *das auf Deutsch?*
　　a. *sagen Sie*
　　b. *sagt man*
　　c. *schreibt man*

18. *Ihre Telefonnummer ist* _____ (3 30 74).
　　a. *drei dreiundzwanzig vierundfünfzig*
　　b. *drei dreissig vierundsiebzig*
　　c. *drei einunddressig achtundsiebzig*

19. _____ (I need) *das.*
    a. *Ich möchte*
    b. *Ich habe davon*
    c. *Ich brauche*

20. *Ich komme* _____ (tomorrow morning).
    a. *nachmittag*
    b. *morgen früh*
    c. *gestern abend*

21. _____ (Must one) *den Hausmeister deshalb sehen?*
    a. *Müssen*
    b. *Muss man*
    c. *Musst du*

22. *Ich* _____ (beg) *Sie um Verzeihung.*
    a. *bitte*
    b. *frage*
    c. *sage*

23. *Wie* _____ (is your name) *Sie?*
    a. *heissen*
    b. *nennen*
    c. *sind*

24. _____ (The check), *bitte.*
    a. *Die Butter*
    b. *Das Geld*
    c. *Die Rechnung*

25. *Könnten Sie mir eine Serviette* _____ (give)?
    a. *bestellen*
    b. *geben*
    c. *gehen*

ANSWERS

1—b; 2—a; 3—c; 4—a; 5—b; 6—b; 7—b; 8—b;
9—c; 10—b; 11—c; 12—b; 13—b; 14—b; 15—b;
16—b; 17—b; 18—b; 19—c; 20—b; 21—b; 22—a;
23—a; 24—c; 25—b.

When you get 100% on this quiz,
you can consider that you have
mastered the course!

SUMMARY OF GERMAN GRAMMAR

1. THE ALPHABET

LETTER	NAME	LETTER	NAME	LETTER	NAME
a	ah	j	yot	s	ess
b	beh	k	kah	t	teh
c	tseh	l	ell	u	oo
d	deh	m	em	v	fauh
e	eh	n	en	w	veh
f	eff	o	oh	x	iks
g	gay	p	peh	y	üpsilon
h	hah	q	ku	z	tsett
i	ee	r	err		

2. THE VOWELS

long **a**	as in *ah*: "father"	*Vater*
short **a**	as in *a*: "matter"	*Ratte*
long **ä**	as in "hair"	*spät*
short **ä**	as in "men"	*Männer*
long **e**	as in "dare"	*gehen*
short **e**	as in "bent"	*Adresse*
e	at end of a word as in "pocket"	*heute*
long **i, ie**	as in "meet"	*Liebe*
short **i**	as in "ship"	*Mitte*
long **o**	as in "lone"	*Bohne*
short **o**	as in "love"	*kommen*
long **ö**	similar to *e* in *geben* but with rounded lips	*König*
short **ö**	similar to *short u* but with rounded lips	*können*
long **u**	as in "mood"	*Buch*

short **u**	as in "bush"	*dumm*
long **ü**	as in *long i* with rounded lips	*früh*
short **ü**	as *short i* but with rounded lips	*Brücke*
y	pronounced as *long u*	*Typ*

3. THE DIPTHONGS

{ **ai**		*Kai*
ei	*y* "by"	*Leine*
au	as in *ou* "house"	*Haus*
{ **äu**		*häufig*
eu	as in *oy* "boy"	*Freund*

4. THE CONSONANTS

b	as in *b* "bed" and at the end of a word as in *p* "trap"
c	as in *k* "keep" and rather rarely like *ts*
d	as in *d* "date" at the end of a word like *t* as in "but"
f	as in *f* "fly"
g	as in *g* "garden"
h	as in *h* "hundred" sometimes not pronounced at all as in *Schuh*—"shoe"
j	as in *y* "York"
k	as in *c* "cut"
l	as in *l* "life"
m	as in *m* "man"
n	as in *n* "never"
p	as in *p* "painter"
q	as in *q* "quality"
r	a little more rolled than in English.
s	at the beginning of a word as in *z* "zoo" at the end of a word or syllable as in *s* "son"

t	as in *t* "tea"
v	as in *f* "fair"
w	as in *v* "vain"
x	as in *x* "mix"
z	like the English combination *ts*

5. SPECIAL LETTER COMBINATIONS

ch	as in *k* "character" *Charakter*
chs	as in *ks Fuchs*—"fox"
ch	a sound near the English *h* in "hue": *Kirche*—church
ch	a guttural sound not existing in English but close to the Scotch "loch"; *e.g. ach!*—"ah!"
ck	in final position pronounced *k*: *Scheck*—check
ig	as sound of *h* in "hue"
sch	as in *sh* "shoe"
sp or st	when placed at the beginning of the word also gives the initial sound of the *sh* as in "shoe" *e.g. Spanien*—"Spain"
ng	as in *ng* "sing"
tz	is similar to the English *ts, e.g. Blitz*—"lightning"

6. THE GERMAN DECLENSION

1. Nominative (subject, noun)

Das Buch ist hier.   The book is here.

2. Genitive (possessive case)

der Name des Lehrers   The name of the teacher

3. Dative (indirect object)

Er gibt dem Kind einen   He gives an apple to the
  Apfel.   child.

4. Accusative (direct object)

Sie hält die Feder.   She is holding the pen.

7. PLURAL OF NOUNS

1. Masculine

a) nominative plus *e*

der Abend   *die Abende*
der Freund   *die Freunde*

b) nominative plus *er*

der Geist   *die Geister*
der Leib   *die Leiber*

c) nominative plus *e* and ¨ (Umlaut) on the last
vowel

der Hut   *die Hüte*
der Fall   *die Fälle*

d) nominative plus *er* and ¨ (Umlaut) on the last
vowel

der Mann   *die Männer*
der Rand   *die Ränder*

e) masculine nouns ending in *el, en, er* do not
change.

der Schlüssel	*die Schlüssel*
der Kuchen	*die Kuchen*
der Maler	*die Maler*

A certain number of masculine nouns, most of them ending in *e*, form all their cases by the addition of an *n* or *en*.

| *der Junge* | *die Jungen* |
| *der Mensch* | *die Menschen* |

2. Feminine

a) Most feminine nouns form their plural by adding *n* or *en*

| *die Tür* | *die Türen* |
| *die Frage* | *die Fragen* |

b) Some add *e* or Umlaut on the last vowel and an *e*.

| *die Kenntnis* | *die Kenntnisse* |
| *die Frucht* | *die Früchte* |

c) Feminine words ending in *in* form their plural in *innen*

| *die Schülerin* | *die Schülerinnen* |
| *die Freundin* | *die Freundinnen* |

3. Neuter

Most neuter nouns form their plural like the masculine, the majority of them in *e* or *er*.

| *das Heft* | *die Hefte* |
| *das Licht* | *die Lichter* |

8. GENDER

German nouns can be either masculine, feminine, or neuter. However, there is no definite rule to determine their gender. Here are a few helpful hints:

1. Masculine are:

   a) designations of trade or profession:
      der Maler, der Arzt, der Künstler

   b) titles of nobility:
      der Fürst, der Graf, der König

   c) nouns ending in *ling:*
      der Sperling, der Jüngling

2. Feminine are:

   a) feminine designations of trade:
      die Malerin, die Ärztin

   b) feminine titles of nobility:
      die Königin, die Fürstin

   c) names of numbers:
      die Drei, die Null

   d) many names of trees:
      die Tanne, die Eiche

   e) nouns ending in *ei, heit, keit, schaft, sucht, ung:*
      die Freiheit, die Gesellschaft, die Ahnung

3. Neuter are:

   a) the diminutives in *chen* or *lein:*
      das Mädchen, das Büchlein

b) many nouns ending in *tum:*
   das Altertum

c) most nouns of metals:
   das Gold, das Eisen

d) most cities:
   das schöne Berlin

e) most countries:
   das Amerika

f) colors:
   das Rot

g) most collective nouns beginning with *ge:*
   das Gebirge (mountains)

THE STRESS: German words generally have one strongly accented syllable or even two if the word is very long.

1. *Short words:* The accent is generally on the first syllable:
   Example: *Vater, Mutter, Bruder*

2. *Long words:* the accent is generally on the root of the word:
   *Emp**fehl**ung Ge**bir**ge Ge**bäu**de*

3. Separable prefixes are always accented:
   abmachen **zu**geben **mit**gehen

4. Inseparable prefixes (*be, emp, ent, er, ge, ver, zer*) are never accented. The accent always falls on the following syllable.
   erhalten   vergessen   zerbrechen

9. THE DEFINITE ARTICLE

1. Unlike English usage, the definite article can be
   used in front of a first name (*familiar*)
   Der Hans und die Margarete John and Margaret

2. In front of a title:
   Ist der Herr Doktor da? Is the (Mr.) doctor at
   home? *Nein, aber die Frau Doktor ist zu Hause.*
   No, but the (Mrs.) Doctor is at home.

Remember the declension of the articles:

MASCULINE	FEMININE	NEUTER
N. *der*	N. *die*	N. *das*
G. *des*	G. *der*	G. *des*
D. *dem*	D. *der*	D. *dem*
A. *den*	A. *die*	A. *das*

PLURAL FOR ALL
N. *die*
G. *der*
D. *den*
A. *die*

10. THE INDEFINITE ARTICLE

Notice that in a negation *ein* becomes *kein*.

Er war kein Arzt, sondern ein Zahnarzt.
He was not a physician but a dentist.

MASCULINE	FEMININE	NEUTER
N. *ein*	*eine*	*ein*
G. *eines*	*einer*	*eines*
D. *einem*	*einer*	*einem*
A. *einen*	*eine*	*ein*

Masculine, feminine, and neuter singular of *kein,* same as
ein.

PLURAL

N. *keine*
G. *keiner*
D. *keinen*
A. *keine*

11. THE ADJECTIVES

Adjectives are declined in three ways:

1. Without article or pronoun (Strong Declension):

MASCULINE	FEMININE	NEUTER
*rot*er *Wein*	*rot*e *Tinte*	*rot*es *Licht*
*rot*en *Weines*	*rot*er *Tinte*	*rot*en *Lichtes*
*rot*em *Wein*	*rot*er *Tinte*	*rot*em *Licht*
*rot*en *Wein*	*rot*e *Tinte*	*rot*es *Licht*

PLURAL (M.F.N.)

Nom. *rot*e *Weine*
Gen. *rot*er *Weinen*
Dat. *rot*en *Weinen*
Acc. *rot*e *Weine*

2. With the definite article (Weak Declension):

SINGULAR

N. *der rot*e *Wein*   N. *die rot*e *Tinte*
G. *des rot*en *Weines*   G. *der rot*en *Tinte*
D. *dem rot*en *Wein*   D. *der rot*en *Tinte*
A. *den rot*en *Wein*   A. *die rot*e *Tinte*

PLURAL

N. *das rot*e *Licht*   N. *die rot*en *Weine*
G. *des rot*en *Lichtes*   G. *der rot*en *Weine*
D. *dem rot*en *Licht*   D. *den rot*en *Weinen*
A. *das rot*e *Licht*   A. *die rot*en *Weine*

3. With the indefinite article, possessive adjective, or (italicized) *kein* words (Mixed Declension):

MASCULINE	FEMININE
N. *ein roter Wein*	N. *seine rote Tinte*
G. *eines roten Weines*	G. *seiner roten Tinte*
D. *einem roten Wein*	D. *seiner roten Tinte*
A. *einen roten Wein*	A. *seine rote Tinte*

NEUTER

N. *kein rotes Licht*
G. *keines roten Lichtes*
D. *keinem roten Licht*
A. *kein rotes Licht*

PLURAL

N. *meine roten Weine*
G. *meiner roten Weine*
D. *meinen roten Weinen*
A. *meine roten Weine*

12. COMPARATIVE AND SUPERLATIVE

1. The comparative and the superlative are formed as in English by adding *er* for the comparative and *st* (or *est*) for the superlative to the adjective.

Some short adjectives also take an Umlaut on their vowels.

schlecht, schlechter, schlechtest	bad, worse, worst
alt, älter, ältest	old, older, oldest

2. There are a few adjectives which have an irregular comparative. Here are the most common ones:

POSITIVE	COMPARATIVE	SUPERLATIVE
gut	*besser*	*der (die, das) beste, am besten*
gross	*grösser*	*der (die, das) grösste, am grössten*
hoch	*höher*	*der (die, das) höchste, am höchsten*
nahe	*näher*	*der (die, das) nächste, am nächsten*
viel	*mehr*	*der (die, das) meiste, am meisten*
gern	*lieber*	*der (die, das) liebste, am liebsten*

13. THE PARTITIVE

1. Generally not translated:

   Example:
   Geben Sie mir Brot!   Give me some bread.
   Geben Sie mir ein Glas Wein.   Give me a glass of wine.

2. *Etwas* can also be used to mean a part of something:

   Example:
   Ich gebe ihm etwas zu trinken.
   I am giving him something to drink.

   Ich gebe ihm etwas davon.
   I give him some of it.

3. The negative *kein* is declined like the indefinite article.

   Example:
   Ich habe ein Messer, aber keine Gabel.
   I have a knife but no fork.

14. POSSESSIVE ADJECTIVES

1. Possessive adjectives agree in gender and number with the thing possessed:

NOMINATIVE

Before Singular nouns:

MASCULINE AND NEUTER	FEMININE	PLURAL	
mein	*meine*	*meine*	my
dein	*deine*	*deine* (*fam.*)	your
sein	*seine*	*seine*	his, its
ihr	*ihre*	*ihre*	her
unser	*unsere*	*unsere*	our
euer	*eure*	*eure*	your (*fam. pl.*)
Ihr	*Ihre*	*Ihre*	your (*polite*)
ihr	*ihre*	*Ihre*	their

2. Examples:

mein Hund	my dog
meine Tante	my aunt
ihr Vater	her father
seine Mutter	his mother
Ihr Buch	your (*polite*) book
ihre Bleistife	their pencils

3. Notice that these adjectives agree in gender not with the possessor as in English, but with the noun they modify. *Sein* and *seine* may therefore mean "his" or "its":

Hans spricht mit seiner Mutter.
John is talking to his mother.

Das Bier hat seinen Geschmack verloren.
The beer has lost its taste.

Sie liest ihren Roman.
She is reading her (their) novel.

15. POSSESSIVE PRONOUNS

	NOMINATIVE		
MASCULINE	FEMININE	NEUTER	
meiner	*meine*	*meines*	mine
deiner	*deine*	*deines*	yours (*fam.*)
seiner	*seine*	*seines*	his
ihrer	*ihre*	*ihres*	hers
Ihrer	*Ihre*	*Ihres*	yours (*form.*)
unser	*unsere*	*unseres*	ours
euer	*eure*	*eures*	yours (*fam.*)
Ihrer	*Ihre*	*Ihres*	yours (*pol.*)
ihrer	*ihre*	*ihres*	theirs

Ist das mein Hut?—Ja, das ist Ihrer. (*deiner*)
Is that my hat?—Yes, that is yours.

Ist das deine Krawatte?—Ja, das ist meine.
Ist that your tie?—Yes, that is mine.

Ist das sein Buch?—Nein, das ist meins.
Is that his book?—No, that is mine.

Ist das ihr Schirm?—Nein, das ist seiner.
Ist that her umbrella?—No, that is his.

16. Demonstrative Adjectives

SINGULAR

N. *dieser*	*diese*	*dieses*	this or that[1]
G. *dieses*	*dieser*	*dieses*	
D. *diesem*	*dieser*	*diesem*	
A. *diesen*	*diese*	*dieses*	

PLURAL (M, F, N)

N. *diese*
G. *dieser*
D. *diesen*
A. *diese*

Examples:

Dieses Haus ist schön.
This (that) house is beautiful

Er sieht diesen Mann.
He sees this man.

Jenes Haus ist hässlich.
That house is ugly.

Er gibt dieser Frau ein Geschenk.
He gives this woman a present.

17. Demonstrative Pronouns

SINGULAR

MASCULINE	FEMININE	NEUTER
N. *derjenige*	N. *diejenige*	N. *dasjenige*
G. *desjenigen*	G. *derjenigen*	G. *desjenigen*
D. *demjenigen*	D. *derjenigen*	D. *demjenigen*
A. *denjenigen*	A. *diejenige*	A. *dasjenige*

[1] *jen* (*-er, -e, -es*) may also be used, but is less common in conversation.

PLURAL
N. *diejenigen*
G. *derjenigen*
G. *denjenigen*
A. *diejenigen*

Mein Buch ist blau. Dasjenige meiner Schwester ist grün.
My book is blue. The one of my sister (My sister's) is green.

18. RELATIVE PRONOUNS

The relative pronoun is like the demonstrative pronoun but its declension varies in the Genitive singular of all genders, and in the Genitive and Dative plural.

SINGULAR

MASCULINE	FEMININE	NEUTER	
N. *der*	N. *die*	N. *das*	who
G. *dessen*	G. *deren*	G. *dessen*	whose
D. *dem*	D. *der*	D. *dem*	to whom
A. *den*	A. *die*	A. *das*	whom

PLURAL

N. *die*	who
G. *deren*	whose
D. *denen*	to whom
A. *die*	whom

Examples:

Der Junge, dessen Vater ich kenne, heisst Richard.
The boy whose father I know is named Richard.

Die Frau, deren Tochter die Universität besucht, arbeitet in einen Kaufhaus.

The woman whose daughter attends the university works in a department store.

Welcher can also be used and is declined in the same way as the article *der*.

Examples:

Der Freund, welcher morgen kommt, heisst Max.
The friend who is coming tomorrow is named Max.

NOTES

1. These pronouns must agree in gender and number with the noun they refer to.

   Das Mädchen, das in der Strasse spielt.
   The little girl who is playing on the street.

2. A comma should always be used before them.

3. The verb is always placed at the end of the clause it introduces.

4. Relative pronouns can never be omitted as in English.

   Das Buch, das ich lese . . .
   The book (that) I am reading . . .

19. PERSONAL PRONOUNS

SINGULAR

N. *ich*	*du*	*er*	*sie*	*es*	*Sie*	(pol.)
G. *meiner*	*deiner*	*seiner*	*ihrer*	*seines*	*Ihrer*	(pol.)
D. *mir*	*dir*	*ihm*	*ihr*	*ihm*	*Ihr*	(pol.)
A. *mich*	*dich*	*ihm*	*sie*	*es*	*Sie*	(pol.)

PLURAL

N. *wir*	*ihr*	*sie*	*Sie*
G. *unserer*	*eurer*	*ihrer*	*Ihrer*
D. *uns*	*euch*	*ihnen*	*Ihnen*
A. *uns*	*euch*	*sie*	*Sie*

Examples:

Wir geben ihr Blumen.
We are giving her flowers.

Du sprichst mit ihm.
You are speaking with him.

Wir sprechen von Ihnen.
We're talking about you (*polite*).

Diese Geschenke sind für dich.
These presents are for you.

20. INDEFINITE PRONOUNS

man	one
jeder(man)	everybody, everyone
jemand	somebody, someone
niemand	nobody
etwas	something, some

Examples:

Jemand steht vor der Tür.
Someone is standing before the door.

Es muss etwas geschehen.
Something has to be done.

Man spricht hier nur Deutsch.
One speaks only German here.

21.　POSITION OF PRONOUNS

In a German sentence the subject pronoun usually comes first and the indirect object pronoun generally precedes the direct object pronoun.

1. *Er　　gibt　　dem Bruder　　einen Roman.*
　　Subj. Pron.　Indir Obj. Pron.　Dir. Obj. Pron.
　　He　　gives　　the brother　　a novel.

2. *Sie schenkt der Mutter eine Ledertasche.*
　　She gives her mother a leather handbag.

Dem Bruder and *der Mutter* are the indirect objects. If we substituted indirect object pronouns for each indirect object, the sentences would read as follows:

Er gibt ihm einen Roman.
He gives him a novel.
(He gives a novel to him.)

Er schenkt ihr eine Ledertasche.
He gives her a leather handbag.
(He gives a leather handbag to her.)

3. If we substituted a direct object pronoun for each direct object, the two sentences would read as follows:

Er gibt ihn dem Bruder.
He gives it to the brother.

Er schenkt <u>sie</u> der Mutter.
He gives it to (his) mother.

4. If we substitute pronouns for both objects in each sentence, we get:

Er gibt ihn ihm.
He gives it to him.

Er schenkt sie ihr.
He gives it to her.

22. THE NEGATIVE

A sentence is made negative by using the word *nicht*, generally following the verb. Words may come between the verb and *nicht*.

Ich weiss.	I know.
Ich weiss nicht.	I do not know.
Ich weiss es nicht.	I don't know it.

The negative of *ein* is *kein*.

23. ADVERBS

1. Almost all adjectives can be used as adverbs.

2. Their comparative is formed the same way as the adjectives.
   Their superlative is preceded by *am* instead of the article, and has the ending *-en*.

Fritz ist ein guter Tänzer.
Fritz is a good dancer.

Fritz tanzt gut.
Fritz dances well.

Karl ist ein besserer Tänzer als Fritz.
Karl is a better dancer than Fritz. Karl dances better
  than Fritz.

Fred Astaire ist der beste Tänzer.
Fred Astaire is the best dancer.

Fred Astaire tanzt am besten.
Fred Astaire dances the best.

3. A few adverbs have an irregular comparative
   and superlative. Here are the most common
   ones:

viel	*mehr*	*am meisten*	much, more, most
gern	*lieber*	*am liebsten*	gladly, preferably, most preferably
bald	*eher*	*am ehesten*	soon, sooner, soonest

4. Adverbs of place:

hier	here
dort	there
fort	away
links	on the left
rechts	on the right
vorne	in front of
nirgends	nowhere
irgendwo	somewhere
weg	aside, away
hinter	behind
unten	underneath

drinnen	inside
draussen	outside
überall	everywhere
nirgendwo, nirgends	nowhere
weit	far
nahe	near
dort	up there
dort drüben	over there

5. Adverbs of time:

heute	today
bald	soon
ab und zu	now and then
gerade	just
morgen	tomorrow
gestern	yesterday
vorgestern	the day before yesterday
übermorgen	the day after tomorrow
jetzt	now
dann	then
vorher	before
damals	once, at that time
einmal, ehemals	once, formerly
früh	early
bald	soon
spät	late
oft	often
niemals, nie	never
immer, je, jemals	always, ever
lang, lange	long, for a long time
sofort	at once, right away
manchmal	sometimes
noch	still, yet
nicht mehr	no longer, no more
nachher	afterwards

6. Adverbs of manner:

deshalb	therefore
fast	almost
genau	exactly
sehr	very
sogar	even
überhaupt	at all
sowieso	anyway
gut	well
schlecht	ill, badly
so, somit	thus, so
ähnlich	similarly
andererseits	on the other hand
zusammen	together
viel	much, very
besonders	above all, especially
absichtlich	on purpose, purposely
ausdrücklich	expressly
gewöhnlich	usually

7. Adverbs of quantity or degree:

viel	much, many
genug	enough
auf einmal	all of a sudden
kaum	not much, hardly
wenig	little
mehr	more
nicht mehr	no more
weniger	less
noch mehr	more, even more
zuviel	too much, too many
soviel	so much, so many

8. Particles and intensifiers

allerdings	certainly
also	so, well
doch	yes, indeed
eben	exactly, just
ja	certainly, to be sure
mal	just, simply
nähmlich	namely
nur	only
schon	already, I (we) suppose
wohl	probably
zwar	to be sure

24. PREPOSITIONS

1. With the Genitive:

während	during
wegen	because of
statt, anstatt	instead of
trotz	in spite of

2. With the Accusative:

durch	through, by
für	for
gegen	against, toward
ohne	without
um	round, about, at (time)

3. With the Dative:

aus	from, out of
bei	at, by, near, with

gegenüber	facing, across from
mit	with
nach	after, to (a place)
seit	since
von	of, from, by
zu	to, at

4. With the Dative or Accusative:

an	at, to
auf	on, upon, in
hinter	behind
in	in, into, at
neben	beside, near
über	over, across
unter	under, among
vor	before, ago
zwischen	between

25. CONTRACTIONS

am	for	*an dem*
ans	for	*an das*
im	for	*in dem*
ins	for	*in das*
beim	for	*bei dem*
vom	for	*von dem*
zum	for	*zu dem*
zur	for	*zu der*
ins	for	*in das*
fürs	for	*für das*
aufs	for	*auf das*

26. PREFIXES

Many German verbs have certain prefixes. They are divided into three groups:

1. *The inseparable prefixes,* which remain attached to the verb and are never accented (just like the English verbs: overthrow, understand, etc.). In the past tense, the past participles of these verbs do not take the prefix *ge.* These prefixes are: *be, emp, ent, er, ge, miss, ver, zer, hinter, wider:* Ex.: *emfehlen, gefallen, verstehen*

2. *The separable prefixes:* These are linked to the verb in the compound tenses; in the other tenses they are separated and generally placed at the end of the sentence. They are always accented. The most common such prefixes are: *ab, an, auf, aus, bei, ein, fort, mit, nach, vor, weg, zu, frei, los, wahr, statt.* There are also compound separable prefixes added to verbs, such as: *hinaus, herauf, hinein, herein, zurück, zusammen:* Ex.: *mitkommen, weggehen, zuschliessen*
her indicates a movement toward the person who is speaking:

Kommen Sie herunter!   Come down.

hin indicates a movement away from the person speaking:

Geh hinaus!   Go out!

The separable prefix is so important in the sentence that the verb is sometimes omitted in short statements:

Herein!   (Come) in!

3. Some prefixes are sometimes separable and sometimes inseparable, depending on the meaning of the verb. They are:

wieder, voll, durch, um, unter, über.

Examples: *Der Schüler wiederholt seine Lektion.*
          The student repeats his lesson.

Holen Sie das wieder!
Take it back!

Die Polizei hat ihm das ganze Hause durchsucht.
The police searched his whole house.

27. THE TENSES OF THE INDICATIVE

SIMPLE TENSES

1. The present tense expresses an uncompleted action in the present. It has several English translations:

ich spreche   I speak, I am speaking, I do speak
ich esse   I eat, I am eating, I do eat

2. The imperfect tense expresses a continued or habitual action in the past. It also indicates an action that was happening when something else

happened. The weak verbs add the following
endings to their stem: *te, test, te, tet, ten.*

The strong verbs usually change their stem
vowel. The first and third person singular have
no ending. The others are as in the present.

Er schlief, als Hans ein- *trat.*	He was sleeping when John entered.
Er sprach oft davon.	He often spoke about that.
Es war dunkel, als er *ausging.*	It was night (dark) when he went out.

3. The future tense is formed by using the auxiliary *werden* plus the infinitive of the verb. It
   indicates a future action:

Er wird morgen ankom- *men.*	He'll arrive tomorrow.
Ich werde ihm morgen *schreiben.*	I'll write him (to him) tomorrow.

4. The past tense is formed by adding the past
   participle to the present indicative of *haben* or,
   in some cases, *sein.* It is used to indicate a past
   action which is completed in the present or
   which happened only once:

Er hat mir nichts gesagt.	He didn't tell me any- thing.
Ich habe meine Arbeit *beendet.*	I finished my work. I have finished my work.
Haben Sie ihn gesehen?	Have you seen him?
Sie sind angekommen.	They arrived.

5. The pluperfect tense is formed by adding the past participle to the imperfect of *haben* or, in some cases, *sein:*

Er hatte es getan.	He had done it.
Als ich zurückkam, war er schon fortgewesen.	When I came back, he had already left.

6. The future perfect tense is formed by adding the past participle to the future of *haben* or, in some cases, *sein.* It translates the English future perfect:

Er wird bald seine Arbeit beendet haben.	He will soon have finished his work.
In zwei Wochen wird er schon in Spanien gewesen sein.	In two weeks he already will have been in Spain.

Sometimes it indicates probability:

Er wird es ihm zweifellos gesagt haben.	No doubt he will have told him.
Er wird krank gewesen sein.	He probably was sick.
Ich werde mich geirrt haben.	I must have been mistaken.

COMPOUND TENSES

1. The compound tenses are made up of *haben* (intransitive verbs use *sein*) and the past participle:

Er hat gesprochen.	He has spoken.
Sie haben gegessen.	You have eaten.

2. Most compound tenses are formed with the auxiliary *haben:*

Ich habe ein Geschenk erhalten.   I received a present.

Er hat zuviel getrunken.   He drank too much.

3. The most common intransitive verbs conjugated with the verb *sein* are:
   gehen, ankommen, absteigen, eintreten, einsteigen, sterben, abreisen, bleiben, kommen, fallen, zurückkommen, laufen

Examples:

Ich bin gekommen.   I have come.
Er ist angekommen.   He has come.
Wir sind abgereist.   We have left.

Er ist durch ganz Europa gefahren.
He traveled through Europe.

The verb *fahren* can also be used as a transitive verb, requiring a direct object.

Er hat den Mercedes nach Hamburg gefahren.
He drove the Mercedes to Hamburg (the Mercedes is the direct object of the verb, *fahren*).

28. THE PAST PARTICIPLE

The first syllable of the past participle of the weak and strong verbs is always *ge* when the verbs have no prefix whatsoever. If they do have a separable prefix, then the syllable *ge* stands between the prefix and the

past participle. If the verbs have an inseparable prefix, the past participle has no additional *ge*.

Infinitive	Past Participle
(strong verb without prefix)	
ziehen to pull	*gezogen*
(strong with a separable prefix)	
vorziehen to prefer	*vorgezogen*
(weak without prefix)	
warten to wait	*gewartet*
(weak with a separable prefix)	
abwarten to wait and see	*abgewartet*
(strong verb with an inseparable prefix)	
verlieren to lose	*verloren*
(weak with an inseparable prefix)	
entdecken to discover	*entdeckt*

In the weak verbs, the part participle ends in *t* or *et*.

arbeiten	*gearbeitet*
lernen	*gelernt*

In the strong verbs the past participle ends in *en*, but the vowel of the infinitive stem generally changes. Therefore when you study the verbs, do not forget to memorize the past participle as well as the other tenses. See table of irregular verbs, page 327.

29. USE OF THE AUXILIARIES *HABEN* AND *SEIN*

Notice that most verbs form the perfect, pluperfect, and future perfect with the auxiliary *haben:*

ich habe gesehen	I have seen
(chiefly transitive & reflexive)	
du hast gesehen	you have seen
ich habe mich gewaschen	I have washed myself.

However, quite a few verbs, chiefly intransitive, form these tenses with the auxiliary *sein:*

1. The verbs *sein, werden, bleiben.*

2. Verbs indicating a change of place (chiefly, verbs of motion, as: *gehen, kommen, eilen, fallen, fliessen, laufen, reisen, rollen, steigen, sinken, aufstehen, fliegen, begegnen,* etc.

3. Verbs indicating a change in the condition of a thing or a person, as: *aufwachen, einschlafen, wachsen, aufbleiben, verblühen, vergehen, verschwinden, sterben, erhalten, platzen, erkranken.*

30. THE SUBJUNCTIVE

Present of *haben, sein, werden* "to have, to be, to become."

ich habe (*hätte*)	*ich sei*	*ich werde* (*würde*)
du habest	*due seiest*	*du werdest*
er, sie, es habe	*er, sie, es sei*	*er, sie, es werde*
wir haben (*hätten*)	*wir seien*	*wir werden* (*würden*)
ihr habet	*ihr seiet*	*ihr werdet*
Sie, sie haben (*hätten*)	*Sie, sie seien*	*Sie, sie werden* (*würden*)

The endings of both weak and strong verbs are *e, est, e, en, et, en.* The strong verbs keep the stem vowel in each person.

When the present subjunctive verb forms are identical to the indicative, the imperfect subjunctive verb forms are used: *Er sagte, dass ich ihn nicht begrüsst hätte* (instead of *begrüsst habe*).

IMPERFECT

ich hätte	*ich wäre*	*ich würde*
du hättest	*du wärest*	*du würdest*
er, sie, es hätte	*er, sie, es wäre*	*er, sie, es würde*
wur hätten	*wir wären*	*wir würden*
ihr hättet	*ihr wäret*	*ihr würdet*
Sie, sie hätten	*Sie, sie wären*	*Sie, sie würden*

Notice that the imperfect tense of the weak verbs is identical in both the indicative and subjunctive. When this occurs, the structure *würde* and a main verb are used. The substitution is therefore with the present conditional tense. Examples:

Indirect Discourse:
Er sagte, dass er es nicht lernen würde.
He said that he would not learn it.

Unreal Conditions:
Wenn er mit mir ins Kino ginge, dann würde ich mich freuen.
If he went with me to the movies, I'd be happy.

Strong verbs have the same endings as the present subjunctive, but take the *Umlaut* if their stem vowel is *a, e,* or *u.*

ich tat   I did   *ich täte*   that I did

The past tenses: The past, pluperfect, and the future are formed with the past participle of the indicative of the verb plus the auxiliaries *haben, sein,* and *werden* in their respective subjunctive forms. The subjunctive is used to express "doubt, wish, eventuality, unreality." It is also used:

1. in indirect discourse

2. after certain conjunctions and expressions, such as:

als ob	as if
es sei denn, dass	unless

Examples:

Er glaubte, dass er käme.	He believed that he was coming.
Wir helfen ihm, damit er gesund werde.	We help him, so that he may be healthy again.

3. A contrary-to-fact condition in reference to present or future time is usually introduced by the conjunction *wenn* (if) and the imperfect subjunctive followed by the result clause in the present conditional:

Example: *Wenn er morgen käme, dann würde ich mit ihm in die Stadt fahren.*
If he came tomorrow, I would go to the city with him.

The "if" clause (*wenn* clause) has transposed word order (verb in last position), and the main clause has

inverted word order (subject after the verb) whenever
it stands after the subordinate clause. The above sentence may also be expressed as follows:

a. *Ich würde mit ihm in die Stadt fahren, wenn er
    morgen käme.*

b. *Ich führe mit ihm in die Stadt, wenn er käme.*

c. *Ich würde mit ihm in die Stadt fahren, wenn er
    kommen würde.*

Sentence "c" is employed less frequently, since it
employs one conditional verb form in each clause.

4. To express a wish:

Mögen Sie glücklich sein!	May you be happy!
Wärest du doch hier!	Wish you were here!

5. Unreal conditions in reference to past time are
   formed by the past perfect subjunctive in the
   wenn clause, followed by the conditional perfect. In modern German, the conditional perfect
   is usually replaced by the pluperfect subjunctive. Note that the helping verb may be a form
   of *haben* or *sein.* Examples:

*Wenn ich Zeit gehabt hätte, wäre ich mit dir zum
    Strand gekommen.*
If I had had the time, I would have come to the beach
    with you.

*Wenn ich die Bahn genommen hätte, (dann) hätte ich
    ihn rechtzeitig getroffen.*
If I had taken the train, (then) I would have met him
    on time.

31. THE CONDITIONAL

The conditional is formed with the auxiliary *werden* in its imperfect subjunctive form.

ich würde	*wir würden*
du würdest	*ihr würdet*
er, sie, es würde	*sie (Sie) würden*

It is generally used in connection with the conjunction *wenn* instead of the subjunctive to express a condition.

Wenn wir Geld hätten, würden wir eine lange Reise machen.
If we had any money, we would go on a long trip.

The past conditional is formed like the past future, but using *würde* instead of *werde*.

32. THE PASSIVE VOICE

The passive voice is formed with the past participle of the verb and the auxiliary *werden* used in the present and in the past.

Die Erde wird von der Sonne beleuchtet.

The earth is lit by the sun. "By" is translated by the German *von* (plus dative):

Amerika wurde von Kolumbus entdeckt.
America was discovered by Columbus.

In the past tense (perfect tense) the participle of the auxiliary *werden, geworden,* drops the prefix *ge-* and becomes simply *worden.*

Example:

Das Buch ist von ihm geschrieben worden.
The book has been written by him.

Er war von ihr gesehen worden.
He had been seen by her.

33. THE IMPERATIVE

The imperative of the verbs is formed from the present indicative tense.

2nd person singular: Drop the ending *n* from the infinitive. However, strong verbs changing the vowel *e* to *i* or *ie* in the present indicative form their imperative by dropping the *st* from this tense.

Lerne! (*du lernst*)
Nimm! (*du nimmst*)

1st person plural: Invert the infinitive form with the personal pronoun:

Singen wir! (*wir singen*)

2nd person plural: Simply insert the second person plural of the present indicative tense and omit the pronoun.

Gebt! (*ihr gebt*)

3rd person plural: Same as the 1st person plural

Nehmen Sie! Geben Sie!

To express the imperative, the verb *lassen* can also be used; it corresponds to the English "let."

Example:

Lassen Sie das sein!   Let it be!

Imperative of *sein* and *haben:*

sein to be	*haben* to have
sei (fam.)! be!	*habe* (fam.)! have!
seid (fam. pl.)! be!	*habt* (fam. pl.)! have!
seien wir! let us be!	*haben wir!* let us have!

34. THE INFINITIVE

The infinitive is usually preceded by *zu* when used in connection with another verb; however, *zu* is omitted when the infinitive is used in connection with the following verbs:

werden, können, dürfen, wollen, mögen, müssen, sollen, lassen, machen, hören, sehen, heissen, helfen, lehren, lernen

Examples:

Er bittet ihn, den Brief zu schreiben.	He asks him to write the letter.
Ich werde ihr schreiben.	I shall write to her (future)
Ich helfe ihm den Wagen waschen.	I'm helping him wash the car.
Er lehrt uns schwimmen.	He teaches us to swim.

The infinitive is also used after certain prepositions in connection with *zu:*

um . . . zu (in order to)
ohne . . . zu (without)   the *zu* can be used alone
anstatt . . . zu (instead of)

Examples:

Wir gehen zur Schule, um zu lernen.	We go to school to learn.
Ich kann nicht essen, ohne etwas zu trinken.	I cannot eat without drinking something.
Er faulenzt, anstatt uns zu helfen.	He is lazy instead of helping us.

Words with a separable prefix have the *zu* between the prefix and the infinitive.

Example: *aufmachen*

Er bittet ihn, die Tür aufzumachen.
He asks him to open the door.

35. COMPLEMENTS OF VERBS

Verbs can be followed by:

a. preposition: their complement should be put in the case required by the preposition; for example: *bedecken mit*—"to cover with" (always dative)

Der Tisch ist mit Staub bedeckt.	The table is covered with dust.

b. an object without a preposition: The genitive, accusative, or dative is used, depending on the verb.

Examples:

Er ist des Mordes beschuldigt. (Genitive)	He is accused of murder.
Sie glauben mir nicht. (Dative)	You don't believe me.
Wir lieben ihn. (Accusative)	We love him.

36. CHANGES IN THE NORMAL SEQUENCE OF WORDS WITHIN A SENTENCE

1. *By Transposition:* putting the verb at the end of a sentence.

In a subordinate clause, that is, a clause beginning with a relative pronoun or a conjunction, the verb is always placed at the end of the clause.

Die Sprache, die wir lernen, ist Deutsch.
The language that we are learning is German.

Ich kann nicht sehen, weil es dunkel ist.
I cannot see because it is dark.

Ich glaube, dass das Essen in diesem Restaurant gut ist.
I believe that the food in this restaurant is good.

Notice also that a comma is always used before the relative pronoun or conjunction. If the verb is in a compound tense the *auxiliary* is placed at the end of the sentence.

Ich glaube nicht, dass es morgen regnen wird.
I do not believe that it will rain tomorrow.

In the case of an indirect question or subordinate clause introduced by an interrogative word, such as the pronouns: *wer, was,* or *welcher,* or the adverbs: *wo, wann,* etc., or the conjunction: *ob,* the verb is also placed at the end of the sentence.

Wir wissen nicht, ob er morgen kommt.
We don't know whether he is coming tomorrow.

Können Sie mir sagen, wie weit es von hier bis zum Bahnhof ist?
Can you tell me how far it is from here to the train station?

2. *By Inversion:* putting the verb before the subject. The inversion is necessary:

  a) usually when a question is asked.

(affirmative)
Er schreibt den Brief. He writes the letter.
(interrogative)
Schreibt er den Brief? Does he write the letter?

  b) in the main clause of any sentence when it is preceded by a subordinate clause.

Wenn wir die Augen schliessen, können wir nicht sehen.
If we close our eyes, we cannot see.

In the above example, however, you have the inversion because the main clause is put after the subordinate clause.

c) whenever the main clause opens with a word other than the subject.

Morgen werden die Kinder ins Kino gehen.
Tomorrow the children will go to the movies.

Here we have inversion because the sentence does not start with its subject, *die Kinder,* but with another word: *morgen.*

Die Kinder werden morgen ins Kino gehen.
The children will go to the movies tomorrow.

The above does not take any inversion because the sentence is started by its subject, *die Kinder.*

37. INDIRECT DISCOURSE

When you want to tell a story or make an indirect quotation in German, you use indirect discourse:

Direct Discourse:
Hans sagt: "Ich gehe zum Bahnhof."
John says: "I am going to the station."

Indirect Discourse:
Hans sagt, dass er zum Bahnhof gehe.
John says that he is going to the station.

Imperfect:
Hans sagte, dass er zum Bahnhof ginge.
John said that he was going to the station.

NOTES

1. The subjunctive should be used (even though you can use the indicative, as many Germans do).

2. The conjunction *dass*—"that" can be used or omitted.

If it is used, the verb should be placed at the end of the sentence, as in the regular case of transposition.

Er sagt, dass er zum Bahnhof gehe.

3. If it is omitted, the order of the words remains unchanged.

Hans sagt, er gehe zum Bahnhof.
John says he is going to the station.

Hans sagte, er ginge zum Bahnhof.
John said he was going to the station.

The tense of the verb in indirect discourse does not affect the tense of the inflected verb form in the indirect statement. Examples:

Er berichtet, er nehme (nähme) den Bus. (action in present)

Er berichtete, er habe (hätte) den Bus genommen. (action in past)

Er erzählte uns, er sei (wäre) eine Meile gelaufen. (action in past with an intransitive verb)

Er habe berichtet, er werde (würde) den Bus nehmen. (action in future)

The subjunctive of indirect discourse is normally used after the following verbs: *behaupten* (to claim), *berichten* (to report), *erklären* (to explain), *glauben* (to believe), *meinen* (to mean), *sagen* (to say), and *schreiben* (to write).

4. Notice that in both instances, a comma is used at the beginning of the second clause.

5. The following sequence of tenses is generally observed in expressing conditional sentences:

For Real Conditions:

The If-Clause (*Wenn-Clause*)	Result Clause
Present Indicative	Future or Present Indicative

For Unreal Conditions in Reference to Present or Future Time:

The If-Clause (*Wenn-Clause*)	Result Clause
Imperfect Subjunctive	Present Conditional or Imperfect Subjunctive

For Unreal Conditions in Reference to Past Time:

The If-Clause (*Wenn-Clause*)	Result Clause
Pluperfect Subjunctive	Pluperfect Subjunctive or Conditional Perfect

38. CONSTRUCTION OF THE SENTENCE

(SUMMARY)

1. Main Clauses or Simple Sentences:

a) Affirmative sentence:

Das Buch ist rot.   The book is red.

b) Interrogative:

Ist das Buch rot?   Is the book red?

c) Negative:

Das Buch ist nicht rot.	The book is not red.

d) Past tenses:

Ich habe ein Gedicht gelernt.	I have learned a poem.
Ich lernte ein Gedicht.	I learned a poem.
Ich hatte ein Gedicht gelernt.	I had learned a poem.

e) Infinitive:

Sie brauchen das nicht zu wissen.	You do not need to know that.

2. Subordinate clauses:

a) Transposition:

Ich sehe, dass das Buch rot ist.	I see that the book is red.
Ich kenne den Schuler, der das Gedicht liest.	I know the student who is reading the poem.

b) Inversion:

Wenn das Wetter schon ist, gehe ich gern spazieren.
(The second clause has inverted word order).
When the weather is fine, I like to take a walk.

c) Indirect discourse:

Sie antwortet ihm, dass sie ein Schülerin $\begin{cases} \textit{sei.} \\ \textit{ist.} \end{cases}$

Sie antwortet ihm, sie $\begin{cases} \textit{sei} \\ \textit{ist} \end{cases}$ *eine Schülerin.*

She answers (him) that she is a pupil.

39. THE MOST COMMON IRREGULAR VERBS

sein   to be

INFINITIVE

PRESENT	PAST
sein	*gewesen sein*

PARTICIPLES

PRESENT	PAST
seiend	*gewesen*

INDICATIVE

PRESENT	PRESENT PERFECT
ich bin	*bin gewesen*
du bist	*bist gewesen*
er, sie, es ist	*ist gewesen*
wir sind	*sind gewesen*
ihr seid	*seid gewesen*
sie (Sie) sind	*sind gewesen*

IMPERFECT	PAST PERFECT
ich war	*war gewesen*
du warst	*warst gewesen*
er, sie, es war	*war gewesen*
wir waren	*waren gewesen*
ihr wart	*wart gewesen*
sie (Sie) waren	*waren gewesen*

FUTURE	PAST FUTURE
ich werde sein	*werde gewesen sein*
du wirst sein	*wirst gewesen sein*
er, sie, es wird sein	*wird gewesen sein*

wir werden sein	werden gewesen sein
ihr werdet sein	werdet gewesen sein
sie (Sie) werden sein	werden gewesen sein

CONDITIONAL

PRESENT	CONDITIONAL PERFECT
ich würde sein	würde gewesen sein
du würdest sein	würdest gewesen sein
er, sie, es würde sein	würde gewesen sein
wir würden sein	würden gewesen sein
ihr würdet sein	würdet gewesen sein
sie (Sie) würden sein	würden gewesen sein

IMPERATIVE

sei!
seien wir!
seid!
seien Sie!

SUBJUNCTIVE

PRESENT	PRESENT PERFECT
ich sei	ich sei gewesen
du seiest	du seiest gewesen
er, sie, es sei	er sei gewesen
wir seien	wir seien gewesen
ihr seiet	ihr seid gewesen
sie (Sie) seien	sie seien gewesen

IMPERFECT	PAST PERFECT
ich wäre	ich wäre gewesen
du wärest	du wärest gewesen
er, sie, es wäre	er wäre gewesen

wir wären	wir wären gewesen
ihr wäret	ihr wäret gewesen
sie (Sie) wären	sie (Sie) wären gewesen

haben   to have

INFINITIVE

| PRESENT | PAST |
| *haben* | *gehabt haben* |

PARTICIPLES

| PRESENT | PAST |
| *habend* | *gehabt* |

INDICATIVE

PRESENT	PRESENT PERFECT
ich habe	*habe gehabt*
du hast	*hast gehabt*
er, sie, es hat	*hat gehabt*
wir haben	*haben gehabt*
ihr habt	*habt gehabt*
sie, Sie haben	*haben gehabt*

IMPERFECT	PAST PERFECT
ich hatte	*hatte gehabt*
du hattest	*hattest gehabt*
er hatte	*hatte gehabt*
wir hatten	*hatten gehabt*
ihr hattet	*hattet gehabt*
sie (Sie) hatten	*hatten gehabt*

FUTURE	FUTURE PERFECT
ich werde haben	*werde gehabt haben*
du wirst haben	*wirst gehabt haben*
er, sie, es wird haben	*wird gehabt haben*
wir werden haben	*werden gehabt haben*
ihr werdet haben	*werdet gehabt haben*
sie (Sie) werden haben	*werden gehabt haben*

CONDITIONAL	PAST CONDITIONAL
ich würde haben	*würde gehabt haben*
du würdest haben	*würdest gehabt haben*
er, sie, es würde haben	*würde gehabt haben*
wir würden haben	*würden gehabt haben*
ihr würdet haben	*würdet gehabt haben*
sie (Sie) würden haben	*würden gehabt haben*

IMPERATIVE

Habe!
Haben wir!
Habt!
Haben Sie!

SUBJUNCTIVE

When the subjunctive forms are identical to the indicative forms, you have to use an alternate subjunctive form. These alternates are in parentheses.

PRESENT	PAST
ich habe	*ich habe (hätte) gehabt*
du habest	*du habest gehabt*
er, sie, es habe	*er, sie, es habe gehabt*
wir haben	*wir haben (hätten)*
	gehabt

| ihr habet | ihr habet gehabt |
| sie (Sie) haben | sie (Sie) haben (hatten) gehabt |

IMPERFECT	PAST PERFECT
ich hätte	ich hätte gehabt
du hättest	du hättest gehabt
er, Sie, es hätte	er, Sie, es hätte gehabt
wir hätten	wir hätten gehabt
ihr hättet	ihr hättet gehabt
sie (Sie) hätten	sie (Sie) hätten gehabt

werden   to become

INFINITIVE

PRESENT	PAST
werden	geworden sein

PARTICIPLES

PRESENT	PAST
werdend	geworden

INDICATIVE

PRESENT	PRESENT PERFECT
ich werde	bin geworden
du wirst	bist geworden
er, sie, es wird	ist geworden
wir werden	sind geworden
ihr werdet	seid geworden
sie (Sie) werden	sind geworden

IMPERFECT	PAST PERFECT
ich wurde	war geworden
du wurdest	warst geworden

er, sie, es wurde   war geworden
wir wurden   waren geworden
ihr wurdet   wart geworden
sie (Sie) wurden   waren geworden

FUTURE	FUTURE PERFECT
ich werde werden	werde geworden sein
du wirst werden	wirst geworden sein
er, sie, es wird werden	wird geworden sein
wir werden werden	werden geworden sein
ihr werdet werden	werdet geworden sein
sie (Sie) werden werden	werden geworden sein

CONDITIONAL	CONDITIONAL PERFECT
ich würde werden	würde geworden sein
du würdest werden	würdest geworden sein
er, sie, es würde werden	würde geworden sein
wir würden werden	würden geworden sein
ihr würdet werden	würdet geworden sein
sie (Sie) würden werden	würden geworden sein

IMPERATIVE

werde!
werden wir!
werdet!
werden Sie!

SUBJUNCTIVE

PRESENT	IMPERFECT
ich werde (würde)	ich würde
du werdest	du würdest
er, sei, es werde	er, sie, es würde
wir werden (würden)	wir würden

ihr werdet   *ihr würdet*
sie (Sie) werden (würden)   *sie (Sie) würden*

können   to be able to

INFINITIVE

PRESENT   PAST
können   *gekonnt haben*

PARTICIPLES

PRESENT   PAST
könnend   *gekonnt*

INDICATIVE

PRESENT	PRESENT PERFECT
ich kann	*habe gekonnt*
du kannst	*hast gekonnt*
er, sie, es kann	*hat gekonnt*
wir können	*haben gekonnt*
ihr könnt	*habt gekonnt*
sie (Sie) können	*haben gekonnt*

IMPERFECT	PAST PERFECT
ich konnte	*hatte gekonnt*
du konntest	*hattest gekonnt*
er, sie, es konnte	*hatte gekonnt*
wir konnten	*hatten gekonnt*
ihr konntet	*hattet gekonnt*
sie (Sie) konnten	*hatten gekonnt*

FUTURE	FUTURE PERFECT
ich werde können	*werde gekonnt haben*
du wirst können	*wirst gekonnt haben*

er, sie, es wird können	wird gekonnt haben
wir werden können	werden gekonnt haben
ihr werdet können	werdet gekonnt haben
sie (Sie) werden können	werden gekonnt haben

CONDITIONAL	CONDITIONAL PERFECT
ich würde können	würde gekonnt haben
du würdest können	würdest gekonnt haben
er, sie, es würde können	würde gekonnt haben
wir würden können	würden gekonnt haben
ihr würdet können	würdet gekonnt haben
sie (Sie) werden können	würden gekonnt haben

SUBJUNCTIVE

PRESENT	PRESENT PERFECT
ich könne	ich (habe) hätte gekonnt
du könnest	du habest gekonnt
er, sie, es könne	er habe gekonnt
wir können (könnten)	wir (haben) hätten gekonnt
ihr könnet	ihr habet gekonnt
sie (Sie) können (könnten)	sie (Sie) (haben) hätten gekonnt

IMPERFECT	PAST PERFECT
ich könnte	ich hätte gekonnt
du könntest	du hättest gekonnt
er, sie, es könnte	er, sie, es hätte gekonnt
wir könnten	wir hätten gekonnt
ihr könntet	ihr hättet gekonnt
sie (Sie) könnten	sie (Sie) hätten gekonnt

dürfen   to be allowed to

INFINITIVE

PRESENT

dürfen

PAST

gedurft haben

PARTICIPLES

PRESENT

—

PAST

gedurft

INDICATIVE

PRESENT

ich darf
du darfst
er, sie, es darf
wir dürfen
ihr dürft
sie, Sie dürfen

PAST

habe gedurft
hast gedurft
hat gedurft
haben gedurft
habt gedurft
haben gedurft

IMPERFECT

ich durfte
du durftest
er, sie, es durfte
wir durften
ihr durftet
sie (Sie) durften

PAST PERFECT

hatte gedurft
hattest gedurft
hatte gedurft
hatten gedurft
hattet gedurft
hatten gedurft

FUTURE

ich werde dürfen
du wirst dürfen
er, sie, es wird dürfen
wir werden dürfen
ihr werdet dürfen
sie (Sie) werden dürfen

FUTURE PERFECT

werde gedurft haben
wirst gedurft haben
wird gedurft haben
werden gedurft haben
werdet gedurft haben
werden gedurft haben

CONDITIONAL	CONDITIONAL PERFECT
ich würde dürfen	würde gedurft haben
du würdest dürfen	würdest gedurft haben
er, sie, es würde dürfen	würde gedurft haben
wir würden dürfen	würden gedurft haben
ihr würdet dürfen	würdet gedurft haben
sie (Sie) würden dürfen	würden gedurft haben

SUBJUNCTIVE

PRESENT	PRESENT PERFECT
ich dürfe	ich habe (hätte) gedurft
du dürfest	du habest gedurft
er, sie, es dürfe	er habe gedurft
wir dürfen (dürften)	wir haben (hätten) gedurft
ihr dürfet	ihr habet gedurft
sie (Sie) dürfen (dürften)	sie (Sie) haben (hätten) gedurft.

IMPERFECT	PAST PERFECT
ich dürfte	ich hätte gedurft
du dürftest	du hättest gedurft
er, sie, es dürfte	er hätte gedurft
wir dürften	wir hätten gedurft
ihr dürftet	ihr hättet gedurft
sie (Sie) dürften	sie hätten gedurft

müssen   to be obliged to, to have to

INFINITIVE

PRESENT	PAST
müssen	gemusst haben

PARTICIPLES

PRESENT

müssen

PAST

gemusst

INDICATIVE

PRESENT

ich muss
du musst
er, sie, es muss
wir müssen
ihr müsst
sie, (Sie) müssen

PRESENT PERFECT

habe gemusst
hast gemusst
hat gemusst
haben gemusst
habt gemusst
haben gemusst

IMPERFECT

ich musste
du musstest
er, sie, es musste
wir mussten
ihr musstet
sie (Sie) mussten

PAST PERFECT

hatte gemusst
hattest gemusst
hatte gemusst
hatten gemusst
hattet gemusst
hatten gemusst

FUTURE

ich werde müssen
du wirst müssen
er, sie, es wird müssen
wir werden müssen
ihr werdet müssen
sie (Sie) werden müssen

FUTURE PERFECT

werde gemusst haben
wirst gemusst haben
wird gemusst haben
werden gemusst haben
werdet gemusst haben
werden gemusst haben

CONDITIONAL

ich würde müssen
du würdest müssen
er, sie, es würde müssen

CONDITIONAL PERFECT

würde gemusst haben
würdest gemusst haben
würde gemusst haben

wir würden müssen	würden gemusst haben
ihr würdet müssen	würdet gemusst haben
sie (Sie) würden müssen	würden gemusst haben

SUBJUNCTIVE

PRESENT	PRESENT PERFCT
ich müsse	ich habe (hätte) gemusst
du müssest	du habest gemusst
er, sie, es müsse	er, sie, es habe gemusst
wir müssen (müssten)	wir haben (hätten) gemusst
ihr müsset	ihr habet gemusst
sie, Sie müssen (müssten)	sie, Sie haben (hätten) gemusst

IMPERFECT	PAST PERFECT
ich müsste	ich hätte gemusst
du müsstest	du hättest gemusst
er, sie, es müsse	er, sie, es hätte gemusst
wir müssten	wir hätten gemusst
ihr müsstet	ihr hättet gemusst
sie, Sie müssten	sie (Sie) hätten gemusst

wissen   to know

INFINITIVE

PRESENT	PAST
wissen	gewusst haben

PARTICIPLES

PRESENT	PAST
wissend	gewusst

INDICATIVE

PRESENT	PRESENT PERFECT
ich weiss	*habe gewusst*
du weisst	*hast gewusst*
er, sie, es weiss	*hat gewusst*
wir wissen	*haben gewusst*
ihr wisst	*habt gewusst*
sie, Sie wissen	*haben gewusst*

IMPERFECT	PAST PERFECT
ich wusste	*hatte gewusst*
du wusstest	*hattest gewusst*
er, sie, es wusste	*hatte gewusst*
wir wussten	*hatten gewusst*
ihr wusstet	*hattet gewusst*
sie (Sie) wussten	*hatten gewusst*

FUTURE	FUTURE PERFECT
ich werde wissen	*werde gewusst haben*
du wirst wissen	*wirst gewusst haben*
er, sie, es wird wissen	*wird gewusst haben*
wir werden wissen	*werden gewusst haben*
ihr werdet wissen	*werdet gewusst haben*
sie (Sie) werden wissen	*werden gewusst haben*

CONDITIONAL	CONDITIONAL PERFECT
ich würde wissen	*würde gewusst haben*
du würdest wissen	*würdest gewusst haben*
er, sie, es würde wissen	*würde gewusst haben*
wir würden wissen	*würden gewusst haben*
ihr würdet wissen	*würdet gewusst haben*
sie (Sie) würden wissen	*würden gewusst haben*

IMPERATIVE

wisse!
wissen wir!
wisst!
wissen Sie!

SUBJUNCTIVE

PRESENT

ich wisse
du wissest
er, sie, es wisse
wir wissen (wüssten)
ihr wisset
sie (Sie) wissen (wüssten)

PRESENT PERFECT

ich habe hätte gewusst
du habest gewusst
er habe gewusst
wir haben (hätten) gewusst
ihr habet gewusst
sie (Sie) haben (hätten)
  gewusst

IMPERFECT

ich wüsste
du wüsstest
er, sie, es wüsste
wir wüssten
ihr wüsstet
sie (Sie) wüssten

PAST PERFECT

ich hätte gewusst
du hättest gewusst
er, sie, es hätte gewusst
wir hätten gewusst
ihr hättet gewusst
sie (Sie) hätten gewusst

gehen   to go

INFINITIVE

PRESENT

gehen

PAST

gegangen sein

PARTICIPLES

PRESENT

gehend

PAST

gegangen

INDICATIVE

PRESENT	PRESENT PERFECT
ich gehe	*bin gegangen*
du gehst	*bist gegangen*
er, sie, es geht	*ist gegangen*
wir gehen	*sind gegangen*
ihr geht	*seid gegangen*
sie (Sie) gehen	*sind gegangen*

IMPERFECT	PAST PERFECT
ich ging	*war gegangen*
du gingst	*warst gegangen*
er, sie, es ging	*war gegangen*
wir gingen	*waren gegangen*
ihr gingt	*wart gegangen*
sie (Sie) gingen	*waren gegangen*

FUTURE	FUTURE PERFECT
ich werde gehen	*werde gegangen sein*
du wirst gehen	*wirst gegangen sein*
er, sie, es wird gehen	*wird gegangen sein*
wir werden gehen	*werden gegangen sein*
ihr werdet gehen	*werdet gegangen sein*
sie (Sie) werden gehen	*werden gegangen sein*

CONDITIONAL	CONDITIONAL PERFECT
ich würde gehen	*würde gegangen sein*
du würdest gehen	*würdest gegangen sein*
er, sie, es würde gehen	*würde gegangen sein*
wir würden gehen	*würden gegangen sein*
ihr würdet gehen	*würdet gegangen sein*
sie (Sie) würden gehen	*würden gegangen sein*

IMPERATIVE

gehe!
gehen wir!
geht!
gehen Sie!

SUBJUNCTIVE

PRESENT	PRESENT PERFECT
ich (gehe) ginge	*ich sei gegangen*
du gehest	*du seiest gegangen*
er, sie, es gehe	*er sei gegangen*
wir (gehen) gingen	*wir seien gegangen*
ihr gehet	*ihr seid gegangen*
sie (Sie) (gehen) gingen	*sie (Sie) seien gegangen*

IMPERFECT	PAST PERFECT
ich ginge	*ich wäre gegangen*
du gingest	*du wärest gegangen*
er, sie, es ginge	*er wäre gegangen*
wir gingen	*wir wären gegangen*
ihr ginget	*ihr wäret gegangen*
sie (Sie) gingen	*sie wären gegangen*

kommen   to come

INFINITIVE

PRESENT	PAST
kommen	*gekommen sein*

PARTICIPLES

PRESENT	PAST
kommend	*gekommen*

INDICATIVE

PRESENT	PRESENT PERFECT
ich komme	*bin gekommen*
du kommst	*bist gekommen*
er, sie, es kommt	*ist gekommen*
wir kommen	*sind gekommen*
ihr kommt	*seid gekommen*
sie, Sie kommen	*sind gekommen*

IMPERFECT	PAST PERFECT
ich kam	*war gekommen*
du kamst	*warst gekommen*
er, sie, es kam	*war gekommen*
wir kamen	*waren gekommen*
ihr kamt	*wart gekommen*
sie (Sie) kamen	*waren gekommen*

FUTURE	FUTURE PERFECT
ich werde kommen	*werde gekommen sein*
du wirst kommen	*wirst gekommen sein*
er, sie, es wird kommen	*wird gekommen sein*
wir werden kommen	*werden gekommen sein*
ihr werdet kommen	*werdet gekommen sein*
sie (Sie) werden kommen	*werden gekommen sein*

CONDITIONAL	CONDITIONAL PERFECT
ich würde kommen	*würde gekommen sein*
du würdest kommen	*würdest gekommen sein*
er, sie, es würde kommen	*würde gekommen sein*
wir würden kommen	*würden gekommen sein*
ihr würdet kommen	*würdet gekommen sein*
sie (Sie) würden kommen	*würden gekommen sein*

IMPERATIVE

komm!
kommen wir!
kommt!
kommen Sie!

SUBJUNCTIVE

PRESENT

ich (komme) käme
dass du kommest
er, sie, es komme
wir (kommen) kämen
ihr kommet
sie [Sie] (kommen)
   kämen

PRESENT PERFECT

ich sei gekommen
du seiest gekommen
er, sie, es sei gekommen
wir seien gekommen
ihr seid gekommen
sie seien gekommen

IMPERFECT

ich käme
du kämest
er, sie, es käme
wir kämen
ihr kämet
sie (Sie) kämen

PAST PERFECT

ich wäre gekommen
du wärest gekommen
er, sie, es wäre gekommen
wir wären gekommen
ihr wäret gekommen
sie wären gekommen

40. OTHER IRREGULAR VERBS

When the present subjunctive form is in parenthesis, it indicates that it is identical to the present indicative. Whenever this occurs, the imperfect or the past perfect subjunctive form is used.

Infinitive: *beginnen* to begin
Pres. Part.: *beginnend*
Present Indicative: *ich beginne, du beginnst, er be-*

*ginnt, wir beginnen, ihr beginnt, Sie beginnen, sie
beginnen*
Present Subjunctive: (*ich beginne*), *du beginnest, er
beginne, wir beginnen, ihr beginnet, (Sie beginnen*), *sie* (*beginnen*)
Imperfect Indicative: *ich begann*
Imperfect Subjunctive: *Ich begänne (begönne)*
Past Part.: *begonnen*
Present Perfect Indicative: *ich habe begonnen*
Past Perfect Indicative: *ich hatte begonnen*
Past Perfect Subjunctive: *ich hätte begonnen*
Future: *ich werde beginnen*
Future Perfect: *ich werde begonnen haben*
Conditional: *ich würde beginnen*
Conditional Perfect: *ich würde begonnen haben*
Imperative: *beginn! beginnen wir! beginnt! beginnen
Sie!*

Infinitive: *bleiben* to remain
Pres. Part.: *bleibend*
Present Indicative: *ich bleibe, du bleibst, er bleibt, wir
bleiben, ihr bleibt, Sie bleiben, sie bleiben*
Present Subjunctive: *ich bleibe, du bleibest, er bleibe,
wir bleiben, ihr bleibet, Sie bleiben, sie bleiben*
Imperfect Indicative: *ich bleib*
Imperfect Subjunctive: *ich bleibe*
Past Part.: *geblieben*
Present Perfect Indicative: *ich bin geblieben*
Past Perfect Indicative: *ich war geblieben*
Present Perfect Subjunctive: *ich sei geblieben*
Past Perfect Subjunctive: *ich wäre geblieben*
Future: *ich werde bleiben*
Future Perfect: *ich werde geblieben sein*
Conditional: *ich würde bleiben*
Conditional Perfect: *ich würde geblieben sein*
Imperative: *bleib! bleiben wir! bleibt! bleiben Sie!*

Infinitive: *bringen* to bring
Pres. Part.: *bringend*
Present Indicative: *ich bringe, du bringst, er bringt, wir bringen, ihr bringt, Sie bringen, sie bringen*
Present Subjunctive: (*ich bringe*), *du bringest, er bringt,* (*wir bringen*), *ihr bringet,* (*Sie bringen, sie bringen*)
Imperfect Indicative: *ich brachte*
Imperfect Subjunctive: *ich brächte*
Past Part.: *gebracht*
Past Indicative: *ich habe gebracht*
Past Perfect Indicative: *ich hatte gebracht*
Present Perfect Subjunctive: *ich habe* (*hatte*) *gebracht*
Past Perfect Subjunctive: *ich hätte gebracht*
Future: *ich werde bringen*
Future Perfect: *ich werde gebracht haben*
Conditional: *ich würde bringen*
Conditional Perfect: *ich würde gebracht haben*
Imperative: *bring! bringen wir! bringt! bringen Sie!*

Infinitive: *denken* to think
Pres. Part.: *denkend*
Present Indicative: *ich denke, du denkst, er denkt, wir denken, ihr denkt, Sie denken, sie denken*
Present Subjunctive: (*ich denke*), *du denkest, er denke,* (*wir denken*), *ihr denket,* (*Sie denken, sie denken*)
Imperfect Indicative: *ich dachte*
Imperfect Subjunctive: *ich dächte*
Past Part.: *gedacht*
Present Perfect Indicative: *ich habe gedacht*
Past Perfect Indicative: *ich hatte gedacht*
Present Perfect Subjunctive: (*ich habe gedacht*)
Past Perfect Subjunctive: *ich hätte gedacht*
Future: *ich werde denken*
Future Perfect: *ich werde gedacht haben*

Conditional: *ich würde denken*
Conditional Perfect: *ich würde gedacht haben*
Imperative: *denk! denken wir! denkt! denken Sie!*

Infinitive: *essen* to eat
Pres. Part.: *essend*
Present Indicative: *ich esse, du isst, er isst, wir essen, ihr esst, Sie essen, sie essen*
Present Subjunctive: (*ich esse*), *du essest, er esse, (wir essen), ihr esset, (Sie essen, sie essen)*
Imperfect Indicative: *ich ass*
Imperfect Subjunctive: *ich ässe*
Past Part.: *gegessen*
Present Perfect Indicative: *ich habe gegessen*
Past Perfect Indicative: *ich hatte gegessen*
Present Perfect Subjunctive: *ich (hatte) habe gegessen*
Past Perfect Subjunctive: *ich hätte gegessen*
Future: *ich werde essen*
Future Perfect: *ich werde gegessen haben*
Conditional: *ich würde essen*
Conditional Perfect: *ich würde gegessen haben*
Imperative: *iss! essen wir! esst! essen Sie!*

Infinitive: *fahren* to drive
Pres. Part.: *fahrend*
Present Indicative: *ich fahre, du fährst, er fährt, wir fahren, ihr fahrt, Sie fahren, sie fahren*
Present Subjunctive: *ich (fahre) führe, du fahrest, er fahre, (wir fahren), ihr fahret, (Sie fahren, sie fahren)*
Imperfect Indicative: *ich fuhr*
Imperfect Subjunctive: *ich führe*
Past Part.: *gefahren*
Present Perfect Indicative: *ich bin gefahren*
Past Perfect Indicative: *ich war gefahren*

Present Perfect Subjunctive: *ich sei gefahren*
Past Perfect Subjunctive: *ich wäre gefahren*
Future: *ich werde fahren*
Future Perfect: *ich werde gefahren sein*
Conditional: *ich würde fahren*
Conditional Perfect: *ich würde gefahren sein*
Imperative: *fahr! fahren wir! fahrt! fahren Sie!*

Infinitive: *fallen* to fall
Pres. Part.: *fallend*
Present Indicative: *ich falle, du fällst, er fällt, wir fallen, ihr fallt, Sie fallen, sie fallen*
Present Subjunctive: *ich (falle) fiele, du fallest, er falle, (wir fallen), ihr fallet, (Sie fallen, sie fallen)*
Imperfect Indicative: *ich fiel*
Imperfect Subjunctive: *ich fiele*
Past Part.: *gefallen*
Present Perfect Indicative: *ich bin gefallen*
Past Perfect Indicative: *ich war gefallen*
Present Perfect Subjunctive: *ich sei gefallen*
Past Perfect Subjunctive: *ich wäre gefallen*
Future: *ich werde fallen*
Future Perfect: *ich werde gefallen sein*
Conditional: *ich würde fallen*
Conditional Perfect: *ich würde gefallen sein*
Imperative: *falle! fallen wir! fallt! fallen Sie!*

Infinitive: *finden* to find
Pres. Part.: *findend*
Present Indicative: *ich finde, du findest, er findet, wir finden, ihr findet, Sie finden, sie finden*
Present Subjunctive: *ich (finde) fände, du findest, er finde, (wir finden), ihr findet, (Sie finden, sie finden)*
Imperfect Indicative: *ich fand*
Imperfect Subjunctive: *ich fände*

Past Part.: *gefunden*
Present Perfect Indicative: *ich habe gefunden*
Past Perfect Indicative: *ich hatte gefunden*
Present Perfect Subjunctive: *ich habe gefunden*
Past Perfect Subjunctive: *ich hätte gefunden*
Future: *ich werde finden*
Future Perfect: *ich werde gefunden haben*
Conditional: *ich würde finden*
Conditional Perfect: *ich würde gefunden haben*
Imperative: *find! finden wir! findet! finden Sie!*

Infinitive: *fliegen* to fly
Pres. Part.: *fliegend*
Present Indicative: *ich fliege, du fliegst, er fliegt, wir fliegen, ihr fliegt, Sie fliegen, sie fliegen*
Present Subjunctive: *ich (fliege) flöge, du fliegest, er fliege, (wir fliegen), ihr flieget, Sie fliegen, (sie fliegen)*
Imperfect Indicative: *ich flog*
Imperfect Subjunctive: *ich flöge*
Past Part.: *geflogen*
Present Perfect Indicative: *ich bin geflogen*
Past Perfect Indicative: *ich war geflogen*
Present Perfect Subjunctive: *ich sei geflogen*
Past Perfect Subjunctive: *ich wäre geflogen*
Future: *ich werde fliegen*
Future Perfect: *ich werde geflogen sein*
Conditional: *ich würde fliegen*
Conditional Perfect: *ich würde geflogen sein*
Imperative: *fliege! fliegen wir! fliegt! fliegen Sie!*

Infinitive: *heissen* to be called
Pres. Part.: *heissend*
Present Indicative: *ich heisse, du heisst, er heisst, wir heissen, ihr heisst, Sie heissen, sie heissen*

Present Subjunctive: *ich (heisse) hiesse, du heissest, er heisse, (wir heissen), ihr heisset, (Sie heissen, sie heissen)*
Imperfect Indicative: *ich heiss*
Imperfect Subjunctive: *ich heisse*
Past Part.: *geheissen*
Present Perfect Indicative: *ich habe geheissen*
Past Perfect Indicative: *ich hatte geheissen*
Present Perfect Subjunctive: *ich (habe) hätte geheissen*
Past Perfect Subjunctive: *ich hätte geheissen*
Future: *ich werde heissen*
Future Perfect: *ich werde geheissen haben*
Conditional: *ich würde heissen*
Conditional Perfect: *ich würde geheissen haben*
Imperative: *heisse! heissen wir! heisst! heissen Sie!*

Infinitive: *helfen* to help
Pres. Part.: *helfend*
Present Indicative: *ich helfe, du hilfst, er hilft, wir helfen, ihr helft, Sie helfen, sie helfen*
Present Subjunctive: *(ich helfe), du helfest, er helfe, (wir helfen), ihr helfet, (Sie helfen, sie helfen)*
Imperfect Indicative: *ich half*
Imperfect Subjunctive: *ich hälfe (hülfe)*
Past Part.: *geholfen*
Present Perfect Indicative: *ich habe geholfen*
Past Perfect Indicative: *ich hatte geholfen*
Present Perfect Subjunctive: *ich (habe) hätte geholfen*
Past Perfect Subjunctive: *ich hätte geholfen*
Future: *ich werde helfen*
Future Perfect: *ich werde geholfen haben*
Conditional: *ich würde helfen*
Conditional Perfect: *ich würde geholfen haben*
Imperative: *hilf! helfen wir! helft! helfen Sie!*

Infinitive: *kennen* to know
Pres. Part.: *kennend*
Present Indicative: *ich kenne, du kennst, er kennt, wir kennen, ihr kennt, Sie kennen, sie kennen*
Present Subjunctive: *ich (kenne) kennte, du kennest, er kenne, (wir kennen), ihr kennet, (Sie kennen, sie kennen)*
Imperfect Indicative: *ich kannte*
Imperfect Subjunctive: *ich kannte*
Past Part.: *gekannt*
Present Perfect Indicative: *ich habe gekannt*
Past Perfect Indicative: *ich hatte gekannt*
Present Perfect Subjunctive: *ich (habe) hätte gekannt*
Past Perfect Subjunctive: *ich hätte gekannt*
Future: *ich werde kennen*
Future Perfect: *ich werde gekannt haben*
Conditional: *ich würde kennen*
Conditional Perfect: *ich würde gekannt haben*
Imperative: *kenne! kennen wir! kennt! kennen Sie!*

Infinitive: *laden* to load
Pres. Part.: *ladend*
Present Indicative: *ich lade, du lädst, er lädt, wir laden, ihr ladet, Sie laden, sie laden*
Present Subjunctive: *ich (lade) lüde, du ladest, er lad, (wir laden), ihr ladet, (Sie laden, sie laden)*
Imperfect Indicative: *ich lud*
Imperfect Subjunctive: *ich lüde*
Past Part.: *geladen*
Present Perfect Indicative: *ich habe geladen*
Past Perfect Indicative: *ich hatte geladen*
Present Perfect Subjunctive: *ich (habe) hätte geladen*
Past Perfect Subjunctive: *ich hätte geladen*
Future: *ich werde laden*
Future Perfect: *ich werde geladen haben*
Conditional: *ich würde laden*

Conditional Perfect: *ich würde geladen haben*
Imperative: *lade! laden wir! ladet! laden Sie!*

Infinitive: *lassen* to let
Pres. Part.: *lassend*
Present Indicative: *ich lasse, du lässt, er lässt, wir lassen, ihr lasst, Sie lassen, sie lassen*
Present Subjunctive: *ich (lasse) liesse, du lassest, er lasse, (wir lassen), ihr lasset, Sie lassen, (sie lassen)*
Imperfect Indicative: *ich liess*
Imperfect Subjunctive: *ich liesse*
Past Part.: *gelassen*
Present Perfect Indicative: *ich habe gelassen*
Past Perfect Indicative: *ich hatte gelassen*
Present Perfect Subjunctive: *ich (habe) hätte gelassen*
Past Perfect Subjunctive: *ich hätte gelassen*
Future: *ich werde lassen*
Future Perfect: *ich werde gelassen haben*
Conditional: *ich würde lassen*
Conditional Perfect: *ich würde gelassen haben*
Imperative: *lass! lassen wir! lasst! lassen Sie!*

Infinitive: *laufen* to run
Pres. Part.: *laufend*
Present Indicative: *ich laufe, du läufst, er läuft, wir laufen, ihr lauft, Sie laufen, sie laufen*
Present Subjunctive: *ich (laufe) liefe, du laufest, er laufe, (wir laufen), ihr laufet, Sie laufen, (sie laufen)*
Imperfect Indicative: *ich lief*
Imperfect Subjunctive: *ich liefe*
Past Part.: *gelaufen*
Present Perfect Indicative: *ich bin gelaufen*
Past Perfect Indicative: *ich war gelaufen*
Present Perfect Subjunctive: *ich sei gelaufen*

Past Perfect Subjunctive: *ich wäre gelaufen*
Future: *ich werde laufen*
Future Perfect: *ich werde gelaufen sein*
Conditional: *ich würde laufen*
Conditional Perfect: *ich würde gelaufen sein*
Imperative: *lauf! laufen wir! lauft! laufen Sie!*

Infinitive: *leiden* to suffer, endure
Pres. Part.: *leidend*
Present Indicative: *ich leide, du leidest, er leidet, wir leiden, ihr leidet, Sie leiden, sie leiden*
Present Subjunctive: *ich (leide) litte, du leidest, er leide, (wir leiden), ihr leidet, Sie leiden, (sie leiden)*
Imperfect Indicative: *ich litt*
Imperfect Subjunctive: *ich litte*
Past Part.: *gelitten*
Present Perfect Indicative: *ich habe gelitten*
Past Perfect Indicative: *ich hatte gelitten*
Present Perfect Subjunctive: *ich (habe) hätte gelitten*
Past Perfect Subjunctive: *ich hätte gelitten*
Future: *ich werde leiden*
Future Perfect: *ich werde gelitten haben*
Conditional: *ich würde leiden*
Conditional Perfect: *ich würde gelitten haben*
Imperative: *leide! leiden wir! leidet! leiden Sie!*

Infinitive: *lesen* to read
Pres. Part.: *lesend*
Present Indicative: *ich lese, du liest, er liest, wir lesen, ihr lest, Sie lesen, sie lesen*
Present Subjunctive: *ich (lese) läse, du lesest, er lese, (wir lesen), ihr leset, (Sie lesen, sie lesen)*
Imperfect Indicative: *ich las*
Imperfect Subjunctive: *ich läse*
Past Part.: *gelesen*

Present Perfect Indicative: *ich habe gelesen*
Past Perfect Indicative: *ich hatte gelesen*
Present Perfect Subjunctive: *ich (habe) hätte gelesen*
Past Perfect Subjunctive: *ich hätte gelesen*
Future: *ich werde lesen*
Future Perfect: *ich werde gelesen haben*
Conditional: *ich würde lesen*
Conditional Perfect: *ich würde gelesen haben*
Imperative: *lies! lesen wir! lest! lesen Sie!*

Infinitive: *liegen* to lie (recline)
Pres. Part.: *liegend*
Present Indicative: *ich liege, du liegst, er liegt, wir liegen, ihr liegt, Sie liegen, sie liegen*
Present Subjunctive: *ich (liege) läge, du liegest, er liege, (wir liegen), ihr lieget, (Sie liegen, sie liegen)*
Imperfect Indicative: *ich lag*
Imperfect Subjunctive: *ich läge*
Past Part.: *gelegen*
Present Perfect Indicative: *ich habe gelegen*
Past Perfect Indicative: *ich hatte gelegen*
Present Perfect Subjunctive: *ich (habe) hätte gelegen*
Past Perfect Subjunctive: *ich hätte gelegen*
Future: *ich werde liegen*
Future Perfect: *ich werde gelegen haben*
Conditional: *ich würde liegen*
Conditional Perfect: *ich würde gelegen haben*
Imperative: *liege! liegen wir! liegt! liegen Sie!*

Infinitive: *lügen* to lie (say something untrue)
Pres. Part.: *lügend*
Present Indicative: *ich lüge, du lügst, er lügt, wir lügen, ihr lügt, Sie lügen, sie lügen*
Present Subjunctive: *ich lüge, du lügest, er lüge, wir lügen, ihr lüget, Sie lügen, sie lügen*
Imperfect Indicative: *ich log*

Imperfect Subjunctive: *ich löge*
Past Part.: *gelogen*
Present Perfect Indicative: *ich habe gelogen*
Past Perfect Indicative: *ich hatte gelogen*
Present Perfect Subjunctive: *ich (habe) hätte gelogen*
Past Perfect Subjunctive: *ich hätte gelogen*
Future: *ich werde lügen*
Future Perfect: *ich werde gelogen haben*
Conditional: *ich würde lügen*
Conditional Perfect: *ich würde gelogen haben*
Imperative: *lüge! lügen wir! lügt! lügen Sie!*

Infinitive: *nehmen* to take
Pres. Part.: *nehmend*
Present Indicative: *ich nehme, du nimmst, er nimmt,
   wir nehmen, ihr nehmt, Sie nehmen, sie nehmen*
Present Subjunctive: *ich (nehme) nähme, du nehmest,
   er nehme, (wir nehmen), ihr nehmet, (Sie nehmen,
   sie nehmen.)*
Imperfect Indicative: *ich nahm*
Imperfect Subjunctive: *ich nähme*
Past Part.: *genommen*
Present Perfect Indicative: *ich habe genommen*
Past Perfect Indicative: *ich hatte genommen*
Present Perfect Subjunctive: *ich (habe) hätte genom-
   men*
Past Perfect Subjunctive: *ich hätte genommen*
Future: *ich werde nehmen*
Future Perfect: *ich werde genommen haben*
Conditional: *ich würde nehmen*
Conditional Perfect: *ich würde genommen haben*
Imperative: *nimm! nehmen wir! nehmt! nehmen Sie!*

Infinitive: *nennen* to name
Pres. Part.: *nennend*

Present Indicative: *ich nenne, du nennst, er nennt, wir nennen, ihr nennt, Sie nennen, sie nennen*

Present Subjunctive: *ich (nenne) nennte, du nennest, er nenne, (wir nennen), ihr nennet, (Sie nennen, sie nennen)*

Imperfect Indicative: *ich nannte*

Imperfect Subjunctive: *ich nennte*

Past Part.: *genannt*

Present Perfect Indicative: *ich habe genannt*

Past Perfect Indicative: *ich hatte genannt*

Present Perfect Subjunctive: *ich (habe) hätte genannt*

Past Perfect Subjunctive: *ich hätte genannt*

Future: *ich werde nennen*

Future Perfect: *ich werde genannt haben*

Conditional: *ich würde nennen*

Conditional Perfect: *ich würde genannt haben*

Imperative: *nenne! nennen wir! nennt! nennen Sie!*

Infinitive: *rufen* to call

Pres. Part.: *rufend*

Present Indicative: *ich rufe, du rufst, er ruft, wir rufen, ihr ruft, Sie rufen, sie rufen*

Present Subjunctive: *ich (rufe) riefe, du rufest, er rufe, (wir rufen), rufet, (Sie rufen, sie rufen)*

Imperfect Indicative: *ich rief*

Imperfect Subjunctive: *ich riefe*

Past Part.: *gerufen*

Present Perfect Indicative: *ich habe gerufen*

Past Perfect Indicative: *ich hatte gerufen*

Present Perfect Subjunctive: *ich (habe) hätte gerufen*

Past Perfect Subjunctive: *ich hätte gerufen*

Future: *ich werde rufen*

Future Perfect: *ich werde gerufen haben*

Conditional: *ich würde rufen*

Conditional Perfect: *ich würde gerufen haben*

Imperative: *ruf! rufen wir! ruft! rufen Sie!*

Infinitive: *schaffen* to create
Pres. Part.: *schaffend*
Present Indicative: *ich schaffe, du schaffst, er schafft, wir schaffen, ihr schafft, Sie schaffen, sie schaffen*
Present Subjunctive: *ich (schaffe) schüfe, du schaffest, er schaffe, (wir schaffen), ihr schaffet, (Sie schaffen, sie schaffen)*
Imperfect Indicative: *ich schuf*
Imperfect Subjunctive: *ich schüfe*
Past Part.: *geschaffen*
Present Perfect Indicative: *ich habe geschaffen*
Past Perfect Indicative: *ich hatte geschaffen*
Present Perfect Subjunctive: *ich (habe) hätte geschaffen*
Past Perfect Subjunctive: *ich hätte geschaffen*
Future: *ich werde schaffen*
Future Perfect: *ich werde geschaffen haben*
Conditional: *ich würde schaffen*
Conditional Perfect: *ich würde geschaffen haben*
Imperative: *schaffe! schaffen wir! schafft! schaffen Sie!*

Infinitive: *schlafen* to sleep
Pres. Part.: *schlafend*
Present Indicative: *ich schlafe, du schläfst, er schläft, wir schlafen, ihr schlaft, sie schlafen*
Present Subjunctive: *ich (schlafe) schliefe, du schlafest, er schlafe, (wir schlafen), ihr schlafet, (Sie schlafen, sie schlafen)*
Imperfect Indicative: *ich schlief*
Imperfect Subjunctive: *ich schliefe*
Past Part.: *geschlafen*
Present Perfect Indicative: *ich habe geschlafen*
Past Perfect Indicative: *ich hatte geschlafen*

Present Perfect Subjunctive: *ich (habe) hätte ge-schlafen*
Past Perfect Subjunctive: *ich hätte geschlafen*
Future: *ich werde schlafen*
Future Perfect: *ich werde geschlafen haben*
Conditional: *ich würde schlafen*
Conditional Perfect: *ich würde geschlafen haben*
Imperative: *schlafe! schlafen wir! schlaft! schlafen Sie!*

Infinitive: *schlagen* to beat, to strike
Pres. Part.: *schlagend*
Present Indicative: *ich schlage, du schlägst, er schlägt, wir schlagen, ihr schlagt, Sie schlagen, sie schlagen*
Present Subjunctive: *ich (schlage) schlüge, du schlag-est, er schlage, (wir schlagen), ihr schlaget, (Sie schlagen, sie schlagen)*
Imperfect Indicative: *ich schlug*
Imperfect Subjunctive: *ich schlüge*
Past Part.: *geschlagen*
Present Perfect Indicative: *ich habe geschlagen*
Past Perfect Indicative: *ich hatte geschlagen*
Present Perfect Subjunctive: *ich (habe) hätte geschla-gen*
Past Perfect Subjunctive: *ich hätte geschlagen*
Future: *ich werde schlagen*
Future Perfect: *ich werde geschlagen haben*
Conditional: *ich würde schlagen*
Conditional Perfect: *ich würde geschlagen haben*
Imperative: *schlage! schlagen wir! schlagt! schlagen Sie!*

Infinitive: *schreiben* to write
Pres. Part.: *schreibend*
Present Indicative: *ich schreibe, du schreibst, er*

*schreibt, wir schreiben, ihr schreibt, Sie schreiben,
sie schreiben*

Present Subjunctive: *ich (schreibe) schriebe, du
schreibest, er schreibe, (wir schreiben), ihr schrei-
bet, (Sie schreiben, sie schreiben)*

Imperfect Indicative: *ich schrieb*

Imperfect Subjunctive: *ich schriebe*

Past Part.: *geschrieben*

Present Perfect Indicative: *ich habe geschrieben*

Past Perfect Indicative: *ich hatte geschrieben*

Present Perfect Subjunctive: *ich (habe) hätte geschrieben*

Past Perfect Subjunctive: *ich hätte geschrieben*

Future: *ich werde schreiben*

Future Perfect: *ich werde geschrieben haben*

Conditional: *ich würde schreiben*

Conditional Perfect: *ich würde geschrieben haben*

Imperative: *schreib! schreiben wir! schreibt!
schreiben Sie!*

Infinitive: *schwimmen* to swim

Pres. Part.: *schwimmend*

Present Indicative: *ich schwimme, du schwimmst, er
schwimmt, wir schwimmen, ihr schwimmt, Sie
schwimmen, sie schwimmen*

Present Subjunctive: *ich (schwimme) schwömme, du
schwimmest, er schwimme, (wir schwimmen), ihr
schwimmet, (Sie schwimmen, sie schwimmen)*

Imperfect Indicative: *ich schwamm*

Imperfect Subjunctive: *ich schwömme (schwämme)*

Past Part.: *geschwommen*

Present Perfect Indicative: *ich bin geschwommen*

Past Perfect Indicative: *ich war geschwommen*

Present Perfect Subjunctive: *ich sei geschwommen*

Past Perfect Subjunctive: *ich wäre geschwommen*

Future: *ich werde schwimmen*
Future Perfect: *ich werde geschwommen sein*
Conditional: *ich würde schwimmen*
Conditional Perfect: *ich würde geschwommen sein*
Imperative: *schwimm! schwimmen wir! schwimmt! schwimmen Sie!*

Infinitive: *senden* to send
Pres. Part.: *sendend*
Present Indicative: *ich sende, du sendest, er sendet, wir senden, ihr sendet, Sie senden, sie senden*
Present Subjunctive: *ich (sende) sendete, du sendest, er sendet, (wir senden), ihr sendet, (Sie senden, sie senden)*
Imperfect Indicative: *ich sandte* (or *sendete*)
Imperfect Subjunctive: *ich sendete*
Past Part.: *gesandt*
Present Perfect Indicative: *ich habe gesandt*
Past Perfect Indicative: *ich hatte gesandt*
Present Perfect Subjunctive: *ich (habe) hätte gesandt*
Past Perfect Subjunctive: *ich hätte gesandt*
Future: *ich werde senden*
Future Perfect: *ich werde gesandt haben*
Conditional: *ich würde senden*
Conditional Perfect: *ich würde gesandt haben*
Imperative: *sende! senden wir! sendet! senden Sie!*

Infinitive: *singen* to sing
Pres. Part.: *singend*
Present Indicative: *ich singe, du singst, er singt, wir singen, ihr singt, Sie singen, sie singen*
Present Subjunctive: *ich (singe) sänge, du singest, er singe, (wir singen), ihr singet, (Sie singen, sie singen)*
Imperfect Indicative: *ich sang*

Imperfect Subjunctive: *ich sänge*
Past Part.: *gesungen*
Present Perfect Indicative: *ich habe gesungen*
Past Perfect Indicative: *ich hatte gesungen*
Present Perfect Subjunctive: *ich (habe) hatte gesungen*
Past Perfect Subjunctive: *ich hätte gesungen*
Future: *ich werde singen*
Future Perfect: *ich werde gesungen haben*
Conditional: *ich würde singen*
Conditional Perfect: *ich würde gesungen haben*
Imperative: *sing! singen wir! singt! singen Sie!*

Infinitive: *sitzen* to sit
Pres. Part.: *sitzend*
Present Indicative: *ich sitze, du sitzt, er sitzt, wir sitzen, ihr sitzt, Sie sitzen, sie sitzen*
Present Subjunctive: *ich (sitze) sässe, du sitzest, er sitze, (wir sitzen), ihr sitzet, (Sie sitzen, sie sitzen)*
Imperfect Indicative: *ich sass*
Imperfect Subjunctive: *ich sässe*
Past Part.: *gesessen*
Present Perfect Indicative: *ich habe gesessen*
Past Perfect Indicative: *ich hatte gesessen*
Present Perfect Subjunctive: *ich (habe) hätte gesessen*
Past Perfect Subjunctive: *ich hätte gesessen*
Future: *ich werde sitzen*
Future Perfect: *ich werde gesessen haben*
Conditional: *ich würde sitzen*
Conditional Perfect: *ich würde gesessen haben*
Imperative: *sitz! sitzen wir! sitzt! sitzen Sie!*

Infinitive: *stehen* to stand
Pres. Part.: *stehend*
Present Indicative: *ich stehe, du stehst, er steht, wir stehen, ihr steht, Sie stehen, sie stehen*

Present Subjunctive: *ich (stehe) stünde/stände du stehest, er stehe, (wir stehen), ihr stehet, (Sie stehen, sie stehen)*

Imperfect Indicative: *ich stand*

Imperfect Subjunctive: *ich stünde* or *stände*

Past Part.: *gestanden*

Present Perfect Indicative: *ich habe gestanden*

Past Perfect Indicative: *ich hatte gestanden.*

Present Perfect Subjunctive: *ich (habe) hätte gestanden*

Past Perfect Subjunctive: *ich hätte gestanden*

Future: *ich werde stehen*

Future Perfect: *ich werde gestanden haben*

Conditional: *ich würde stehen*

Conditional Perfect: *ich würde gestanden haben*

Imperative: *steh! stehen wir! steht! stehen Sie!*

Infinitive: *stehlen* to steal

Pres. Part.: *stehlend*

Present Indicative: *ich stehle, du stiehlst, er stiehlt, wir stehlen, ihr stehlt, Sie stehlen, sie stehlen.*

Present Subjunctive: *ich (stehle) stöhle/stähle, du stehlest, er stehle, (wir stehlen), ihr stehlet, (Sie stehlen, sie stehlen)*

Imperfect Indicative: *ich stahl*

Imperfect Subjunctive: *ich stöhle/stähle*

Past Part.: *gestohlen*

Present Perfect Indicative: *ich habe gestohlen*

Past Perfect Indicative: *ich hatte gestohlen*

Present Perfect Subjunctive: *ich (habe) hätte gestohlen*

Past Perfect Subjunctive: *ich hätte gestohlen*

Future: *ich werde stehlen*

Future Perfect: *ich werde gestohlen haben*

Conditional: *ich würde stehlen*

Conditional Perfect: *ich würde gestohlen haben*

Imperative: *stiehl! stehlen wir! stehlt! stehlen Sie!*

Infinitive: *springen* to jump
Pres. Part.: *springend*
Present Indicative: *ich springe, du springst, er springt, wir springen, ihr springt, Sie springen, sie springen.*
Present Subjunctive: *ich (springe) spränge, du springest, er springe, (wir springen), ihr springet, (Sie springen, sie springen)*
Imperfect Indicative: *ich sprang*
Imperfect Subjunctive: *ich spränge*
Past Part.: *gesprungen*
Present Perfect Indicative: *ich bin gesprungen*
Past Perfect Indicative: *ich war gesprungen*
Present Perfect Subjunctive: *ich sei gesprungen*
Past Perfect Subjunctive: *ich wäre gesprungen*
Future: *ich werde springen*
Future Perfect: *ich werde gesprungen sein*
Conditional: *ich würde springen*
Conditional Perfect: *ich würde gesprungen sein*
Imperative: *spring! springen wir! springt! springen Sie!*

Infinitive: *tragen* to carry
Pres. Part.: *tragend*
Present Indicative: *ich trage, du trägst, er trägt, wir tragen, ihr tragt, Sie tragen, sie tragen*
Present Subjunctive: *ich (trage) trüge, du tragest, er trage, (wir tragen), ihr traget, (Sie tragen, sie tragen)*
Imperfect Indicative: *ich trug*
Imperfect Subjunctive: *ich trüge*
Past Part.: *getragen*
Present Perfect Indicative: *ich (habe) hätte getragen*
Past Perfect Indicative: *ich hatte getragen*

Present Perfect Subjunctive: *ich habe getragen*
Past Perfect Subjunctive: *ich hätte getragen*
Future: *ich werde tragen*
Future Perfect: *ich werde getragen haben*
Conditional: *ich würde tragen*
Conditional Perfect: *ich würde getragen haben*
Imperative: *trag! tragen wir! tragt! tragen Sie!*

Infinitive: *treffen* to meet
Pres. Part.: *treffend*
Present Indicative: *ich treffe, du triffst, er trifft, wir treffen, ihr trefft, Sie treffen, sie treffen*
Present Subjunctive: *ich (treffe) träfe, du treffest, er treffe, (wir treffen), ihr treffet, (Sie treffen, sie treffen)*
Imperfect Indicative: *ich traf*
Imperfect Subjunctive: *ich träfe*
Past Part.: *getroffen*
Present Perfect Indicative: *ich habe getroffen*
Past Perfect Indicative: *ich hätte getroffen*
Present Perfect Subjunctive: *ich (habe) hätte getroffen*
Past Perfect Subjunctive: *ich hätte getroffen*
Future: *ich werde treffen*
Future Perfect: *ich werde getroffen haben*
Conditional: *ich würde treffen*
Conditional Perfect: *ich würde getroffen haben*
Imperative: *triff! treffen wir! trefft! treffen Sie!*

Infinitive: *trinken* to drink
Pres. Part.: *trinkend*
Present Indicative: *ich trinke, du trinkst, er trinkt, wir trinken, ihr trinkt, Sie trinken, sie trinken*
Present Subjunctive: *ich (trinke) tränke, du trinkest, er trinke, (wir trinken), ihr trinket, (Sie trinken, sie trinken)*

Imperfect Indicative: *ich trank*
Imperfect Subjunctive: *ich tränke*
Past Part.: *getrunken*
Present Perfect Indicative: *ich habe getrunken*
Past Perfect Indicative: *ich hatte getrunken*
Present Perfect Subjunctive: *ich (habe) hätte getrunken*
Past Perfect Subjunctive: *ich hätte getrunken*
Future: *ich werde trinken*
Future Perfect: *ich werde getrunken haben*
Conditional: *ich würde trinken*
Conditional Perfect: *ich würde getrunken haben*
Imperative: *trink! trinken wir! trinkt! trinken Sie!*

Infinitive: *tun* to do
Pres. Part.: *tuend*
Present Indicative: *ich tue, du tust, er tut, wir tun, ihr tut, Sie tun, sie tun*
Present Subjunctive: *ich (tue) täte, du tuest, er tue, (wir tun), ihr tuet, (Sie tun, sie tun)*
Imperfect Indicative: *ich tat*
Imperfect Subjunctive: *ich täte*
Past Part.: *getan*
Present Perfect Indicative: *ich habe getan*
Past Perfect Indicative: *ich hatte getan*
Present Perfect Subjunctive: *ich (habe) hätte getan*
Past Perfect Subjunctive: *ich hätte getan*
Future: *ich werde tun*
Future Perfect: *ich werde getan haben*
Conditional: *ich würde tun*
Conditional Perfect: *ich würde getan haben*
Imperative: *tue! tun wir! tut! tun Sie!*

Infinitive: *vergessen* to forget
Pres. Part.: *vergessend*
Present Indicative: *ich vergesse, du vergisst, er ver-*

gisst, wir vergessen, ihr vergesst, Sie vergessen, sie vergessen

Present Subjunctive: *ich (vergesse) vergässe, du vergessest, er vergesse, (wir vergessen), ihr vergesset, (Sie vergessen, sie vergessen)*

Imperfect Indicative: *ich vergass*

Imperfect Subjunctive: *ich vergässe*

Past Part.: *vergessen*

Present Perfect Indicative: *ich habe vergessen*

Past Perfect Indicative: *ich hatte vergessen*

Present Perfect Subjunctive: *ich (habe) hätte vergessen*

Past Perfect Subjunctive: *ich hätte vergessen*

Future: *ich werde vergessen*

Future Perfect: *ich werde vergessen haben*

Conditional: *ich würde vergessen*

Conditional Perfect: *ich würde vergessen haben*

Imperative: *vergiss! vergessen wir! vergesst! vergessen Sie!*

Infinitive: *verlieren* to lose

Pres. Part.: *verlierend*

Present Indicative: *ich verliere, du verlierst, er verliert, wir verlieren, ihr verliert, Sie verlieren, sie verlieren*

Present Subjunctive: *ich (verliere) verlöre, du verlierest, er verliere, (wir verlieren), ihr verlieret, (Sie verlieren, sie verlieren)*

Imperfect Indicative: *ich verlor*

Imperfect Subjunctive: *ich verlöre*

Past Part.: *verloren*

Present Perfect Indicative: *ich habe verloren*

Past Perfect Indicative: *ich hatte verloren*

Present Perfect Subjunctive: *ich (habe) hätte verloren*

Past Perfect Subjunctive: *ich hätte verloren*

Future: *ich werde verlieren*

Future Perfect: *ich werde verloren haben*
Conditional: *ich würde verlieren*
Conditional Perfect: *ich würde verloren haben*
Imperative: *verlier(e)! verlieren wir! verliert! verlieren Sie!*

LETTER WRITING

A. THANK-YOU NOTES

Berlin, den 6. Januar 1993

Sehr geehrte Frau Zimmermann,

   Ich möchte Ihnen herzlich für Ihr wunderbares Geschenk danken. Das Bild entspricht ganz meinem Geschmack und passt so gut zu den neuen Möbeln in meinem Wohnzimmer.
   Meinen allerherzlichsten Dank.

Mit verbindlichen Grüssen
Lotte Schäfer

Berlin, January 6, 1993

Dear Mrs. Zimmermann,

   I should (would) like to thank you for your delightful present. The picture is entirely to my taste and matches the new furniture in my living room perfectly.
   Thank you ever so much.

Sincerely yours,
Lotte Schäfer

B. BUSINESS LETTERS

H. Molz
Kantstrasse 16
1000 Berlin 14

Berlin, den 2. Mai 1993

Verlag Peter Basten
Kurfürstendamm 10
1000 Berlin 20

Anbei übersende ich Ihnen einen Scheck über DM 23. für ein Jahresabonnement Ihrer Zeitschrift „Merkur."

Hochachtungsvoll!
Heinrich Molz

ANLAGE

H. Mulz
16 Kant Street
1000 Berlin 14

May 2, 1993

Peter Basten Press
10 Kurfürstendamm
1000 Berlin 20

Gentlemen:

Enclosed please find a check for 23 marks for a year's subscription to your magazine *Merkur.*

Very truly yours,
Heinrich Molz

(Encl.)

Schwarzkopf & Co.
Breite Strasse 6
1000 Berlin 16

Berlin, den 30. Sept. 1993

Firma
Paul Gerber & Co
van Groothestrasse 20
1000 Berlin 22

Ihre Anfrage 8.8.93

Sehr geehrte Herren,

   In Beantwortung Ihrer Anfrage vom 10. ds. bestäti-gen wir Ihnen gerne nochmals die Aufgabe der Sen-dung per Postpaket am 13. August.

Hochachtungsvoll
Ernst Schwarzkopf

6 Broad Street
1000 Berlin 16

Sept. 30, 1993

Paul Gerber & Co.
20 van Groothe Street
1000 Berlin 22

Re: Inquiry of 8.8.93

Gentlemen:

   In reply to your letter (''inquiry'') of this month,

we wish to confirm once more that the merchandise
was mailed to you parcel post on August 13.

Very truly yours,
Ernest Schwarzkopf

C. INFORMAL LETTERS

7. *März 1993*

Lieber Helmut,

*Ich habe mich sehr über Deinen letzten Brief ge-
freut. Zunächst habe ich eine gute Nachricht für Dich.
Anfang April beabsichtige ich, zwei Wochen in Berlin
zu verbringen. Ich freue mich schon sehr darauf, mit
Dir und Deiner Familie zusammenzukommen und
hoffe, dass es Euch allen gut geht.*

*Irene begleitet mich auf dieser Reise. Sie freut sich
sehr, nun endlich Deine Frau kennenzulernen. Auf
diese Weise wird es uns gelingen die beühmten Se-
henswürdigkeiten des alten und des neuen Berlins zu
besichtigen. Wir beide können uns lange unterhalten,
wie wir es in der Schule immer getan haben.*

*Meine Praxis läuft ganz gut zur Zeit. Ich werde
versuchen, nicht zu viele neue Patienten während des
Monats Aprils anzunehmen, obwohl ich glaube, dass
es sehr schwierig sein wird. Neulich habe ich mich
mit Müller getroffen. Er hat nach Dir gefragt und
lässt Dich herzlich grüssen. Man kann es kaum
glauben, dass der ,,kleine Fritz'' zwei Kaufhäuser
und mehrere Restaurants besitzt.*

*Fast hätte ich die Hauptsache vergessen. Ich wäre
Dir sehr dankbar, wenn Du mir ein Zimmer im Hilton
Hotel für den fünften April reservieren könntest. Du
tätest mir einen grossen Gefallen.*

Ich hoffe bald von Dir zu hören. Grüsse an Deine Frau.

Dein
Klaus

March 7, 1993

Dear Helmut,

I was very happy to receive your last letter. First of all, I have some good news for you. I intend to spend two weeks in Berlin at the beginning of April. I'm already looking forward to getting together with you and your family and hope you are all well.

Irene is going to accompany me on this trip. She is looking forward to meeting your wife. That way we will be able to visit the sights of the old and new Berlin. The two of us will be able to chat as we always used to in school.

Presently, my practice is going quite well. I'll try not to take on too many patients during the month of April, although I believe that to be somewhat difficult.

Recently I met with Müller. He asked for you. He sends you his best. One can hardly believe that "little Fritz" owns two department stores and several restaurants.

I almost forgot the most important thing. I would be very grateful if you were able to reserve a room for me at the Hilton Hotel for the fifth of April. You would be doing me a big favor.

I hope to hear from you soon. Regards to your wife.

Yours,
Klaus

D. FORMS OF SALUTATIONS AND COMPLIMENTARY CLOSINGS

SALUTATIONS:

FORMAL

Sehr geehrter Herr Professor,	Dear Professor (Smith),
Sehr geehrter Herr Bürgermeister,	Der Mayor (Smith),
Sehr geehrter Herr Rechtsanwalt, *Sehr geehrter Herr Doktor,*	Dear Lawyer (Smith), (Lawyers are often addressed as *"Doktor"* in Germany.)
Sehr geehrte Frau Schmitt,	Dear Mrs. Schmitt,
Sehr geehrte Herren,	Gentlemen:
Sehr geehrter Herr Pulver,	Dear Mr. Pulver,

INFORMAL

Mein lieber Karl,	Dear Karl,
Meine liebe Franziska,	Dear Frances,
Mein Liebling,	My darling (*m.* and *f.*),
Mein Liebster,	My darling (*m.*),
Meine Liebste,	My darling (*f.*),
Lieber Franz,	Dear Frank,
Liebe Paula,	Dear Paula,
Meine Lieben,	My dear ones,

COMPLIMENTARY CLOSINGS:

FORMAL

1. *Hochachtungsvoll!*[1]   Very truly yours,
   ("Most respectfully")
2. *Mit vorzüglicher Hochach-*   Very truly yours,
   tung!
   ("With the most excellent
   and highest regard")
3. *Mit besten Grüssen,*   Yours truly,
   ("With best greetings")
4. *Wir empfehlen uns*   Yours truly,
   mit besten Grüssen,
   ("We commend ourselves
   with best regards")

INFORMAL

1. *Mit herzlichem*   Very sincerely, love
   Gruss
   ("With hearty
   greeting")
2. *Bitte grüsse Deine*   Please give my regards
   Mutter von mir   to your mother
3. *Meine besten Grüsse*   Give my regards to your
   an die Deinen   family
4. *Grüsse und Küsse*   My love to everybody
   an Euch alle
   ("Greetings and
   kisses to you all")

---

[1] Exclamation point is optional

E. FORM OF THE ENVELOPE

Schwartzkopf & Co.
Breite Strasse 6
1000 Berlin 16

                    Firma
              Schiller & Kramer
               z. Hd. Fr. Berger
             Kurfürstendamm 75
               1000 Berlin 22

Letters to an individual are addressed:

Herrn   *Hrn. Franz; Hrn. Müller*   (Mr.)
Frau   *Fr. Else Schneider; Fr. Schneider*   (Mrs.)